Trouble

What Every Christian Should Know About Trials, Tribulations, and Troublesome Times

By K. Sheldon Bailey

First Edition: October 2013

ISBN 978-0-9897826-0-9

Printed in the United States of America
For Worldwide Distribution

Unless otherwise noted, Scripture quotations are from the New King James Version of the Bible.

Quotations marked (AMP) are from the Amplified version of the Bible.

Quotations marked (NAS) are from the New American Standard version of the Bible.

All emphasis within quotations is the author's addition.

Disciples' Pen Publishing
320 Pine Ave. Suite 803
Long Beach, CA 90802
(562) 363-5470

"Taking the Word, Teaching the World"

K. Sheldon Bailey Ministries
www.ksheldonbailey.org

Cover Photo Courtesy of Smotherman Images
E-mail: smothermanimages@gmail.com

All glory, honor, praise, and thanksgiving to my Heavenly Father, His Son Jesus, and His Holy Spirit for the irreplaceable role they play in my life and in the writing of *Trouble*.
Thank you Lord. Great is Your faithfulness!

In Loving Memory of My "Moms"

Adrienne Florence Bailey

(1935-1991)

Whose life of holiness and commitment
To Christ was a living epistle.

What we, your children, saw in you
Became a seed in us—seed that has
Brought forth fruit after its own kind.

Who was the first to see and tell me of
"The vision" of my being in a pulpit
While I was yet in the world, entangled in sin.
Whose effectual fervent prayer has availed
much in my life and that of her other
Children—Terrence, Lashonne and baby Jamie.

Whose sacrificial love; endurance of difficulty, personal tragedy
and trouble served as an example; an inspiration; and the
reasons for my everlasting honor,
admiration and appreciation!

Thanks, Moms.
May the fruit of my life on Earth
Be credited to your account in Heaven.

Dedication

This book is dedicated to the loving memory of my mother, Adrienne F. Bailey who overcame more trouble than anyone I have personally known.

This book is also dedicated to:

- † Christians in every nation who are experiencing difficulty of different sorts.
- † Christians near and far who are wondering whether the struggle of walking with God and waiting on the good of His Word to be fulfilled is worth the trouble they are encountering.
- † Those who have given up on God after coming back again and again.
- † Those who have confused falling with failing but are willing to get back up and give it one more try.
- † Those who are without hope and who feel as if they are also without help.
- † Believers who are physically, emotionally or spiritually beaten, worn, tattered, and torn.
- † Believers who feel like it is better to turn back than it is to continue trusting God.
- † Believers who wonder if life is worth living and quietly wishes life would end.

- † The beloved of God who feel as if no one cares about them as they secretly and silently shed tears inside and out.
- † The beloved of God who are broken and bleeding, and whose pain goes unnoticed and unspoken.

This book is dedicated to the Christian who has yet to experience the good he has been expecting—the good that is real and that is awaiting his arrival.

Acknowledgments

Special People

Adrienne F. Bailey, my mother, my friend, my first example of true Christianity, and the person who first prophesied to me my calling in Christ. Ronald J. Hart, my father. Dad, thank you for your contributions to my life, and for being not only a father, but a friend as well. I love laughing with you. Terry L. Bailey, my older brother. You have been used by God to be a blessing to me in ways you are probably unaware of. Thank you TB, I love you "Bro". Lashonne Christine, my little sister. Thank you for letting me break your arm everyday growing up. I am grateful to God for what He has done in your life, and what He has yet to do. Marc Hart, my younger brother. I am proud of the intelligent and good hearted man you are. I believe that the best is yet to come for you. To my nephews and niecy-poos: Brandon, Alora, Brett, Makayla, and Amber, the Uncman loves you all and I am proud of who you all are, and are becoming! And to my entire family, I love the wonderful times we have together. May there be more such times!

Acknowledgments

Special Partners

Valerie Gerrard Browne, Pastors Tom and Heather Flores, Patricia Paige, Angie Marquez, Jeff Haynes, Jr., Artel Dyer, John Dixon, Jeff Washington, Lola DuCree, Minnie James, Richard James, Pastor James and Terri Cooper, Lydia Dunn, Cynthia Davenport. Thank you all for your financial support and partnership in helping to make *Trouble* possible. Special thanks to Kathy Curtis of Christian Book Production Services (www.christianbookformat.com). I am grateful to have benefited from your wisdom, experience, and expertise in typesetting *Trouble*. I thank you also for helping me to right the wrongs in writing *Trouble*, and teaching me along the way.

Acknowledgments

Mentors

With great gratitude, I also acknowledge men of God who have played a significant role in my Christianity, and in the life of my Christian ministry.

(The late)

Pastor John Nix-McReynolds

Second Baptist Church – Santa Ana, California

My pastor, the one who acknowledged my gift of teaching, calling into the Word ministry, and gave me the first opportunity to minister to the people of God.

Dr. Robert L. Wilks, Jr.

Vine-Life Christian Fellowship – Riverside, California

Thank you for sowing the seed of worship into me. Worship has tremendously impacted both my life and ministry in ways that are immeasurable!

Pastor Edward A. Smith, Sr.

Zoe Christian Fellowship – Whittier, California

Thank you for showing me the importance of reaching the nations. Your commitment to missions is remarkable. I look forward to learning more from you.

Valerie Gerrard Browne
"Auntie V"

No amount of words could adequately express what you mean to me and have meant to my life over the past 10 years. I have always known that belief was a powerful tool, but I did not learn that belief shown in another's ability was just a powerful until your belief in me taught me that lesson.

My appreciation for your support of me could not be greater. You have been there for me at every turn, helping to meet every need. And your words to me in the most difficult times of my life helped me immensely by putting a voice to the words God wanted me to hear during those times.

You have played a role in my life over these past years that no one else has played. You have been encouraging, uplifting, assuring and reassuring. You saw in me what others were blinded to; and you continued to see when others had lost focus. For these reasons, and because of the sweet, loving and kind, and caring person you are, my love and gratitude for you shall never shallow! Thank you Auntie V. Thank you so very, very much!!

May God's best, and increased blessings forever find you!

Nephew K

Table of Contents

Introduction xix

Chapter 1
Ye Shall Have Tribulation 21

Chapter 2
In the Time of Trouble 35

Chapter 3
Trouble: A Weapon or a Tool? 53

Chapter 4
Why Does the Lord Allow Trouble? 71

Chapter 5
Where in the World Is God
When I Am in Trouble? 119

Chapter 6
Trouble, Brokenness, and
the Spirit of Suicide 131

Chapter 7
The Importance of the Word
in the Time of Trouble 157

Chapter 8
The Importance of Prayer in the Time of Trouble 175

Chapter 9
The Importance of Praise in the Time of Trouble 193

Chapter 10
The Importance of Church Attendance in the Time of Trouble 209

Chapter 11
The Importance of Patience in the Time of Trouble 233

Chapter 12
Equipped to Endure 249

Chapter 13
The Helpfulness of Hopefulness 275

Chapter 14
The Voice of God in the Time of Trouble 293

Chapter 15
This Is Only a Test 309

Chapter 16
Trustful in Trouble 335

Conclusion 357

Introduction

The teaching of Jesus the Christ reveals to us that every disciple and follower of His will encounter trouble of some sort at some point in life. The one thing shared by every Bible character that walked with God is that each one encountered trouble during the course of their relationship with the Lord.

From Adam to Jesus, in between and after the ascension of Jesus to be with the Father, we find children of God of different ethnicities, ages, economic classes, and levels of spiritual maturity facing trials and tribulations of all types. Be it the loss of close family members or loved ones, the struggle or failure of a marriage, financial devastation, sickness, disease, abuse, betrayal, abandonment, unfair treatment or the target of ill intentions, the ruin of a reputation or misfortune of some other sort—indiscriminately trouble uninvitedly visits the life of every person. No one escapes unscathed from days of difficulty and times of trials!

I thank God for the Holy Bible for a number of reasons, among which is the fact that His Word grants us access into the lives of people past—those children of God who lived centuries before us and dealt with tragedy, mishap, and disaster. For it is from the all-encompassing view of reading their stories from beginning to end that we gather understanding of what trouble is and is not and what trouble does and cannot do. As the Word of God escorts us into the trying times of their lives, we are also permitted to gather understanding, to gain strength, and to glean encouragement from their triumph over trouble. Their encouragement enables us to weather the storms of our own difficulty-drenched days.

Five years after receiving the inspiration to write this book on trouble in the life of the Christian, I finally completed it. Not because it actually took me five years to write it, but because the Lord took me through a time of trouble that would enable me to write this book with an *inside-the-storm* perspective. I believe sometimes with some things that an *outside-looking-in* perspective allows us to see things those on the *inside looking out* simply cannot see. However, when it comes to *trouble*, certain lessons can only be learned in the eye of the storm.

For example, no civilian can write about war the way a soldier can, even if the civilian is an on-the-ground reporter or photographer. The personal experience of the soldier provides an emotion, insight, and a sensitivity acquired from actually being *in* battle that is not known by the civilian—no matter how much he has interviewed veterans or read their stories. Their stories are *their* stories and cannot be told in the same manner, with the same emotion. We all hope never to have to go to war or be a part of any of its battles. However, should we have to, we certainly want to be sided with the soldier whose *in-war* experience and insight will serve us better in surviving the battle. I trust that the lessons I have learned, and the practices I have applied during my time of trouble, will serve you well as you seek to overcome the obstacles you are confronted with.

I am grateful that the Lord has led you to this book. I believe with all of my heart that it will be a *tremendous* blessing to you! So, without further ado, get ready to get into *Trouble!*

Chapter 1
Ye Shall Have Tribulation

"In the world
you shall have tribulation:
but be of good cheer;
I have overcome the world."
John 16:33

Trouble is an ordinary part of life for every human being. If you live in this world, you can expect to come face-to-face with some kind of adversity at some point. This is especially true if you are a Christian.

In speaking to His disciples in John 16:33, Jesus is also speaking to us as modern-day disciples, informing us that we too shall encounter trouble. Even for the believer, trouble of some sort is unavoidable. At some point during the course of our Christian walk, we will experience things or people that cause us difficulty or distress. Sooner or later in our sold-out, hardcore, committed relationship with God, even we, like so many other Godly people, both in and outside of the pages of the Bible, will meet face-to-face with troublesome times.

Some of the trouble we will encounter is common to the human experience. However, some troubles are exclusive to our existence as Christians living in a world that is growing evermore hostile toward Christianity and the God Whom we represent. Decades after Jesus prophetically introduced this insight about the world, trouble, and the disciple, the apostle Paul would convey this truth to Timothy, his spiritual son.

Yes, all who live godly in Christ Jesus will suffer persecution. But evil men and impostors will grow worse and worse, deceiving and being deceived.
2 Timothy 3:12, 13

There are also troubles that are distinct to us as Christians because they contribute to our spiritual growth and our preparation for spiritual service. This means that trouble isn't always a sign that the Christian has done wrong; rather, it often signifies that God is at work.

The assertion that we as Christians will be faced with things that are difficult to deal with is not a negative confession; it is merely a restating of what has already been declared by the Christ. And the words Jesus spoke are not words of pessimism; they are words of proven truth—communicated by Him Who is wisdom and knowledge incarnate.

I recognize the concern over what is confessed with our mouth. I also endorse the idea of our need to be mindful and careful of what we say because our words carry the weight of influence as well as the creative ability to build up, and the destructive ability to tear down. We learn this truth throughout the Bible, including the following passages:

He who guards his mouth preserves his life; but he who opens wide his lips shall have destruction.
Proverbs 13:3

Death and life are in the power of the tongue...
Proverbs 18:21

Whoever guards his mouth and tongue keeps his soul from troubles.
Proverbs 21:31

Jesus was aware of and even spoke such passages. Nevertheless, He tells us, **"In the world you *shall have tribulation....*"** The Master did not make this statement to be negative, neither for the sake of alarming us; nor is He seeking to sabotage our faith by sowing seeds of cynicism into our heart. Jesus is simply telling us about trouble so that we will not be caught unaware of this aspect of the Christian life.

The words of Jesus and others in the Bible who speak to us about times of difficulty should be embraced because their aim is to aid us in understanding not only the realism of trouble, but also its accomplishing purpose.

A look through the pages of God's Word reveals that everyone who had a relationship with God also had an encounter with trouble at some point during the course of that relationship. Godly characters, from Adam in Genesis to John in the book of Revelation, as well as everyone in between, experienced trouble of some sort in one season or another. Jesus the Savior was no exception. Even before His arrest in the Garden of Gethsemane and the countless other times people sought His life, Jesus experienced trouble of different sorts. In fact, Jesus had an encounter with trouble even before He was old enough to know what trouble was, or *that* He was in trouble. Not long after the birth of Jesus, Herod sought the death of Jesus because he was afraid the King of the Jews was born to replace *him* as king of the Jews.

From the time of His birth, Jesus occasionally experienced trouble until His death on the cross, including His death on the cross. Because Jesus experienced trouble throughout His life is not to say that we should expect trouble our entire life. That's not the plan of God. God's plan in sending His only begotten Son is for us to have eternal life in Heaven *and* a good quality of life on Earth before we get to Heaven. But, be that as it may, like our Savior, we too will meet with a little adversity on the road to abundant life. And as it was with our Savior in overcoming every episode of trouble He ever encountered, including death on the cross, it is also in the plans of the Father for us to overcome trouble as well. This is what Jesus in the opening verse to this chapter goes on to make known.

These things I have spoken to you,
that in Me you may have peace.
<u>In the world you will have tribulation;</u>
<u>but be of good cheer, I have</u>
<u>overcome the world.</u>
John 16:33

Jesus is saying that living in the world will be accompanied by trouble. However, He then uses the word "but." Following bad news, "but" is a breath of fresh air because it changes the direction and turns the table right when it appears trouble has the last say. "But" signifies that the trouble we encounter is not the end, nor the victor, neither the last man standing. Instead, trouble is a defeated foe on the path to abundant life.

With the confidence that accompanies having all power and authority, Jesus prophesies of overcoming the world and the trouble found therein—just as He would soon after overcome death, Hell, and the grave. And with the same authoritative voice and power to fulfill prophecy, His words are purposed to encourage our peace, cheer, and optimism by assuring us that. just as He has overcome the world's trouble in His life, He has also overcome the world's trouble in ours.

For this reason we need not fret, fear, doubt, or be dismayed in our season of trouble. As it was with the Christ, so shall it be with the Christian!

Jesus overcame trouble so that we could overcome trouble.

"Beloved [Christians], think it not strange concerning the fiery trials [trouble] which is to try you, as though some strange thing has happened unto you."
1 Peter 4:12

In saying, **"think it not strange,"** the apostle Peter is also saying we should not be surprised by the experience of trouble. In fact, he writes these words under the inspiration of the Holy Spirit, meaning it was the Lord who prompted Peter to pen these words. But also, Peter was among the original disciples whom Jesus told, **"...ye shall have tribulation."** Therefore, in his epistle to Christians, Peter was not writing words that were intended to incite dread or discouragement; he was simply obeying the Spirit and teaching other believers what he himself had been taught by the Master, and what he had been instructed by the Master to do. In Matthew 28:19 and 20, Jesus told Peter and the other disciples to **"go and make disciples...teaching them to observe whatsoever things I have commanded [or taught] you."** In his writings, Peter was merely echoing the words and teachings he received from Jesus years earlier, which is exactly what disciples are supposed to do.

Peter, like Jesus, was warning believers about the coming of trouble so that at trouble's arrival they would not be caught off guard by thinking they are exempt or off-limits to trouble because they are saved, set apart, and Spirit-filled. This truth is important to understand because unexpected trouble has a way of alarming people, leaving them dazed and confused. It is also capable of impairing their focus, disarming their faith, and crippling their progress in the process.

The words by Jesus and Peter by no means suggest that we should go forth with a gloom-and-doom perspective, expecting trouble around every corner, or to come knocking any minute. That perspective would not allow us to enjoy life as God desires. However, their words are purposed to prevent us from being naïve about trouble and the Christian life, and to help us prepare for trouble in the Christian life.

Although rainstorms, typhoons, and hurricanes are not humanly preventable, our awareness of their pending arrival affords us the opportunity to prepare for what we cannot prevent. Therefore, we value the words of warning from meteorologists and other weather professionals. Giving us a *heads up*, or a word of warning, is exactly what Jesus is doing when He says, **"ye shall have tribulation."** Knowing we **"shall have tribulation"** and that it is an ordinary part of the Christian life provides us with an opportunity to prepare ourselves so that *when* the storm comes, it does not do the damage it is capable of when we are *not* prepared.

People who live in areas where rainstorms, typhoons, and hurricanes occur on a somewhat regular basis don't wait until their arrival to prepare for them. They prepare beforehand by boarding up windows and doors, securing outdoor valuables, and by stocking up on water, food, and other essentials. Having previous knowledge that a storm is coming provides them with an opportunity to prepare for the storm. Preparation *before* the storm increases the likelihood of surviving the storm.

Such is the case with us and the stormy times of the Christian life. Knowing we will encounter trouble at some point during our faith walk provides us with the time necessary to develop a plan of action *before* its arrival. This way, when trouble does come, the surprise of its presence will not paralyze our faith and cause us to doubt or give up on seeking and serving God. Jesus foretells us of trouble so that its appearance upon the shores of our life will not catch us off guard, or find us spiritually or psychologically unprepared.

Satan's aim is for trouble to weaken us to the point of *giving up*; however, God's aim is for the same trouble to strengthen and prepare us for *going up*. This is the second reason Jesus foretells us of trouble; so that we may know that trouble is a part of ***His plan*** to prepare us for ***His purpose***. There is training for the future that takes place in trouble. There is also a spiritual education provided by the stormy seasons of life that is not offered by seasons of smooth sailing.

Every good sailor needs to be trained on rough and stormy seas before he can become a master sailor who is capable of great accomplishments. Lessons are to be learned during troublesome training conditions that the sailor cannot be taught in the safety of the seashore. It is during the storms that a sailor gains a greater knowledge about the sea, his vessel, and himself. And it is this deeper, more valuable knowledge that prepares him to succeed in life as a master sailor.

In the same way, troublesome, stormy times in life prepare us for the plans and purposes of God like no other times can. They are both difficult and undesirable, but they do a work in us that is unaccomplished by any other season in life.

There is training for the future that takes place in times of trouble that we cannot receive in seasons of ease.

The book of Genesis tells the history of a man named Joseph, the eleventh son of the patriarch Jacob, whose name was later changed to Israel. The heart of the story of Joseph's life begins in Genesis chapter 37 when he was seventeen years old. The story reveals that God had a tremendous purpose for Joseph's existence and a plan to bring that purpose to pass. God's plan called for Joseph to cross paths with trouble. This plan may sound strange but, the trouble God *allows* is sometimes the trouble He summons. Often, if not always, when trouble *comes,* it's because it has been *called* for by God for some reason of significance—to accomplish a specific purpose or to do a *readying* work in us.

Everything without free will must immediately submit to the voice and the call of God. The Bible says God calls for the waters, they answer, and He sends them on assignment to water Earth. God calls lightning, it comes, and God commands when and where lightning is to strike. God calls for the morning and it comes with the rising of the sun to begin the dawning of each new day.

In the same way these tangibles come in response to the call of God, trouble also answers the call of God, accepting the assignment of God to prepare us for His purpose and His good plan for our life. And this was the case with the trouble that visited the life of Joseph. Joseph learned lessons during and *from* his times of trouble that were a part of God's plan to prepare him for who and what God had purposed and destined him to be.

Joseph's trouble began when, out of envy and hatred, nine of his eleven brothers decided to be rid of him. Their original desire was to murder Joseph, but Reuben, the oldest brother, persuaded the others to place him in a pit instead. Reuben later planned to rescue Joseph and return him to Jacob, their father. However, as God would have it, even Reuben's plan to later deliver Joseph from the pit was not in the plan of God for Joseph. Before their eldest brother could return and execute the rescue mission, the other brothers had staged Joseph's death and sold him to a group of people called the Ishmaelites for 20 shekels of silver. Joseph would later be taken into Egypt and sold into slavery to an Egyptian officer named Potiphar.

I am intrigued by the fact that God didn't allow Reuben to return in time to rescue Joseph from the pit. This detail says that sometimes God doesn't permit people to help us—even during the most trying and needful times of our life. I believe one reason God doesn't always allow people to aid us is because He calls and ordains certain seasons of difficulty from which He Himself desires and plans to deliver us.

In the process of our maturity and God's fulfilling of His perfect plan for our lives, at some point, He begins to wean us from the dependence of people, causing and positioning us to be dependent on Him, and Him alone. Nothing compels us to pray and seek the face of God like our need for help when no one can or will help us. Nothing causes us to turn to God like the turning away of other people when we turn to them for help. Nothing causes us to draw from the deep well of Living Water like the dryness of the people pool. If God always permitted people to help us in our trouble, we would not come to know Him personally as Jehovah-shama-natsal, the Lord Who *hears and delivers* **(Psalm 34:17).**

The Lord allowing Joseph's brother to throw him into a pit allows us to know two facts: Firstly, the plan of the brothers to do away with Joseph was used by God for good. This makes sense in light of **Romans 8:28** which says **"… all things work together for good to those who love God, to those who are the called according to His purpose."** Secondly, Joseph not being delivered by Reuben meant that the pit was God's plan for Joseph that was simply carried out by his ill-intentioned brothers.

When we consider the fact that God is our Protector, our Helper, and our Deliverer, it seems odd and seemingly out of character for Him to sit back, but sometimes He does indeed allow our enemies to bring trouble and cause problems for us.

However, it is out of this trouble and these problems that God gives birth to some of the biggest blessings of our life! Joseph, David, and Job are all excellent examples of this reality, and later we will look at their stories of trouble in greater detail in order to gather some excellent insight, instruction, and encouragement. If you have read even the opening chapter of the book of Job, you would recall that the Lord permitted Satan, Job's enemy *(and no one's friend),* to cause him possibly the worse trouble any one person has encountered in such a short period of time:

And the Lord said to Satan, "Behold, all that He has is in your power; only do not lay a hand on his person." So Satan went out from the presence of the Lord.
Job 1:12

Now there arose a day when Job's sons and daughters were eating and drinking wine in their oldest brother's house; and a messenger came to Job and said, "The oxen were plowing and the donkeys feeding beside them, when the Sabeans raided them and took them away—indeed they have killed the servants with the edge of the sword; and I along have escaped to tell you!"
Job 1:13-15

***While he was still speaking*, another also came and said, "The fire of God fell from heaven and burned up the sheep and the servants, and consumed them; and I alone have escaped to tell you!"**
Job 1:16

***While he was still speaking,* another also came and said, "The Chaldeans formed three bands, raided the camels and took them away, yes, and killed the servants with the edge of the sword; and I alone have escaped to tell you."**
Job 1:17

***While he was still speaking,* another Also came and said, "Your sons and daughters were eating and drinking wine in their oldest brother's house, and suddenly a great wind came from across the wilderness and struck the four corners of the house, and it fell on the young people, and they are dead; and I alone have escaped to tell you!"**
Job 1:18, 19

In just a matter of what may have been an hour, Job lost all of his children, his livestock (and source of income), and all but three of his employees. That's a great deal for a person to deal with in one year—having to deal with all of that in one hour is unfathomable! If these tragedies were not bad enough, not long after, the Lord allowed Satan to strike Job with a sickness in his body. And to top it all off, his wife, *Jobetta, was backsliding*!

However, at the end of Job's time of trouble he experienced blessings unequaled by what he enjoyed before his trouble began. It has been said that, *"Job received double for his trouble."* A comparison with Job's before-and-after-trouble life reveals how God did more than restore him:

(Before)

"...his possessions were seven thousand sheep, three thousand camels, five hundred yoke of oxen, five hundred female donkeys..."
Job 1:3

(After)

"And the Lord restored Job's losses when he prayed for his friends. Indeed the Lord gave Job twice as much as he had before.
Job 42:10

"...the Lord blessed the latter [after trouble] days of Job more than his beginning [before trouble days]; for he had fourteen thousand sheep, six thousand camels, one thousand yoke of oxen, and one thousand female donkeys."
Job 42:12

It's true. Job received *double for his trouble*! Despite his enemy's aim to forever rob him of everyone and everything of meaning in his life, the Lord made certain that at the end of trouble, Job ended on top! And this is one reason why we cannot become sinfully angry when enemies or adversities of any sort seem to get the best of us. God uses what appears to be the worst for us as a part of His plan to bless us and bring about His *best for us*!

God is so strong,
He wrings right out of wrong;
and brings the best of times
out of the worst of times.

After being delivered from the pit and sold as a slave into the house of Potiphar, Joseph was eventually given authority over all Potiphar owned, as well as his fellow servants. During this time of trouble Joseph would receive hands-on training in managing the affairs of Potiphar's house and overseeing people.

I'm certain that Joseph was honored by the trust and responsibility bestowed upon him, but he probably had no idea that God was using his season of trouble to train and prepare him for what the Lord had ultimately planned for him—a position greater than what he held with Potiphar.

After a while in Potiphar's house where things were going extremely well, Potiphar's wife falsely accused Joseph of sexually harassing her. The charge enraged Potiphar and caused him to have Joseph wrongfully imprisoned. Joseph was not aware of it at the time and probably felt let down by God; but as it turned out, that trouble signified the end of his training in Potiphar's house and moved him a step closer to living in God's best for him.

I will address this issue in greater detail in a later chapter, but sometimes we misunderstand the trouble the Lord says we ***"...shall have."*** I am convinced that this misunderstanding is because the word *trouble,* by nature, carries a negative connotation that doesn't allow Christians to realize that trouble often gives birth to good. To make this case, consider these two passages of Scripture:

And Joseph found
favor in [Potiphar's] sight, and he served him:
<u>and he made him overseer over his house,</u>
<u>and all that he had he put into his hand.</u>
Genesis 39:4

"[Aside from Potiphar]) There is none greater
in this house than I...."
Genesis 39:9

Notice next what Pharaoh would later say to Joseph after leaving Potiphar's house, spending some time in prison, and coming into God's plan for his life:

"You shall be over my house, and according to your word
shall all my people be ruled: only in the throne will I
be greater than you." And Pharaoh said unto Joseph,
"See, I have set thee over all the land of Egypt."
Genesis 41:40, 41

What is visible from Joseph's life is that the Lord allowed his brothers to trouble him because that trouble would ultimately lead him to Potiphar's house where Joseph would be trained on a *lesser level* to do the same things on a much *greater level* at a later time in Pharaoh's palace. By the time Joseph arrived at his purpose of serving under Pharaoh, he had already been trained and well learned in the area of assignment to which he would be appointed. But this could not have been the case had Joseph not encountered the trouble of the pit from his brothers, or the trouble of prison from Potiphar's wife which positioned him to be found by Pharaoh.

The point here is that God has purpose for the trouble He permits, and He uses our troublesome times to prepare us for greater times. After Joseph had become governor of Egypt, had been reunited with his family, and had forgiven his brothers, he made a statement that I believe captures every Christian's encounter with trouble—regardless of its type or point of origin. Following the death of Jacob, his father, and in response to his brothers' fear of revenge against them, Joseph offers the most powerful and telling words about the trouble they had caused him:

"But as for you, you meant evil against me, but God meant it [trouble] for good, in order to bring it about as it is, this day, to save many people alive."
Genesis 50:20

God always has a greater purpose for our trouble than what we are able to see or understand. God will either foil our enemies' plans against us, or use them to bless us. In either instance, we must continue to trust Him and be assured that whatever trouble we are experiencing, God is with us.

Yes, **"in the world you shall have trouble, but be of good cheer…"** God is using your trouble for your good!

Chapter 2
In the Time of Trouble

"In the time of trouble
He shall hide me in His pavilion…."
Psalm 27:5

There is a difference between trouble and *the thing* trouble seeks to accomplish. If this statement sounds strange, it is because we often see trouble as *the end of a thing* instead of a means by which a particular end is achieved. In other words, we sometimes give trouble credit for accomplishing the devastation that it seeks to accomplish even before devastation has actually occurred.

God uses our times of trouble to prepare us for our destiny. However, it is likewise true that Satan has his own aim and agenda for the trouble every Christian encounters. But what we as Christians must realize is that trouble and its intended agenda are not one and the same thing. Though related, there is a significant difference between the two. For example, the bark of a dog and the bite of a dog are not the same. The bark of the dog may suggest that a person is in trouble, but the bark does not automatically mean the person will be bitten.

There is a story about a young man who was walking down a busy street and heard a dog barking. Although he saw the dog was behind a tall fence, he still decided to cross the street. Upon crossing the busy street, he was struck by a car and suffered a broken leg. This accident happened because the young man automatically assumed that the *troubling* bark would lead to a painful bite, when in fact the bark was not capable of accomplishing what the young man thought it would accomplish.

I think we are sometimes like that. At the first sound of trouble, we believe the worst-case scenario will follow, and we make decisions that do us more harm than the trouble is capable of doing.

Many have experienced sickness and instantly assumed that illness would lead to death when it could actually lead to a greater quality of life. Many more people recover and live strong lives after sickness than those who actually die from their sickness. But the *worry* about the destiny of sickness can do more damage than the sickness itself. Whereas being sick can mean trouble, it is not an automatic death sentence because trouble does not always successfully complete its assignment.

Another example and one that many can identify with during these times, is the loss of a job. Losing a job can certainly be troublesome. However, losing a job does not necessarily mean that you are going to starve, be hungry, be homeless, or forever without employment. In fact, it is still true that God does not **"...forsake the righteous, nor allow his seed to beg for bread" (Psalm 37:25)**. Sometimes the loss of a job can actually be favorable because the job or the environment can sometimes be more harmful than helpful. As troubling as losing a job or having a failing business seems, neither guarantees the results we sometimes dread. The end of a job is not the end of the road; neither does a failed business mean that we have failed in life. Someone insightfully said,

"A curve in the road is not the end of the road unless we fail to make the turn." In the same way, a curve in the road of our employment or business endeavors is not the end of the road. In fact, failing in a business or losing a job have often been the events in life that have catapulted people into greatness from the platform of mediocrity. Think about it—Joseph lost his job in Potiphar's house because Potiphar's wife told an untruth about him. Her lie, which was allowed by God, led Joseph away from the lesser to the greater.

I have learned that the trouble which appears to destine us for the worst is actually steering us toward the best—a "*best*" to which we would not be led were it not for trouble. As crazy as it may sound, the trouble we think is *terribly harmful* often turns out to be *tremendously helpful.* More than we are able to realize when the chaos of trouble clouds our mind, that which is *better* follows that which is *bad.*

The point is, there is a difference between trouble and the thing trouble seeks to accomplish. Although acts of misfortune occur, it does not automatically mean the absolute worst is destined to follow. Our ability to understand this truth will help us defeat the fear that accompanies troubling news—fear that is capable of doing more harm than the trouble itself.

If you are on a road that has taken you to trouble of any kind, know that that trouble isn't necessarily the end of the road. Other roads lead to an even better, more lucrative, and less stressful life. Trust God, and make the turn!

**Trouble is not sovereign.
It is limited in its ability. It can
only do what the Lord allows it to
do. And oftentimes God *makes*
trouble do His children good.**

Many Bible characters came to learn the truth about trouble's limited ability. Joseph is one such person. Remember, the story that began in Genesis 37 revealed that Joseph's brothers "hated" him, and out of their hatred toward him, the majority of them wanted to kill him.

NEWS FLASH: Any time someone desires to, or is trying to kill you...*YOU ARE IN TROUBLE!* But that does not mean that trouble is going to have its way:

"Now when they saw him afar off, even before he came near them, they conspired against him to kill him. Then they said to one another, 'Look, this dreamer is coming! Come therefore, let us now kill him and cast him into some pit; and we shall say, "Some wild beast has devoured him." We shall see what will become of his dreams!' But Reuben heard it, and he delivered him out of their hands, and said, 'Let us not kill him.'"
Genesis 37:18-21

According to these verses, Joseph was in trouble, and trouble's aim was to kill him. Nevertheless, there was a difference between what trouble *intended* to do and what trouble was *permitted* to do by God.

In the life of the Christian, every intention from every source needs God's cooperation in order to be successful. Early in the book of Job, Satan had to seek permission from God to trouble Job. Although God granted Satan permission to trouble Job, God restricted trouble from killing Job. The trouble Satan caused Job did not accomplish what the devil had in mind; instead, trouble accomplished what God had in mind—the increase of Job's life. Accordingly, regardless of trouble's intention, without God's permission, the best trouble can do is fail at accomplishing its objective—whatever that may be—and accomplish the good will of God—whatever *that* may be.

As with Job, trouble's goal was to kill Joseph, but God did not grant trouble *permission* to do so. Instead, God raised up someone to thwart trouble's cruel intentions, and God used trouble to accomplish His own plan for Joseph's life:

"And Reuben said to them, 'Shed no blood, but cast him into this pit which is in the wilderness, and do not lay a hand on him"—that he might deliver him out of their hands, and bring him back to his father.'"
Genesis 37:22

Evil purposes cannot be accomplished without God's permission. Whatever evil God permits He uses to prosper us according to what He has planned for us.

Again, trouble sought to kill Joseph, but God did not authorize trouble to do what it set out to do. Trouble could only place Joseph in a pit from where he would be delivered to embark on the tremendous plan God had for his life. This example teaches us that whatever trouble *does* accomplish is permitted by God and is being used to bring to pass His great plan for our life.

Such was the case with Joseph. Remember, in a dream God had shown him a plan for his life that involved his brothers bowing before him. The story goes on to reveal that God's plan for Joseph's life was for him to become the governor over Egypt and to save many lives during a famine that would plague the entire region. The trouble that was intended to do Joseph *harm* ended up doing him *good,* and led to the Lord's desire for his life coming to pass.

Joseph was not the only Bible character who came to understand that trouble could not automatically accomplish the destruction it sought to accomplish; David understood this reality as well. David may have faced more trouble than any other person in the Bible. In fact, he may have been in more trouble than all the other Bible characters combined! Okay… maybe not…but David was seemingly *always* in trouble. For many reasons, many people wanted a piece of David. They didn't just want to injure him; they wanted to kill him! At one point, even the men who trusted and followed him talked about stoning him. *(You know your life is full of trouble when even your closest friends are talking about taking your life!)*

Early in his life, no one caused David more trouble than Saul, Israel's first king, a man who was driven by envy to put David to death. David was number one on King Saul's *Top Ten List of People to Kill Before I Die.* In fact, David occupied all ten spots. Saul was so obsessed with killing David that his plan *after* killing David, was to kill David.

Although David was in trouble with King Saul, others, and even entire armies, none of them could kill him. They could not kill him because there is a difference between the trouble they caused him and what God allowed trouble to succeed in doing. They caused David trouble, but the trouble they *caused him* could not *kill him* as intended. Just because trouble intends to accomplish something, trouble has no guarantee of success. Instead, what trouble accidentally succeeds at is playing a role in the fulfillment of God's good for our life.

David's understanding of this truth was expressed when he wrote Psalm 27:5, which says, **"In the time of trouble He shall hide me…."**

Here's a question: if the presence of David's trouble automatically meant his destruction, from what was God *hiding* or protecting David? If the presence of trouble automatically meant destruction, it would have been pointless to try to help

David by hiding him. God was not hiding David *from* trouble itself because, by David's own admission, he was already "in" trouble. **"In the time of trouble..."** means that David was already in the middle of difficulty. Therefore, God must have been hiding him from something else. That *something else* was the *destruction* trouble sought to accomplish in David's life. More specifically, that something else was his *death* at the hands of the army that had risen up against David.

"Though an host should encamp against me,
my heart shall not fear."
Psalm 27:3

Although David was confronted by an innumerable quantity of enemy troops (signifying the seriousness of his trouble), he did not equate their presence with his demise. He knew he was in trouble, but he also knew that trouble's ability was limited and therefore not guaranteed to succeed. David also knew God would shelter him from the death trouble came to bring or intended to accomplish. In **Psalm 59:16**, he expressed this knowledge:

"But I will sing of Your power;
Yes, I will sing aloud of Your mercy
in the morning; for You have been my
defense and refuge in the day of my trouble."

Again, although David was already in trouble, he spoke of God being his **"defense...in the day of [his] trouble."** You may ask, *"If David was already in trouble, from what was God defending him?"* Good question. Here's the answer: God obviously was not protecting David from trouble altogether because David was already in trouble. Therefore, God *must have* been protecting him from trouble's ultimate aim, whatever it was!

The experiences and statements of David clearly communicate to us that God will allow us to encounter trouble, but He will also defend us from trouble's plan to do us in completely.

The trouble enemies cause us unintentionally works to help us.

The difference between trouble and the total destruction it seeks to accomplish can probably be seen in each of our lives. Think back to a time when you received troubling news. What probably followed in your mind was the worst possible outcome of that news. However, think about the times you received troubling news and assumed the worst would come of it, only to look back after trouble had passed to notice that it did not turn out as badly as you thought it would.

This means that the trouble you encountered and what that trouble accomplished by the time the dust settled and the smoke cleared were entirely different. It also means that although God allowed the trouble to come, He did *not* allow it to be accompanied by the carry-on luggage of total destruction. Instead, God hid you from serious harm, and He defended you from the damage trouble intended.

I don't know if any single passage better speaks of this protection in a time of trouble than **Isaiah 54:17** wherein God says, **"No weapon that is formed against you shall prosper…."** Typically, when one forms a weapon against another person, it includes plans for severe injury. It is therefore fair to say that the person against whom the weapon has been formed is in trouble. Nevertheless, God is speaking in this verse from an *after-the-weapon-has-already-been-formed* standpoint, and He declares that though the weapon that has been designed to bring about destruction, it will not have the success it seeks or was created to accomplish.

God did not prevent the weapon from being formed, but He does promise to prevent it from prospering. In the same way, God permits trouble to be formed against us, but He protects us from the ultimate aim and desire of trouble so that it cannot prosper.

God permits, but He also protects, so that what He permits cannot prosper beyond accomplishing *His* good, acceptable, and perfect purpose.

Again, it is important to understand trouble's limited ability, because without this understanding, there is a tendency for us to live in fear of the worst-case scenario. And when this happens, the *fear* of the worst occurring often does more damage to us than the actual outcome of the trouble. Automatically fearing the worst outcome when we receive troubling news is like being afraid of the bark of that old bad-breath dog. Dog barks can trouble us, but they do not mean serious harm is on the horizon.

In 1933 during his inaugural address, President Franklin D. Roosevelt offered these words in the ear of a country that was experiencing a very difficult time:

> *"So first of all, let me assert my firm belief, that the only thing we have to fear is, fear itself. Nameless, unreasoning, unjustified terror which paralyzes needed efforts to convert retreat into advance."*

How powerful, poignant, and presently applicable is the reality of these words for the times with which we are faced! We need not fear the outcome of our trouble because our *fear* of the worst outcome will not only paralyze and prevent our making progress; it will do us more harm than the actual outcome of the trouble. The fear of a certain outcome can cause us to do things and even make hasty decisions that ultimately do more damage than trouble's worst-case scenario.

I remember the time when I was about seven years old growing up in the Ickes housing projects on Chicago's south side. My older brother Terry (who is nearly six years my senior) was talking to a young girl who I assume was about his age. Being as mischievous as the average boy my age would be, I decided to pick up a rock and throw it at the girl in a playful sort of way. *(I chose not to throw it at my older brother for the obvious reason of avoiding the certainty of physical trauma being inflicted upon my small and undeveloped body.)*

When I threw the rock at her, to my astonishment, she caught it! And seemingly in the same motion, she acted as if she was going to throw it back. At that very moment fear gripped me, causing the playful grin on my face to turn immediately into a look of terror! In *fear* I turned to run away from what I thought was sure to be a boomerang-rock coming in my direction from a 13-year-old girl who could catch rocks and probably throw them with greater velocity than the 7-year-old kid who had thrown it to begin with.

As I turned to make my getaway—my great escape—I must have forgotten my bearings and that there was a *big tree* only two or three feet behind me. When I turned to run, I ran face first into that *big tree! (Ouch!)* Instantly everything went black, and I was knocked out cold! Right then and there I learned where cartoonists envision the images of their characters seeing stars when they are hit by something. I felt like the Hubble Space Telescope because I saw stars of all shapes and sizes! If you have never run face first into a tree, trust me, it's an overrated experience!

Later that day after coming home from the hospital, and the local branch office of the Astronomers of America, I remember seeing my face in a mirror. It looked as if someone had placed half of a pomegranate over the place where my right eye was! The rest of my face was fine, but my eye was swollen shut! I think I started to cry—from the other eye!

The girl who caught the rock never actually threw it back. She merely pretended she was going to throw it. However, out of *fear,* I turned to run. And it was my *fear* that led to an injury the rock could not have caused because it was still in her hand.

My point is that sometimes our fear can do us more harm than the trouble of which we are fearful. Like that rock—regardless from where it comes—trouble is still in the hand and under the authority of God, and it can only accomplish what He permits it to accomplish. Therefore, we need not be fearful, because whatever the Lord allows or licenses, He uses it to perform something other than what it was formed for.

(How dare she catch my rock! And who put that stupid tree behind me when I wasn't looking?!)

In fourth verse of Psalm 23, David wrote:

"Yea, though I walk through the valley of the <u>shadow</u> of death, I will <u>fear</u> no evil."

In this verse David is speaking of another time he was in trouble. But again his words draw a definite line between trouble and what it sought to accomplish. In this famed psalm, David likens trouble to a "shadow." We understand shadows to be images of things that have intercepted or obstructed the flow of light. Although shadows can project intimidating images, shadows are not that image which they project. Therefore, no matter how legitimately threatening the actual *thing* is, its shadow does not carry the same harmful ability. David understood this about *things* and their *shadow.* And in recognizing this difference, he knew the *trouble* was the thing; but the threat of its killing him was merely a *shadow.* This realization prompted him to sing that he would not fearfully assume the worst just because he was in trouble.

This is one reason why the devil wants to cause us to fear and to keep us in fear. He knows that fear causes a trouble all its own—a trouble that may not even be related to the *thing* that caused the fear. And this is also one reason why **"God has not given us the spirit of fear" (2 Timothy 1:7).** He doesn't want us to be harmed, hindered, or held back by fear. Instead, God wants us to go forth in faith, and in confident expectation of His help and deliverance—*especially* in the time of trouble!

If we automatically assume the worst when trouble visits, *fear* may do to us what *shadows* cannot.

"Be not afraid of sudden fear...."
Proverbs 3:25

This portion of Scripture is very interesting and telling because it indicates to us that fear itself is capable of causing us harm. God would not warn us to **"not be *afraid of... fear*"** if being afraid of fear was of no consequence. God tells us not to be afraid of fear because if we allow it to exist within our mind, fear can, in fact, have a damaging effect on us in a number of ways.

Not only can fear cause us to make bad, hasty decisions and have to deal with the trouble they produce, but fear also causes us to worry. And worry that lives long enough produces stress, and stress has been linked to high blood pressure, anxiety attacks, insomnia, and other sicknesses, diseases, emotional dysfunctions, and even death in some instances.

We should strive to be free of fear in every regard. But we should particularly not fear the outcome of trouble—even before we know what that outcome will be. If we do *(I stress),* the fear of what trouble *will bring* can do us more harm than what the trouble *does bring*. Instead, we must adopt the helpful mind-set that is expressed by the words of David, who was no stranger to trouble. We must believe of God that **"in a time of trouble"** He will hide us from whatever trouble's ultimate intention is. And He will.

The Lord can hide us from the ultimate aim of trouble, but we have to fend off the fear trouble brings.

Other good examples of God hiding His people **"in the time of trouble"** and from trouble's intentions include the young Hebrew friends: Shadrach, Meshach, Abed-nego, and Daniel.

You may or may not be familiar with the story of Shadrach, Meshach, and Abed-nego in the book of Daniel and how they refused to bow down to worship an idol created by Nebuchadnezzar, the king of Babylon. Their refusal to bow down to a false god was born out of their commitment to the true and living God. However, their commitment to the true and living God would land them in the middle of a "*burning fiery furnace.*"

The king was so angry at their unwillingness to worship his god that before he ordered them to be thrown into the furnace, he commanded his servants to make it seven times hotter than necessary. In fact, the fire was so hot that it killed the king's servants who threw them in. *(Talk about hazardous duty!)* Still, Shadrach, Meshach, and Abed-nego found themselves in trouble in the form of the furnace they had hoped to avoid.

The following passage reveals what happens after the boys were already in the trouble that was undoubtedly purposed to destroy them:

"Then King Nebuchadnezzar was astonished; and he rose in haste and spoke, saying to his counselors, 'Did we not cast three men bound into the midst of the fire?' They answered and said to the king, 'True, O king.' 'Look!' he answered, 'I see four men loose, walking in the midst of the fire; and they are not hurt, and the form of the fourth is like the Son of God.' Then Nebuchadnezzar went near the mouth of the burning fiery furnace and spoke, saying, 'Shadrach, Meshach, and Abed-Nego, servants of the Most High God, come out, and come here.'
Then Shadrach, Meshach, and Abed-Nego came from the midst of the fire.
27 And the satraps, administrators, governors, and the king's counselors gathered together, and they saw these men on whose bodies the fire had no power; the hair of their head was not singed nor were their garments affected, and the smell of fire was not on them."
Daniel 3:24-27

Here is the point: there's no question about the fact that these young men were in serious trouble. Neither is there any question about the fact that trouble's intention was to kill them. However, in being delivered by the **"Son of God,"** we plainly see that trouble was not *able to achieve* what it was *aiming to achieve*. Not only was trouble unable to put them to death, it had no effect on them whatsoever—no first-, second-, or third-degree burns; their clothes did not catch fire; they did not smell of smoke; and neither was their hair burnt! This was all because God did something spiritually special in protecting them—even after they were in trouble, and He demonstrated His power and authority over trouble and its wicked intentions.

Aside from the power of God, it is impossible for any person to be in a 2800° fire and come out alive and uninjured.

But this is the point: we can find ourselves in a type of trouble that by all accounts should have a devastating effect on us; but while God permits trouble to come, He causes it to leave without accomplishing its goal. Instead, trouble is only allowed to accomplish that which God uses to help, develop, and bless us.

Trouble does not have the authority to guarantee its agenda; neither does it have the omnipotence to perform it.

Daniel, another child of God, found himself in a similar situation for refusing not to pray for 30 days. His refusal placed him in violation of a recently passed decree that carried the penalty of being thrown into a den of lions—obviously a death sentence. Daniel defied the decree, prayed to God anyway, and soon afterward found himself in the midst of a few hungry lions. I think it's fair to assume that Daniel was in *trouble*.

But what followed with Daniel is what followed with his three friends; the Lord showed up to help him:

"Then the king arose very early in the morning and went in haste to the den of lions. And when he came to the den, he cried out with a lamenting voice to Daniel. The king spoke, saying to Daniel, 'Daniel, servant of the living God, has your God, whom you serve continually, been able to deliver you from the lions?' "

"Then Daniel said to the king, 'O king, live forever! My God sent His angel and shut the lions' mouths, so that they have not hurt me, because I was found innocent before Him; and also, O king, I have done no wrong before you.'

Now the king was exceedingly glad for him, and commanded that they should take Daniel up out of the den. So Daniel was taken up out of the den, and no injury whatsoever was found on him, because he believed in his God."
Daniel 6:19-23

Notice four powerful lessons in this passage:

1) Although Daniel was in trouble, that trouble did not do what it was designed to do. In fact, as in the case with Shadrach, Meshach, and Abed-nego, the trouble in which Daniel found himself did not harm him at all.

2) Daniel was delivered from trouble's intention because **"...he believed in his God."** Daniel expected God to deliver him from his time of trouble without allowing trouble to fulfill its agenda. What he believed about God not only delivered him, but it also allowed him to live without fear. When Daniel was confronted with compromising in an area of his relationship with God, his confidence in God kept him from compromising, even when the consequences were supposed to be death.

3) After his trouble was prevented from accomplishing its purpose, and was defeated, Daniel was promoted in the kingdom. Daniel's situation is similar to that of his friends in that they were also increased.

"[God] delivers and rescues; and He works signs and wonders in heaven and on earth, Who has delivered Daniel from the power of the lions. So this Daniel <u>prospered</u> in the reign of Darius and in the reign of Cyrus the Persian."
Daniel 6:27-28

"Then the king <u>promoted</u> Shadrach, Meshach, and Abed-nego in the province of Babylon."
Daniel 3:30

The fulfillment of God's planned good is the common occurrence at the end of trouble's season. Remember, Job received double for his trouble; Joseph possessed the promise God had shown him in a dream; David became king of Israel as Samuel had prophesied; Shadrach, Meshach, and Abed-nego were all promoted; and Daniel prospered.

4) If Daniel, Shadrach, Meshach, and Abed-nego had been fearful of the outcome of their trouble, their fear would have been an obstacle to the faith they had in God. They would have never lived to experience the Lord's delivering power, nor the blessings that awaited their arrival on the other side of their trouble.

In the time of trouble,
faith and fear duel.
The winner determines what we expect,
and what we expect
determines what we experience.

It is important to understand that the blessings these men encountered after their season of trouble ended had already been prepared for them by God—even before their season of trouble began. God had already promised, prophesied, and planned to bless them in the way they were eventually blessed. They only had to trustfully weather the storm of troublesome times in order to possess the blessing. Such is the case with us.

"...eye has not seen, nor ear heard, nor has entered into the heart of man the things God *has prepared* for [all of] those who love Him."
1 Corinthians 2:9

Your trouble serves as a sign that God has prepared great things for you, and He has only permitted trouble to prepare you for those great things.

The undeniable reality for us as believers is that there is a difference between trouble and the thing or the *things* trouble seeks to accomplish. Throughout history, situations that have appeared to hold the worst for God's people have been turned around and used by God to bring about His best for them! It doesn't matter what we go through as Christians because God is not a respecter of persons; rather, He is a respecter of principles, patterns, and the plans He has for us. Just as He protected, delivered, and promoted His people in their time of trouble in times past, we can expect God to follow past patterns in fulfilling the future plans He has for you and me because He changes not. God is the same, yesterday, today, and forever!

Hang in there. You can do it! The Lord will help you because He loves you, and He has promised to never leave or forsake you. Don't give up and don't get weary in well doing because there is before you a season that holds a harvest of blessings that is yours to have when your season of trouble comes to a close.

Be encouraged. God is going to bless you too!

Chapter 3
Trouble:
A Weapon or a Tool?

"No weapon formed against you shall prosper…."
Isaiah 54:17

You may have heard it said that this verse does *not* say weapons would not be formed against us, suggesting instead (if not actually indicating), that weapons will be formed against us despite our being children of God. In fact, some weapons are formed against *because* we are children of God and because we are on assignment for God. As we have already seen this reality, we thereby know it comes with the territory.

However, the promise is that although weapons formed against us are allowed by God, these same weapons will not be permitted by God to prosper or to succeed in their purpose against us. One of the remarkable reasons for this is seen in verse 16, a verse that is often (if not always) overshadowed by the promise of verse 17. In verse 16 God says,

"Behold, I have created the blacksmith who blows the coals in the fire, who brings forth an instrument for his work; and I have created the spoiler to destroy."
Isaiah 54:16

In this verse, God reminds us that He is the Boss! Because God is the Creator of everything and everyone, He is also Lord, Master and Controller of everything and everyone—including "**the spoiler**" who forms the weapons that are designed to destroy us. God is saying, "**no weapon formed against (us) shall prosper**" because He has power and authority over those who formed the weapon, *and* the weapon itself. God will not permit it to prosper or even accomplish its purpose for being created.

Trouble can be either a weapon or a tool depending on who is using it and what it ultimately accomplishes. Most people understand that weapons are designed to cause harm of some sort or even to destroy. Tools, on the other hand are used to build, repair or to rebuild. Whether trouble is a weapon or a tool depends on whose hand holds the trouble. In the hand of Satan, every Christian's adversary, trouble is a *weapon* he uses in an effort to "**steal, kill, and destroy.**" But the same *trouble* in the hand of God is a *tool*—a tool He uses to build up His child in preparation for the great plan He has for his life, or to build bridges that lead the Christian to His purpose, or that plan.

During a time of trouble, the Lord said to the children of Israel who were being held in captivity to the Babylonians:

"I know the plans I have for you… plans of good and not of evil; to bring you a hope and a future."
Jeremiah 29:11

While the children of Israel were in trouble, God was speaking of the plans He had for their future—good plans that would accomplish great things. Even though they were in trouble, God was using their trouble to fulfill His plans for their life. The same is true with you and me and whatever trouble we encounter.

As Christians, we can sometimes underestimate, undervalue or even be unaware of the significant role trouble plays in the plans of God for our life. All throughout the Bible trouble is used either as a weapon in the hand of the enemy or as a tool in the hand of God. God takes the trouble the enemy intended as a weapon and *makes* it into a tool.

"He shall judge between the nations;
and rebuke many people; they shall
beat their swords into plowshares,
and their spears into pruning hooks...."
Isaiah 2:4

Obviously *swords* and *spears* are weapons, and *plowshares* and *pruning hooks* are tools. Isaiah the prophet was saying that a time was coming when warring would cease, and the weapons people once used to hurt would be turned into tools that would be used to help. The point is, if man can take *weapons* that damage and destroy and mold them into *tools* that restore and rebuild, surely God can do the same with the weapons that are formed against His children. And He does.

Just as little becomes much
in the hand of the Master;
weapons become tools.

As a tool, God also uses troublesome times to accomplish a work *in us* and through us that easy-going times are not capable of accomplishing. A spiritual strengthening and *toughness* is created by overcoming the trouble of difficult times that cannot be created by anything else.

This *toughness* and *spiritual strengthening* are necessities that prepare us to conquer and to overcome the obstacles that await us on the path toward a fulfilled purpose. Some obstacles are smaller forms of trouble that God allows us to encounter at one stage in life. From these obstacles we gain wisdom, experience and strength so that we can conquer a greater trouble during a later stage of life—a trouble that stands between who we are now and *who* God has destined us to be.

A good example of this spiritual strengthening is seen in the popular story of David and Goliath, which is found in 1 Samuel 17.

And Saul said to David, You are not able to go against this Philistine to fight with him; for you are a youth, and he a man of war from his youth." But David said to Saul, "Your servant used to keep his father's sheep, and when a lion or a bear came and took a lamb out of the flock, I went out after it and struck it, and delivered the lamb from its mouth; and when it arose against me, I caught it by its beard, and struck and killed it. Your servant has killed both lion and bear; and this uncircumcised Philistine will be like one of them, seeing he has defied the armies of the living God." Moreover David said, "The LORD, who delivered me from the paw of the lion and from the paw of the bear, He will deliver me from the hand of this Philistine."

1 Samuel 17:33-37

"Therefore David ran and stood over the Philistine, took his sword and drew it out of its sheath and killed him, and cut off his head with it."
1 Samuel 17:51

This story of great triumph teaches that overcoming trouble in one stage of life helps the Christian to conquer greater trouble in a later stage of life and positions the Christian for God's ultimate plan.

God allowed David to encounter trouble in the form of a lion and a bear at one stage in his life (and helped him overcome them) so that he would be confidently equipped to conquer the giant later in his life. Had God not permitted David to encounter the lion or the bear, David would not have been equipped with the confidence he needed to face and defeat Goliath, who stood between the future king and his destiny. Conquering the giant helped position David to become the next king of Israel; however, it was overcoming the trouble of the lion and bear that *prepared* him to conquer the giant!

Overcome obstacles create, not an outward, physical strength, but an inward strength, of character. That inward strength of character is called *confidence* which enables the Christian to confront and conquer greater challenges later in life. David may not have been capable of overcoming these challenges without first having been battle-tested and strengthened and made ready for war.

Let me encourage you by telling you that if you are going through a difficult time at the present, there are *at least* three reasons why you can overcome it:

1) As with David, previous victories have prepared you to be victorious in this situation.

2) God would not permit you to be in a battle you are incapable of winning or that He has not planned to win for you.

"Then all this assembly shall know
that the Lord does not save with
sword and spear; for the battle
is the Lord's, and He will
give you into our hands."
1 Samuel 17:47

It's good to know and to be reminded that *our battles* are really not *our battles*—even though we are in them. According to this verse, *our battles* are really God's battles. We should be glad about this fact because it means the Lord is on our side in battle and because the Lord has *never* lost a battle! He is, **"the Lord strong and mighty, the Lord mighty [champion] in battle."**

3) God promises you the victory.

"Now thanks be to God
Who always leads us
in triumph in Christ...."
2 Corinthians 2:14

This passage promises that God, the Champion of every battle He has ever entered and exited, will *cause* you to be triumphant over your trouble.

God leading us to triumph means that He is battling with us in our trouble because He cannot *lead us* unless He is *with us*. And God *leading* us means He is going before us to make a path not only to victory, but also to destiny!

It is important to remember that God never permits His children to experience more than they can handle. If you are experiencing a difficult time, you can handle it. You can handle it because you are not in the battle by yourself. And as

God did for Joseph, David and dozens of others, He will also bring you through your battle victoriously.

The same trouble the devil is using for a weapon against you, God is using as a tool to build an overcoming character in you that toughens and strengthens you to take hold of what He has promised you.

Overcome trouble creates a confidence that enables the Christian to confront and conquer greater challenges on the path to fulfilled purpose, prophesies, and promises.

We saw God use trouble in Joseph's life in the same way. Joseph found himself in trouble with his envious brothers who hated him. Joseph was hated because he was his father's favorite son—and maybe also because he was somewhat of a tattletale, goody-two-shoes. *(Being goody-two-shoes is bad enough, but to be a tattletale on top of that is just completely unacceptable! I think little "Joey" was asking for trouble!)*

Out of their hatred, nine of his eleven brothers wanted to kill him. But thanks to Reuben, they would instead settle for a lesser crime of selling Joseph into slavery.

Psalm 105:18 says, **"They hurt [Joseph's] feet with fetters and he was laid in irons."** The fact that Joseph was "in" chains clearly relays that he was *in trouble*. In addition to being in trouble when one is in a burning fiery furnace, or in a den of lions, anytime anyone finds himself in chains, be it justly or unjustly, he is also *in trouble*.

But before his trouble began, Joseph had been given a glimpse of God's plan through two prophetic dreams for his life. A part of preparing Joseph for the plan God had for him was the trouble that confronted him. The trouble he encountered from his brothers and others along the way prepared Joseph to be the person God had shown him in the dreams.

After coming into his destiny, Joseph came also into the understanding that the trouble he encountered was a tool in the hand of God—a tool that helped shape him into what he needed to be in order to function effectively in his God-given purpose. Joseph's knowledge of this truth is revealed when he stated to his brothers of the trouble they caused him…

"…you meant it [trouble] evil against me,
but God meant it [the same trouble] for good,
in order to bring it about as it is this day,
to save may people…."
Genesis 50:20

From the illustration of Joseph, we find yet again how the trouble we encounter is allowed by God, but it is ultimately purposed to be a blessing for us and to others as well. Most of the men and women of God who have blessed us a great deal spiritually have gone through a tremendous amount of trouble—trouble that has helped them become who they are in God and is helping us become who we are in God.

Without question, Genesis 50:20 offers one of the most profound insights to trouble in the entire Bible because it undeniably reveals that the *same* trouble with which enemies intend to *do us in*, God uses to *do us good*!

Again, **Isaiah 54:17** says, **"No weapon** [trouble of any sort] **formed against you shall prosper…."** The reason behind this promise is that, *before* trouble can fulfill its purpose of evil, God intercepts it and uses it for our good.

"All things [including trouble of all sorts] **work**
together for good to them that love God and are the
called according to His purpose."
Romans 8:28

The point is that trouble is a weapon in the hand of the enemy that God uses as a tool. A tool that shapes us, molds us, and makes us into the mighty (champion) men and women He created, called and destined for us to be!

Trouble that seeks to do us in ultimately does us good!

It is important that we are able to see trouble as God sees it and not as the enemy would have us see it. Trouble in and of itself can certainly be discouraging, and the enemy uses it to distract us from focusing on God, the things of God, the ways of God, and the promises of God. However, realizing and *remembering* that God uses trouble to accomplish positive results in us and for us can take some of the sting out of the trouble we're experiencing.

It's like the pain that follows exercising our muscles. We don't like it, but that pain is easier to accept because we know it's accomplishing something good with us. It is the same with the trouble. We don't like experiencing trouble because it doesn't feel good, but if we hang in there, that same trouble will undoubtedly lead to something good. Remember, God *makes* all things, including trouble, work together for our good!

James, the younger half-brother of Jesus wrote:

**My brethren, count it all joy when you fall into [encounter] various trials knowing that the testing of your faith produces patience.
James 1:2, 3**

The subject of patience will be addressed more extensively in a later chapter, but notice that James 1:3 says that trouble "**produces patience.**" Throughout the Bible, we are taught that patience is a good thing. In fact, in **Galatians 5:22** the

Bible says that patience is one of the fruit of the Spirit; therefore, it *must* be a good thing because all fruit is good—all fruit except tomatoes!

(Now don't get me wrong, I love tomatoes—just not as fruit! Somebody surely got that wrong! Having seeds and growing on a vine should not be the criteria for being classified as fruit. Taste should be a big part of the classification process. If taste were a criterion for being classified as fruit, tomatoes would not make the cut because they definitely taste like a vegetable! Just as normal people don't slice bananas and put them on burgers, we don't slice tomatoes and put them in cereal!)

The point is that trouble produces the spiritual fruit of patience which plays a tremendous role in our living in and possessing the good God has planned. Be it the good of being used by God to help other people or the good of being personally blessed by Him; the times of trouble we patiently endure are followed by the good God has ordained.

Anytime God allows something that creates something else, He uses that "something else" to lead us to things for which we've prayed or things He has planned for us. Listen to this:

> **But let patience** [the good thing created by trouble] **have its perfect work, that you may be perfect and complete, <u>lacking nothing.</u>**
> **James 1:4**

Notice that the good end of "lacking nothing" begins with trouble; which as a tool creates or builds patience. It is appropriate to say that without trouble creating patience we would be left lacking many of the great things God has in store for us.

Seeing trouble in this light allows us to know that we do not serve a purposeless God Who randomly allows trouble without using it for our good. Instead, we serve a God Who exercises His power, authority and lordship over adversities and uses them as tools to build us and our lives into that which brings pleasure to both Him and us!

Trouble leads us to being left without lack.

Not only does trouble create intangibles *inside of us* like patience, trouble also creates tangibles *outside of us* like opportunities.

I said in chapter 1, losing a job or failing at a business is not the end of the road as far as being successful is concerned. This is because, as you may have heard it said, "*When one door closes, another one opens.*" The *other* door that opens is the opportunity that has been created outside of us by the trouble of a job loss or a failed business.

When Joseph's brothers took him from his home and sold him into slavery, that trouble provided him with the opportunity to learn some lessons in Potiphar's house—things he would ultimately need to be successful in serving Pharaoh as governor over Egypt. But it was the act of seeming misfortune that provided Joseph with the new opportunity the opportunity that escorted him to his destiny.

When the devil is up to something bad through trouble, God, through the same trouble, is up to something good! And because God is *so much more* powerful than the devil and anything he can throw at us, God takes every negative thing, and every act of trouble, and by His power He *makes* them turn out for our betterment!

This is exactly what is meant in **Romans 8:28** where the apostle Paul wrote:

"And we <u>know</u> that all things [including trouble] work together for <u>good</u> to those who love God, to those who are the called according to His purpose."

There are some great points of which to take note in this verse. The first is, again, God has so much power He takes and makes trouble bless us regardless of what its original intention may have been—or the purpose for which it was *formed*.

The second point is that God is Lord of all, meaning He is Master over everything and everyone. And as Master, He is in control of all things, and everything is servant to Him—either by choice or by His sovereign will. This is relevant to the verse because the word ***"work"*** also means to *serve*. It doesn't matter how tough it is or appears to be, our trouble is a servant of our God. And since trouble works for God, God uses trouble to do us good. Our Lord has so much power He can literally take the worst of things and *make* the best of things come out of them. He takes our time of trouble and *commands* it to work toward blessing us! And because He is Lord of all, trouble *must* obey Him!

What the devil designs for our detriment, God uses for our betterment.

From verse 31 of this same eighth chapter of Romans, consider these words from the apostle Paul:

"If God is for us, who can be against us?"

This rhetorical question communicates to us that no one or no thing has more power than God. And because the omnipotent God is on our side, pulling for our good, no one or no thing can keep Him from using trouble to bless us and fulfill His good desire for us. The combination of God's power and love for us cannot be stopped from bringing to pass that which is best for us.

Listen to this:

Who shall separate us from the
love of Christ? Shall tribulation,
Or distress, or persecutions, or famine,
Or nakedness, or peril, or sword?
As it is written: "For Your sake we are
killed all day long; we are accounted
As sheep for the slaughter." Yet in
all these things we are more than
conquerors through Him Who loved us.
Romans 8:35-37

This passage makes it plain that there isn't anything that can come between us and the love God has for us. And it is out of God's love for us that He has created a plan of good for us to be blessed by Him and a purpose for us to be a blessing to others.

Trouble, the Tool of Blessing

The trouble we encounter also creates sensitivity in us toward others who experience trouble of any sort. Our trouble creates a sensitivity that not only enables us to identify with people in their time of trouble, but a sensitivity that also better equips us to minister and help them through that time.

In **2 Corinthians 1:3** and **4** the beautifully spoken words of Paul expresses this very truth:

"Blessed be the God and Father of our Lord
Jesus Christ, the Father of mercies and God of all
comfort, Who comforts us in all our tribulation,
that we may be able to comfort those who are in
any trouble, with the comfort with which we
ourselves are comforted by God."

From this passage of Scripture, I learned years ago that God never does anything for us that is *only* for us. Whatever God does or has done for us is purposed to be a blessing at some point for other people as well. We find this, "*not-for-us-only*" principle at work also in our salvation. In **Matthew 4:19** Jesus said to Peter and his brother Andrew: **"Follow Me, and I will make you fishers of men."**

"**Follow Me**" was a call or an invitation to salvation, while the "...**make you fishers of men**" statement tells us that the plan of God was not to save them for their sakes *only*, but to save them and use them to lead others to salvation also.

It is in this spirit and context that Paul was inspired to write:

> **"God...<u>comforts us</u> in all of our tribulation [trouble], <u>so that we may be able to comfort those [others] who are in any trouble</u>, <u>with</u> the [same] comfort which we ourselves are comforted by God."**
> **2 Corinthians 1:3, 4**

The point is that the trouble we encounter in which God comforts us, helps us through, and ultimately delivers us from, creates sensitivity in us toward others who are experiencing trouble. And it is that *created sensitivity* that God uses as a tool to help bless, and encourage others in *their* time of trouble—just as the Lord did for us in *our* time of trouble.

God never does anything for us that is *only* for us. Every good thing He does for us, He plans to withdraw from us to bless others.

When or if God has already delivered you from trouble of any sort, be a good steward of what He has done to help you by helping someone else who is experiencing difficulty.

If the Lord sent someone to bless you when you were in trouble, it is in keeping with the conscience of the kingdom to be a blessing to someone else experiencing trouble. It could be with a monetary blessing or some other sort of tangible blessing. Or it could simply be the blessing of a phone call or a few minutes of company.

Spending time with people who are experiencing days a difficulty is an extreme blessing to them because often family members and folks who were friends before their time of trouble no longer answer the phone or are nowhere to be found. But merely spending a little time with someone and occupying that person's mind with a time of fellowship will be a tremendous blessing.

If God sent someone to speak words of encouragement to you in your time of challenge, withdraw from those words and deposit them into the heart of someone else who needs to be encouraged. You may not think you have the right words to say, but you do. If you will respond to the Spirit and reach out to someone who is struggling, He will give you words to say that will bless them. They may be words that someone spoke to you during your difficult time that proved to be true, or they may be words from your own experience of what God is doing or will do.

Don't allow the fear of not knowing what to say keep you from encouraging someone. You will know what to say because the Spirit of God will make certain of it.

Also be careful not to allow your time of trouble to render you insensitive to others in their time of trouble. I've learned that even during our own time of trouble, the Lord will cause us to cross paths with people He wants to use us to encourage. There have been times when I was going through some things and someone would call me, or I would learn of something going on with some else. And as I would begin to minister and encourage the person with the words the Spirit of God gave me, in the *same moment* the Spirit of God would use those *same words* to minister to me! It was pow-er-ful! But it would not have happened, or been helpful if I had been only focused on myself in my time of trouble. In those situations I've learned, and been reminded that God rewards encouragement with encouragement. When we are in dire straits, if we encourage others, God will encourage us with the words He gives us to encourage others. That is one of the few times when there is an *immediate* reaping of what we're sowing.

Helping others despite the problems we may be experiencing personally will not only be a help for us, but it's also how the Word of God teaches us to be.

Let each of you look out not only
for his own interests, but also
for the interests of others.
Philippians 2:4

Let each of us please his
neighbor for his [neighbor's]
good, leading to edification.
Romans 15:2

During the time that we need help or encouragement, it is important to be sensitive to situations where others may need help or encouragement because in placing their need above our own we are not only obeying the Word of God, we are also operating in the spirit of sacrifice—the same spirit in which the Father operated when He "**gave His only begotten Son,**" and in the same spirit the Son operated when He gave His life as a sacrifice for our sin.

When Jesus laid down His life for our sins, He wasn't looking out for His own interests; He was looking out for ours. And in sacrificing for us in our time of need the Father didn't leave Him suffering, He raised Him up. It will be the same for us when we allow ourselves to be a tool of God in helping others even while we're struggling. God uses us to help them and then He also raises us up in the process.

And though the enemy has sought to use trouble as a weapon against us, God is using the same trouble as a tool to bless us, help us, and build us up to be a blessing to others in the same way He is a blessing to us.

No weapon that is formed against you will prosper because that which is a weapon in the arsenal of the enemy is a tool in the kingdom of God!

Chapter 4
Why Does the Lord Allow Trouble?

"...O my lord, if the Lord is with us, why then has all this befallen us?"
Judges 6:13

No matter how mature we are in our relationship with the Lord, when we encounter trouble there is an indiscriminate tendency to want to know why. We may not pose this question outwardly to God or anyone else but inwardly we often wonder, *"What in the world is going on?! Why is this happening to me?"*

Sometimes we may have an idea of why certain things are happening, but even in those instances we can be found wondering whether the punishment fits the crime, or we find ourselves asking about the whereabouts of God's grace and mercy.

There are also times we find ourselves in trouble and have absolutely no idea why. When we take inventory of our lives, it appears we have dotted all of the "Is" and crossed all of the "Ts." We are, therefore, baffled as to why we're going through what we're going through. I am certain that others, including

Job, must have felt like this considering the fact that Job was **"...an upright man who avoided evil."**

There is a natural tendency to wonder *why* we're experiencing difficulty. Logic suggests if we can learn *why* we can then make adjustments to correct the wrong and everything will be all right. Sometimes that is in fact the case—but not always. As with Job, sometimes our trouble is not the result of any wrongdoing on our part. And in instances like this wondering why can be a trap because we fall into the idea of thinking we're being dealt with unfairly by God. Even if we do not attribute the trouble to Him, we can think it is unfair of Him to allow it.

By nature, traps are tricky; they are purposed to paralyze us and keep us from moving forward. When we don't understand why we are going through what we are going through, if we are not careful, we will spend a great portion of our day and mental energy owning the words of Gideon and trying to figure out, "...**why has this evil befallen me**?"

Instead of focusing on that which we need to focus, our focus is spent on trying to find out where it all went wrong, why it all went wrong, and what can we do to right the wrong! Consequently we are kept from moving forward in life and even in our daily affairs—which can cause additional problems.

Also, when we have no answers, there is a void or an emptiness that exists because of the absence of an answer. Voids can be dangerous because they are purposed to be occupied. And voids do not care with what they are occupied; they just exist to be filled with *something*, be it good or bad, right or wrong, truth or untruth.

Because voids do not have filters or the ability to decipher right from wrong and reject the wrong, the devil often steps in to fill the mental void with his "fiery darts"—thoughts of untruthfulness.

In order to avoid being trapped by wondering why or falling prey to the enemy's filling of the void, it is important that we *know* something and *do* something. What we want to *do* are the things we were doing before trouble came knocking—going to church, reading the Word of God, praying, fasting, serving, living right and giving right. These are just a few of the areas where we cannot allow ourselves to be trapped and be kept from going forward in.

The thing to *know* is that despite the trouble or what may have caused it (if anything), God still loves us and His plan of blessing us has not changed one iota—though the enemy through his void-filling efforts will try to make us think the worst of God and serving Him.

But stay true to God in every regard and trust that even in your absence of understanding of what is going on, and why it's going on, God is still with you and He will cause everything you are experiencing to *work together for your good!*

Having an understanding of trouble helps keeps us from becoming victims of the void.

As stated in the previous chapter, trouble is a tool God puts to work in creating things in us that cannot be created by the easy, trouble-free times of life.

In the scope of trouble being a tool in the hand of God, there are a number of reasons why He allows trouble to visit His people. One such reason is for the sake of getting us back on track with our relationship with Him after falling away.

This was exactly the case when Gideon posed the question of Judges 6:13 to the angel whom the Lord had sent to deliver them from the trouble God had used to draw them back into relationship with Him. Consider what the Bible says in the verses that precede Gideon's question:

> **Then the children of Israel did evil in the sight of the Lord. So the Lord delivered them into the hand of Midian for seven years, 2 and the hand of Midian prevailed against Israel. Because of the Midianites, the children of Israel made for themselves the dens, the caves, and the strongholds which are in the mountains. 3 So it was, whenever Israel had sown, Midian would come up; also Amalekites and the people of the East would come up against them. 4 Then they would encamp against them and destroy the produce of the earth as far as Gaza, and leave no sustenance of Israel, neither sheep nor ox nor donkey.5 For the would come up with their livestock and their tents, coming in as numerous as locusts; both they and their camels were without number; and they would enter the land to destroy it. 6 So Israel was greatly impoverished because of the Midianites, and the children of Israel cried out to the Lord. 7 And it came to pass, when the children of Israel cried out to the Lord because of the Midianites, 8 that the Lord sent a prophet to the children of Israel, who said to them, "Thus says the Lord God of Israel: 'I brought you up from Egypt and brought you out of the house of bondage; 9 and I delivered you out of the hand of the Egyptians and out of the hand of all who oppressed you, and drove them out before you and gave you their land. 10 Also I said to you, "I am the Lord your God; do not fear the gods of the Amorites, in whose land you dwell." But you have not obeyed My voice."**
>
> **Judges 6:1-10**

In these verses we find both the reason and the cause of the trouble the people of God experienced. The reason for their trouble was their disobedience to God—a disobedience that was responsible for their getting off track in their relationship with Him. The cause of their trouble was God Himself.

To some, that reason may sound somewhat unkind or even errant. However, consider this portion of verse one, which says, **"...the Lord delivered them into the hand of Midian...."** The fact that the Lord was responsible for delivering them into the hand of the Midianites means that He had caused their trouble. He did not do it because He isn't a loving God. Instead, He caused their trouble because He *is* a loving God Who was using trouble as a tool to fix their broken relationship with Him. Remember, tools are used to repair that which is broken.

I realize that the idea of God using trouble as a tool to repair and get His people back on track with their relationship with Him is unpopular in some Christian circles. Some believe that God only does good to His people all of the time, and I would wholeheartedly agree. But we must realize that even the trouble God uses as a tool of discipline is good. It's good not because of how it feels when we are experiencing it, but because of what trouble ultimately accomplishes—the repair of our relationship with Him, and our being back on track for His blessings.

Consider further the words of Solomon, the wisest king to have ever lived:

"My son, do not despise the chastening of the Lord, nor detest His correction; for whom the Lord loves He corrects, just as a father the son in whom he delights."
Proverbs 3:11, 12

This verse is powerful and appropriate in proving the point that our Heavenly Father lovingly deals with us as children *through* chastening, or "disciplining" us by orchestrating troublesome times that are designed to get us back to the obedience wherein lies His best for our lives.

The writer of the New Testament book of Hebrews also understood this truth and used it to remind the Jewish people who had converted to Christianity of the same point.

5 And you have forgotten the exhortation
which is addressed to you as to sons:
'My son, do not regard lightly the
discipline of the Lord, nor faint
when you are reproved by Him;
6for those whom the Lord loves He
disciplines and He scourges
every son He receives.'
7 It is for discipline that you endure;
God deals with you as with sons; for what son is
there whom His father does not discipline?
8 But if you are without discipline,
Of which all have become partakers, then
you are illegitimate children and not sons."
9 Furthermore, we had earthly fathers to
discipline us, and we respected them; shall we
much not rather be subjected to the Father of
spirits, and live?" 10 For our earthly fathers
disciplined us for a short time as it seemed best to
them, but <u>our Heavenly Father disciplines us for</u>
<u>our good</u>, that we may share His holiness. 11 All
discipline for the moment seems not to be joyful,
but sorrowful; yet to those who have been
trained by it, afterwards <u>it yields peaceable</u>
<u>fruit of righteousness."</u>
Hebrews 12:5-11 (RSV)

The fact that the writer of Hebrews reminded New Testament Christians of this Old Testament truth makes it clear that how God deals with His children has not changed in New Testament times. And in the above passage, the writer teaches and/or puts us in remembrance of at least three facts:

1) God disciplines us.
2) It doesn't feel good when He does so.
3) Discipline (trouble) accomplishes good in the end.

There are a few things in life that don't *feel* good but are good. No one likes the pain that sometimes accompanies visiting the doctor, or the dentist's office. But that pain, be it from a shot or another medical procedure, is purposed to accomplish good in the end. And often it does. Such is the case with the painful trouble God allows, or sometimes causes in the life of His people. As a tool, it brings forth good in the end.

Solomon wasn't the only child of God to understand this principle. The writer of Psalm 119 was able to recognize trouble's role in his return to relationship with the Lord.

"You have dealt well with Your servant,
O Lord, according to Your Word.
66 Teach me good judgment and knowledge, for I
believe Your commandments.
67 Before I was afflicted [troubled], I went astray,
but now I keep Your Word.
68 You are good, and do good."
Psalm 119:65-68a

In verse 67 the psalmist uses hindsight in stating that his going "**astray**" or *wandering away from God,* preceded his being **"afflicted."** But he credits his trouble with being back on track with God by saying "…**<u>but now</u> I keep your Word**."

In verse 65 the psalmist acknowledges the role played by the Lord in either causing or allowing the affliction to enter his life as a tool and to do the necessary repairs by saying, **"You have dealt well with Your servant…."** He said this not because he enjoyed his season of affliction and couldn't wait for it to return again. No! The psalmist was saying that God had dealt well in allowing the affliction because of what was ultimately accomplished.

In verse 68 the psalmist actually praises God for the trouble and their restored relationship by proclaiming, **"You are good, and <u>do</u> good...."** What did God "**do**" that was so **"good"** that it warranted praising Him? He had caused, or had allowed His servant to be afflicted. And it was the trouble of the affliction that brought about the **"good"** of their relationship being repaired.

When God recognizes that our relationship—not just our fellowship, but our actual relationship—with Him is in jeopardy; or that we are off the path of promise, purpose or blessings He has for us, He will use trouble to help repair the relationship, restore the fellowship, and get us back on track.

For me (and thousands of others like me), it was "pre-God" trouble that drove me to God to begin with. So God understands that trouble can drive us to Him because it has driven many of us to Him. And He takes advantage of His knowledge of this particular ability of trouble and, His lordship over trouble, and He uses trouble for the good of getting His children back into relationship with Him. And I, for one, am happy that He does so! And I'm not the only one.

Behold, happy is the man whom God corrects;
Therefore do not despise the chastening
of the Almighty.
Job 5:17

You may be experiencing a season of trouble as you read this book. Your trouble could be caused, or allowed by the Lord to be used as a tool to fix a breach in your relationship with Him, and to get you back on track with the plans of good He has for your life. Or, your trouble could be a weapon that the enemy has formed against you that, though formed, will not prosper but will be used by God for your good.

But how can we tell what the cause, the reason or the source of our trouble is? It can be difficult to tell sometimes because a certain type of trouble is not always associated with the reason for the trouble. For example, living in sin won't always cause God to use the trouble of financial hardship to get people back on track. God may choose to use some other form of trouble.

On the other hand, our relationship with the Lord may be fine. We can be living right and giving right and still experience the trouble of financial turmoil. Whereas no type of trouble is exclusive to the reason for it, the one thing all trouble has in common is the fact that every type of trouble are tools in the hand of the Master Craftsman. And they are tools that are purposed either to repair our relationship with Him and prepare us for His plans or to build a bridge to our places of promise and purpose.

The question comes: "But Mr. Bailey, can you please answer the question of how one can tell what the cause, the reason or the source of their trouble is?"

Yes, I can. However, in doing so one must be willing to make an honest personal assessment of their life. Every person must ask themselves, *"Is there something, someone or some activity in my life that is contrary to the Word of God and what He requires of me?"* If the answer is "*Yes*," *that* could very well be the reason for your trouble. It is very likely that the Lord Himself has either caused or allowed the trouble because He loves you and is using that trouble as His tool to get you back on track.

We have read what the writers in Job, Psalms, Proverbs and the book of Hebrews had to say about God and His *chastening* (disciplining) of us with trouble, but take a look at what John, the writer of the book of Revelation, quotes God as saying about the matter:

"As many as I love, I rebuke and chasten.
Therefore be zealous, and repent."
Revelation 3:19

If you are sensing that God could be using trouble in your life, and the Holy Spirit has brought to your mind something, someone, or some activity that is against God's Word and desire for you, *now* is the time to repent (turn away) from whatever it is that is causing the trouble you're experiencing.

Now is the time to seek the Lord, acknowledge your wrong before Him, ask for His forgiveness, receive His forgiveness, and let Him restore your broken relationship with Him, and place you *back* on the blessing track!

What we experience nowadays as children of God is no different from what the children of God went through in their relationship with Him in the yesterdays of history. The way God dealt with them is no different from how He deals with us. And how God used trouble to help and bless them is *exactly* how He uses it to help and bless us. Remember, God changes not. **"Jesus Christ is the same yesterday, today, and forever." (Hebrews 13:8)**

Consider in the following verse how Isaiah reveals God's use of trouble to lead His people back into a relationship with Him after they had gotten off track through disobedience:

"Lord, in <u>trouble</u> they have visited You,
they poured out a prayer when <u>Your</u>
chastening was upon them."
Isaiah 26:16

In this Scripture two of the previous truths are spelled out:

1) The Lord chastened His people by using trouble as a tool.

2) Trouble worked in repairing the relationship with Him because it caused them to visit, seek or return to Him.

The Hebrew word for *visit* in the verse also means "to want" or "to remember." When there is a return to God, it is because there is first a *remembrance* of the goodness shared with Him when our relationship was whole and unbroken by the sin of disobedience.

The book of Luke tells the story of the prodigal son (who represents any child of God), who had chosen to break the relationship with his father (who represents God) by leaving and living in a way that was neither good for him nor pleasing to his father. But after encountering a time of trouble, it triggered something in his mind that changed something in his life.

"But when he came to himself [remembered],
he said, 'How many of my father's hired servants
have bread enough to spare, and I perish with
hunger! I will arise and go [return] to my father
and will say to him "Father, I have
sinned against heaven and before you…."
Luke 15:17, 18

The point is that the prodigal son's trouble caused him to *remember* how good things were when he was in close relationship with his father. And what followed his remembering was his returning. In the same way, trouble has a way of causing us to *remember* and making us *want* to return to our Father and once again enjoy the fruits of our fellowship and relationship with Him.

"And he arose and came to his father.
But when he was still
a great way off, his father saw him
and had compassion,
[I love this part!]
and ran and fell on his neck and kissed him!"
Luke 15:20

This is great! But, it gets even better!

"...the father said to his servants, 'Bring out the best robe and put it on him, and put a ring on his and sandals on his feet. And bring the fatted calf bring here and kill it, and let us eat and be merry; for this my son was dead and is alive again; he was lost and is found. And they began to be merry.' "
Luke 15:22-24

The point is that trouble was the consequence for the prodigal son leaving his father and living outside of a relationship with him. But trouble was also used as a tool to remind him of his father's goodness, rebuild that relationship, and restore the son to the type of life his father desired for him.

Not only did the prodigal son and the children of Israel in Isaiah both experience a time of trouble that God used as a tool to repair their broken relationship, God also used their trouble to restore them to the quality of life He had planned all along.

When there is a return to God, it is because there is first a remembrance of the good that was shared with Him when the relationship was whole.

From this Biblical account, we have seen the remembrance, the return, and the restoration of the prodigal son, but Isaiah 26:15 speaks of the state of the children of Israel after their trouble had caused them to remember, return, and be restored to the Lord.

"Lord, in trouble they have visited You,
they poured out a prayer when Your
chastening was upon them."
Isaiah 26:16

Please understand that this verse was written after God had used the tool of trouble to restore the children of Israel's damaged relationship with Him. We can ascertain this fact because of the past tense words of "visited," "poured," and "when," which all speak of a time past.

But not only did God use trouble to get them back on track with their relationship with Him, He also used trouble to get them back on track with the plan for good and blessings He had for their life—as was the case with the prodigal son.

"You have increased the nation, O Lord,
You have increased the nation;
You are glorified; You have expanded
All the borders of the land."
Isaiah 26:15

Increasing the nation and expanding the borders of the land both speak of God restoring them to the plan and blessings He had for them before they got off track and encountered trouble.

The lesson that can be found in this verse and in a number of other places in the Bible is that when the Christian falls away from God and/or begins to live contrary to what He requires of us, God will either allow or cause us to experience trouble. But in doing so, He uses that trouble as a tool to repair our relationship with Him and returns us to the path of purpose, promise and blessing. And as crazy as it may sound, *this* makes the trouble worth it!

Remember, repent and return, and receive repair and restoration!

Trouble: The Great Character Creator

Another reason why God allows trouble to visit our life is to create certain characteristics in us that are compatible with our purpose, and necessary for His plans for our life.

Character is a broad word that includes a number of different attributes. Depending on the type of trouble God allows and when He allows it, trouble could be purposed to create one attribute in one season and a different one in another season.

One attribute or Christ-like characteristic that trouble creates in the child of God is that of *humility*. Take note of what God said to the children of Israel as Moses was leading them to the Promised Land that the Lord had purposed and planned for them to occupy:

> **"And you shall remember that the Lord your God led you all the way these forty years in the wilderness, <u>to humble you</u> and test you, to know what was in your heart, whether you would keep His commandments or not.**
>
> **So He humbled you, allowed you to hunger, and fed you with manna which you did not know nor did your fathers know, that He might make you know that man shall not live y bread alone; but man lives by every Word that proceeds from the mouth of the Lord."**
>
> **Deuteronomy 8:2, 3**

Before I continue addressing the needful humility God sometimes uses trouble to create in the believer, let me pause for a moment to explain that for the children of Israel the wilderness represented a place and a season of trouble, but it was different from the trouble they had suffered while in Egypt. The trouble they suffered in Egypt at the hand of Pharaoh led them to God and the deliverance He provided.

However, the post-deliverance trouble of the wilderness was designed to prepare them for purpose and promise in Canaan—the blessed land that flowed with milk and honey.

It is extremely important not to confuse pre-God trouble with post-God trouble. Doing so can cause us to question the purpose of turning our life over to God. After all, if we are only going to continue to experience trouble as we did *before* coming to Him, why bother?

Although pre-God and post-God troubles can sometimes feel the same, they are different in purpose. Pre-God trouble is purposed to lead us to the Lord, while the trouble we experience *after* coming to know God is purposed to grow us, groom us, and prepare us for His plan for creating us. We must be mindful of this fact because the devil has a way of trying to trick us into thinking that there is no sense in serving God if trouble is the only reward for doing so. We must be careful to not allow ourselves to be tricked into losing sight of the fact that the primary purpose of coming to God is salvation through Jesus Christ.

It is extremely important not to confuse pre-God trouble with post-God trouble.

Regardless of the level, length or type of trouble we encounter after coming to God, the *primary* purpose of doing so is not to escape earthly experiences of trouble but to one day enjoy the eternal experience of Heaven. This future enjoyment of eternity is one of the reasons why the Bible encourages to:

**"Set your mind on things above [Heaven],
not on things on the Earth."
Colossians 3:2**

Trouble is an earthly issue—not a heavenly one. In fact, the Bible teaches us that in Heaven there will be no trouble whatsoever! *(Can you say, "Hallelujah! Amen!", and do 15 back flips?)*

**"And God will wipe away every tear from their eyes; there shall be no more death, nor sorrow, nor crying. There shall be no more pain, for the former things have passed away.
Revelation 21:4**

No death, no sorrow, no crying, and no more pain mean no more trouble! Hallelujah!

There will be no trouble in Heaven (but plenty of it in Hell), and this is why the primary focus and purpose of our coming to God must be the blessing of Heaven and not the benefits on Earth. Please don't misunderstand me. We most certainly do not want to ignore the fact that there are indeed earthly benefits for serving God. The Bible makes this fact plain in a number of places, but nowhere is it clearer than in **Psalm 103:2-5,** which says:

"Bless the Lord, O my soul; and <u>forget not all of His benefits</u>: Who forgives all your iniquities, Who heals all your diseases, Who redeems your life from destruction, Who crowns you with lovingkindness and tender mercies, Who satisfies your mouth with good things, so that your youth is renewed like the eagle's."

This and other passages of Scripture all make it crystal clear that there are earthly benefits in coming to God that He undoubtedly wants His children to enjoy. But again, the earthly benefits of God cannot and should not be the primary reason for coming to Him. Anyone who has come to God solely or primarily for the sake of enjoying earthly benefits or for escaping earthly trouble, has missed the main point. That person is in danger of departing from the Lord once trouble subsides.

Although pre-God trouble may have driven us to God, the *main* reason He drew us was to save us from Hell and not *just* to deliver us from our difficulties on Earth.

The enemy's aim is to cause us not to know or to lose sight of the most important factor in coming to God, which again is salvation. And the enemy will try to use our trouble to discredit the goodness of God or the legitimacy of life being better in coming to Him. But life with God and earthly troubles is much better than a life with no troubles and no God!

And regardless of the trouble we encounter we must remember two separate, but related, facts: 1) we must *always* remember that this earthly journey is much more about eternal life in Heaven than the troubles we will experience on earth. The apostle Paul in 2 Corinthians 4:17 and 18 wrote:

"For our light affliction, which is but for a moment, is working for us a far more exceeding and eternal weight of glory, while we do not look at things which are seen, but at the things which are not seen. For the things which are seen are temporary, but the things which are not seen are eternal."

The primary purpose of our coming to God must be the blessing of Heaven and not the benefits on Earth.

The second fact to remember, or to know, and of which to be assured is, that as we continue to walk with God and not permit trouble to get us off track, after trouble has accomplished its purpose, God will indeed free us from that which afflicts us.

Consider these statements by David in Psalm 34 as evidence of God's faithfulness to deliver us from our trouble:

"I sought the Lord, and He heard me, and delivered me from all my fears."
Psalm 34:4

"This poor man cried out, and the Lord heard him, and saved him out of all his troubles."
Psalm 34:6

"The righteous cry out, and the Lord hears, and delivers them out of all their troubles."
Psalm 34:17

"Many are the afflictions of the righteous, but the Lord delivers him out of them all."
Psalm 34:19

These verses provide us with ample evidence to support that fact that God will deliver us from "all" of our troubles! Hallelujah!

What is also noteworthy about these verses is that they took place before the prophecy of David becoming king was fulfilled, which means a number of things:

1) Problems in the form of trouble can precede the fulfillment of prophecy.

2) The problems that precede the fulfillment of prophecy are purposed to prepare us for the prophecy.

3) Though the problems that precede the fulfillment are purposeful; they are not permanent.

We know the problems that prepared David for the prophecy of becoming king were purposeful but not permanent because God delivered him out of them all. The fact that David says "all" clearly means that there wasn't just one thing that was troubling him.

As we wait for the fulfillment of prophecies or promises, it is not uncommon to be troubled by a number of different things at once. James 1:2 supports this fact by stating, "**... count it all joy when you fall into <u>various</u> trials....**" *Various* and its first-cousin *variety* means that we can experience more than one episode, or type of trouble at a time. We can have family problems and financial problems at the same time. We can experience trouble with our boss while having a problem with our best buddy. We can have problems paying for the house and heating the house. The wash, the dryer and the dresser can all break at the same time. The car can blow a fan belt while the truck has four flat tires. Or there can be trouble at work while there are problems at church.

Despite the *various* or the variety of trouble we may encounter, the Spirit of God inspired James to write, "**... count it all joy...**" when we encounter such trouble because the Lord of trouble is purposefully using it to produce the patience that leads to the promises and that leaves us "lacking nothing."

"My brethren, count it all joy when you fall into various trials, knowing that the testing of your faith produces patience, But let patience have its perfect work, that you may be perfect and complete, lacking nothing."
James 1:2-4

The point is not to be tricked into thinking that trouble means God isn't good, or that walking with Him isn't worth it. Also, we must not allow earthly trouble to cause us to lose sight of our eternal perspective—a perspective that includes

God using trouble to prepare us for a plan and a purpose that positively affects our life, and the lives of others.

Regardless of the level, length or type of trouble we encounter after coming to the Lord, the primary purpose of coming to Him is not to escape earthy experiences of trouble, but to one day enjoy the eternal experience of Heaven.

A look at the trouble people of the Bible encountered after coming to God allows us to know that trouble is not uncommon; neither is it a sign that we do not have a real relationship with God or that our relationship with Him is meaningless. Our relationship with the Lord is by no means meaningless. Neither is the trouble we face after coming to know Him.

Remember, God said that He led the children of Israel into the wilderness, (the place of trouble) "to humble" them. The preposition "to" used in this verse introduces us to the purpose of God's allowing or leading them to that time of trouble. The trouble was purposed to "humble" His people. It was purposed to humble them because humility would prepare them for the things God had promised them.

God promises us many things for which He must first prepare us. One of the ways God makes us ready to possess certain promises is by humbling us. And certain troubles are given that specific assignment by God.

Consider these verses and how God uses humility to prepare us for His plans for us:

"...the humble {God} teaches His way."
Psalm 25:9b

There is a depth of spiritual truth, revelation, insight and wisdom given by God to the humble that the proud cannot receive from Him. Remember, one of the reasons God led the children of Israel into the wilderness—the place of trouble—was to *humble* them and to *test* them. But before He *tested* them He *taught* them.

We know this because *teaching* always precedes *testing*. No orderly teacher *tests* their students until after they have *taught* their students. We know this also because God didn't begin to teach and give Israel the Word until *after* He had led them into the wilderness where they were first humbled.

This doesn't mean that they didn't learn *anything* before then because certainly they did. They learned that God was a loving, strong, kind, miracle-working God Who provided for them even in their time of trouble. However, they didn't begin to receive the Word of God until after they were troubled and humbled by their wilderness experience. The lessons learned in their time of humility causing trouble was purposed to prepare them for life in the Promised Land.

"The humble will inherit the land,
And will delight themselves in abundant prosperity."
Psalm 37:11 (NAS)

"...with the humble [those who are lowly, <u>who have been pruned or chiseled by trial</u>, and renounce self] is skillful and Godly wisdom...."
Proverbs 11:2 (AMP)

The Hebrew word for *wisdom* in this verse also means "skillful." *Skill* is "the ability that comes from knowledge." When we are humbled by the trouble God allows, there is an impartation of spiritual wisdom, skill, and ability that is supernaturally imparted, and enables one to operate effectively in the plan of God for their life.

**"Now the man Moses was very humble,
more than all men who were on
the face of the Earth."
Numbers 12:3**

God chose Moses *not* because he was the only person He could have used to deliver the children of Israel out of the hand of Pharaoh and the Egyptians. God chose Moses as the first pastor of the largest congregation in history because his humility made him the best candidate to be the very first man to receive the Word of God that included the Ten Commandments and the Law that God wanted to get to the people.

It is not difficult to understand why certain plans God has for us would require a level, (or even a high level) of humility in order to operate effectively. If God has a plan to bless us with great positions of authority, tremendous financial blessings, or to entrust us with a high level of anointing, it would not be unlike God to allow humility creating trouble to visit our lives before He appoints us to that position, increases us with those finances, or entrusts us with that anointing.

**"...be clothed with humility, for 'God resists the proud, but gives grace [favor] to the humble.' Therefore <u>humble yourselves</u> under the mighty hand of God, that <u>He may exalt you</u> in due time."
1 Peter 5:5, 6**

These verses teach us that there is another, higher level of grace and favor that is rewarded *"to the humble."* Also revealed in these verses is the association between *humility* and the *exalting,* or the *elevating* that comes from God.

A humbling of ourselves takes place when we submit ourselves to God through obedience to His Word and to the authority He has placed in our lives. But there is also a humbling that is accomplished by the trying times in life. And whether it is the humbling of ourselves through obedience or through the troubles we encounter, God rewards and elevates the humble, *"in due time."*

Due time is "a time that is certain to come." When a bill is *due,* it means that it is time for that bill to be paid. Well, in the same way, when we walk in humility—however it is created—there is a time when increased favor and exaltation will be paid into our lives.

"By humility and fear of the Lord
are riches and honor and life."
Proverbs 22:4

The word *"by"* means "the way of travel or the way in which something arrives." For example, one can travel *by* train and arrive in Chicago (the second greatest city in the world behind the New Jerusalem). In the same way, we arrive at the place of "**riches and honor and life** [more abundantly]" when we travel "**by humility**."

Consider the amplified rendering of this same verse:

"The <u>reward</u> of humility and the reverent and
worshipful Fear of the Lord
is riches and honor and life."

Many of the promises and plans of God naturally come to pass. But there are some promises, plans and purposes with which we are rewarded that must be prepared for. And humility is the great preparer of these things.

The Lord allows or leads us into times of trouble because nothing creates the character of humility in His children like trouble. However, the humility that is created by trouble is that which is necessary for us to arrive at the place of purpose and greater promise, and for us to receive the rewards that await us there.

Patience Producing Trouble

"My brethren, count it all joy when you fall into various trials, knowing that the testing of your faith produces patience, but let patience have its perfect work, that you may be perfect and complete, lacking nothing."
James 1:2-4

Another Christ-like characteristic the tool of trouble builds in us is that of patience. In the above passage James, the half-brother of Jesus, associated the "various trials" with patience.

Typically, when we think about patience, we think of it in terms of being something we should have but not something that is produced in us by trouble. We are more likely to think patience is what we need to weather the storms of trouble—not something that trouble is capable of creating in us. However, that is exactly what James is teaching!

As a tool, trouble has patience-producing ability because we encounter some seasons of trouble that completely tie our hands and render us powerless to bring about change. I don't know whether or not you have ever been in a season wherein *nothing* you tried worked to bring that season to an end. No amount of prayer or praise could bring deliverance. No fast or amount of faith freed you from the fix in which you found yourself. No length or loudness of crying caused God to be so sympathetic that He abandoned the purpose of the trouble and brought a premature end to the season. We cannot claim an end to some seasons, or financially give our way out of them. We just have to wait. But it is in the *wait* that patience is being produced in us.

Patience is produced by the trouble we encounter because patience has a purpose; it has a "perfect work" that only *it* can accomplish. Just as humility is an elevator of sorts that causes God to take us to higher levels, patience is a key that grants us access to certain promises of God and certain places in His kingdom.

"That you be not slothful, but followers of them who through faith and <u>patience</u> <u>inherit the promises</u>."
Hebrews 6:12

The word "inherit" means "to come into possession." By that definition, some promises are only possessed by the key of patience that gets us *through* the door of that particular promise. Take a look at what this passage goes on to say:

"For when God made promise to Abraham, because He could swear by no greater, He swore by Himself, saying, 'Surely blessing I will bless you, and multiplying I will multiply you.' And so, <u>after</u> (Abraham) had <u>patiently</u> endured, he <u>obtained the promise."</u>
Hebrews 6:13-15

Notice the structural order of verse 15 (as well as verse 12). The promise followed the patience. This is because the patience was the *key* to accessing the promise. Access always follows the key. When there is no key, there will be no access. But when we have patience, we have the key, and that key grants us access through the door wherein awaits us "... **exceeding great and precious promises." (2 Peter 1:4)**

What we find in these verses that applied to Abraham, the father of faith, applies also to us as children of faith. This is why verse 12 admonishes us to be "followers." If we are followers of them that possessed the promises of God by using the *key* of patience, we will therefore be granted the same access if we use the same key.

"But from where cometh this key?" you may be asking. It cometh from the trouble God allows to visits our life. As unnerving as trouble often is, it is also purposeful in that

it produces patience—patience that is the *key* to promise possession.

"Therefore do not cast away your confidence which has great reward. For you have need of patience, that, after you have done the will of God, you may receive the promise."
Hebrews 10:35, 36

Verse 36, Amplified
"For you have need of steadfast patience... So that you may perform and fully accomplish the will of God, and thus receive and carry away [and enjoy to the full] what is promised.

God allows trouble because quite frankly trouble gives us what we need to get what He has promised!

Patience is a key that grants us access to certain promises of God and certain places in His kingdom.

Although patience is being produced in us by the trouble we're waiting to get out of, *waiting* in and of itself is not patience. In fact, it's possible to be waiting and *not* be patient while waiting.

Listen to what David said during one of his many times of trouble:

"I waited patiently for the Lord; and He inclined to me, and heard my cry. He also brought me up out of a horrible pit, out of the miry clay, and set my feet upon a rock and established my steps."
Psalm 40:1, 2

Can I tell you something? Anytime we are in a "horrible pit," or stuck in "miry clay," it means we are in *trouble!*

But notice, David doesn't just say he "waited" for the Lord; he says he "*patiently* waited." It's possible to wait for the Lord and not do so patiently, but *impatiently*.

The problem with impatient waiting is that it prolongs, or it can deprive us of possessing the promise. You may remember that the Lord promised the children of Israel the land of Canaan—a land that "flowed with milk and honey," which represented a much better quality of life.

God put His plan in motion by using Moses to deliver His people, and by leading them through the wilderness which was purposed to humble them, thereby preparing them for possession of the Promised Land.

Certainly the wilderness, the desert, and the difficult times could symbolize the "**horrible pit and the miry clay**" of which David spoke hundreds and hundreds of years later. But unlike David, most of the children of Israel never make it out of the horrible pit and the miry clay and into the land of promise. The reason for this was their murmuring. Murmuring is "manifested impatience."

The Hebrew word for murmur also means "to constantly complain." People who constantly complain are impatient. No doubt you have seen one before. Maybe it was today. They complain that the line at the grocery store is too long and the clerk is moving too slow; they complain that the traffic signal "must be broken because I've been at this red light for 15 minutes!"

Impatient Christians murmur about their jobs, and for that reason cannot get better ones. They complain about their pastor, and for that reason cannot receive the blessings their pastor is purposed by God to lead them into. And they complain about not having this and not having that, and this is wrong and that is wrong, etc. Consequently, because of their constant complaining, they never get out of the horrible pit or the miry clay. And like the children of Israel, they never possess the good God promised them.

Impatience is revealed in constant complaining.

From the book of First Samuel through the book of Psalms, we see David doing a great deal of worshiping, singing, running, fighting, a little trash talking ("this uncircumcised Philistine shall be as one of them"), and even a lot of crying. But the one thing we don't find David doing is complaining about his situation or the condition of his life.

Despite the difficulty of his days we don't find David murmuring because he knew the prophecy and the plan of God held promise for better days ahead. David also knew that God was honorable, faithful, and powerful enough to bring every plan, promise, and prophecy to pass.

You may be thinking, *"Well, I don't have a prophecy from God about a good future for my life."* Oh, but you do! You're just not aware of it. *Every* promise of God for good made to His people is a prophecy for *your* life. You must understand that the Bible is the *living* Word of God. It is *living* meaning that what is written therein is alive and still applies to the people of God—who or wherever we are.

The promise of a land that flowed with milk and honey for the children of Israel is a prophecy for a Promised Land for you and me. The "plans of good" that God had for His people in Jeremiah 29 are prophecies of the plans of good He has for us in our lives. The promises to deliver David out of "all his troubles" are prophecies to deliver us out of all of our troubles too. Remember,

"Whatever things were written before were written for our learning, that we through the patience and comfort of the Scriptures might have hope."
Romans 15:4

Many of the promises of the past are prophecies of the present. Just as God was faithful to fulfill them in the lives of His people in the yesterdays of history, He does so yet today!

David was delivered from the horrible pit, the miry clay, and his every time of trouble—not simply because he waited for God to deliver him, but because he *patiently waited* on the Lord to do so. He waited without complaining.

Maybe you are in a *horrible pit,* or *miry clay* type of situation and you have been waiting on God to bring your time of trouble to an end. But you recognize that you haven't been *patiently waiting,* or you have not been waiting without complaining.

If you acknowledge that you can go before the Father, admit your mistake, and simply ask His forgiveness. God will forgive you, and from this point forth He will act as if you had never murmured, grumbled, or complained about anything. We know God operates in this way because His Word says,

"If we confess our sins, He is faithful and just to forgive us our sins and to cleanse us from all unrighteousness."
1 John 1:9

If you feel inspired to go before the Father, take just a moment to do so. You can simply say something like, *"Father, I come before You acknowledging the fact that I've murmured and complained instead of trusting and patiently waiting on You. Please forgive me, Father. This very moment, I repent and turn from complaining. In the name of Jesus, Father, I ask that You would cleanse me forever from distrust and impatience, so that patience can do its perfect work in me. Thank You, Father. Amen!*

The point is that God sometimes allows trouble because it produces patience. And patience is a key that opens the doors to prophecies and promises, and brings us into possession of the great good God desires for us to possess. Glory!

It is in the *wait* that patience is produced.

Although the Lord may have permitted trouble to visit your life, know that its presence is not without significance. Trouble's presence has brought a present.

I love gifts. If you're anything like me, and you probably are, you also like receiving gifts. If someone wants to *make our day,* it's easy! Just give us a gift and our day will be made!

In the olden days (maybe even now in some places), it was customary for visitors to bring a gift when they visited the king. An individual could not come into the presence of the king without bringing a present—unless being beheaded was the goal of that person's visit. Other than that, gifts were mandatory!

Having been made **"kings and priests"** by Jesus Christ (Revelation 1:6), when God allows trouble to visit our life He forces it to follow the custom and bring to us a gift.

You may have been thinking that trouble has only brought you misery. But besides, and more important than the misery, is the *patience* trouble is producing. It may be true that trouble has visited your life, but it hasn't come empty-handed. Trouble has come bearing a gift—a gift that opens the door to a greater goodness of God than you have ever before experienced!

"My brethren, take the prophets, who spoke in The name of the Lord, as an example of suffering and patience. Indeed we count them blessed who endure. You have heard of the patience of Job and seen the end intended by the Lord—that the Lord is very compassionate and merciful."
James 5:10, 11

Most Christians know all too well about the troubles of Job. The truth is that we hear far more about the trouble than we do about his *intended end.* The statement, "**the end intended by the Lord**" is extremely encouraging, and equally as powerful and promising.

It is extremely encouraging because it tells us that there is an "end" to our troublesome times—no matter how troubling they are or how long they have been troubling us. You may have heard it said before that, "Trouble don't last always." That idiom may not necessarily be true for the unrepentant, but it is most certainly true for the righteous.

That statement is extremely powerful because it is not only saying that there is *an end* intended by God, but that there is a *specific,* ("the") *end* intended by Him. And that specific *end* has to do with the beginning of a new and greater good from God!

How do I know this? I know this for two reasons:

1) The "end" of one thing marks the beginning of a new thing that is the opposite of what is ending. For example, pain is the opposite of comfort; and it is when pain ends, that comfort begins. In the same way, *happiness* is the opposite of trouble. Therefore, *the end* of trouble marks the beginning of happiness, and better days.

2) Secondly, I know Job's (and our) specific end to trouble has to do with the beginning of a new and greater good from God because the Bible reveals this fact.

"And the Lord restored Job's losses when he prayed for his friends. Indeed the Lord gave Job twice as much as he had before."
Job 42:10

This is "the end" of which James spoke. And notice that the "end" of Job's trouble was also the beginning of his happiness and a good from God that was greater than any he had ever experienced!

Guess what? God also has "a happiness and a greater good" in store for you at *"the end"* of your trouble—a trouble God indeed intends to bring to an end. Just be patient. You're going to be blessed!

God allows trouble to visit our life, but He forces it to follow the custom and bring us an unexpected gift!

Positioned by Trouble

The Lord allows us to experience trouble—not only because it prepares us for the plans, purpose and fulfilled prophecies by creating Christ-like characteristics in us. The Lord also allows trouble because it *positions* us for plans, promises and purpose. In fact, *positioning* is a part of the preparation process.

Just as I like gifts, I also like moving. I don't like the *process* of moving—but I love the idea, the excitement, and the anticipation of a new home and a new neighborhood! And although I do *not* like the packing, the lifting, and all the inconveniences that accompany moving, after it's all said and done, and I'm settled, I'm happy I went through the *process* because the reward was worth it.

Well, trouble is like moving. It relocates, or it repositions us to a better place; but the process is a pain! However, few things *position* us to possess the blessings of God, live out the plan of God, and fulfill the purpose of God, like trouble does.

When we consider again the life of Joseph, and the final destination of God's plan and purpose for his life, we notice that the *ending place* was different from the *beginning place*—both geographically and spiritually speaking.

"Now Jacob dwelt in the land where his father was a stranger, in the land of Canaan. This is the history of Jacob. Joseph, being seventeen years old...."
Genesis 37:1, 2a

"And Pharaoh said to Joseph, 'See, I have set you over all the land of Egypt.'"
Genesis 41:41

The *ending place* where the purpose and plan of God for Joseph's life was fulfilled was Egypt. But the *beginning place* was Canaan. It was in Canaan that Joseph's purpose was *revealed*, but in was in Egypt that his purpose was *fulfilled*. In order to get from *revealed* to *fulfilled,* there had to be *movement* from Canaan to Egypt.

How did Joseph make the *move* from Canaan to Egypt? You might say it was by camelback or buggy. Some might say it was by foot. And while the natural mode of transportation may have been any, or all of these, spiritually speaking, Joseph was transported by trouble!

His trouble came by way of the hatred of his brothers, and trouble *moved* Joseph from his father's house to Potiphar's house where he received on-the-job training, and the experience that prepared him for God's ultimate purpose for him.

"Now when they saw him afar off, even before he came near them, they conspired against him to kill him."
Genesis 37:18

Can I tell you something? Anytime your brothers, or sisters, or anyone is conspiring against you to kill you, you are in *trouble!* Run! Run really fast! Call the police and catch the next thing headed out of town—even if it's not smoking! I don't care if you see a hairy hippo with an Afro and one hump, hop on that hump and hightail it out of town!

"Then they said to one another, 'Look, this dreamer is coming! Come therefore, let us now kill him and cast him into some pit; And we shall say, 'Some wild beast has devoured him.' We shall see what will become of his dreams! But Reuben heard it, and he delivered him out of their hands, and said, 'Let us not kill him…Shed no blood but cast him into this pit which is in the wilderness, and do not lay a hand on him….' "
Genesis 37:19-22

"Come and let us sell him to the Ishmaelites, and let not our hand be upon him, for he is our brother and our flesh. And his brothers listened. Then Midianite traders passed by; so the brothers pulled Joseph up and lifted him out of the pit, and sold him to the Ishmaelites for twenty shekels of silver. And they took Joseph to Egypt."
Genesis 37:27, 28

The point is that the trouble God allows not only has a way of *preparing* us for purpose; it also has a way of *positioning* us for purpose. Movement is often a sign that God is positioning us for fulfilled purpose.

And sometimes the movement isn't always upward. Sometimes God orchestrates a backward move to position us for forward progress. Arrows are launched further forward when they are pulled back further in the bow.

Often, regression is a precursor to progression. Things will take place in the period/season of seeming regression that are significant to progression and fulfilled purpose.

After being sold into slavery and landing in Potiphar's house, Joseph probably believed he had landed in the place of fulfilled purpose. After all, Potiphar had placed him in charge of all the other workers; surely he thought this was what he saw in his dreams!

But one lie from Potiphar's wife wiped out what he believed to be the final stop of his unconscious prophetic encounter. When people lie on us, or when life happens and it *moves* us from a particular place, don't be dismayed—just understand that *that* place was not the place of fulfilled purpose; rather, it was the place of preparation for fulfilled purpose!

Sometimes the place that *prepares* us for purpose resembles the place of purpose because some elements and experiences in the place of preparation are consistent with what we understand our purpose to be.

Joseph may have confused Potiphar's house for the place of ultimate purpose because he knew his ultimate purpose, (as revealed in his dreams) was to rule over men. And because he *was* ruling over men he may have thought that was the place of ultimate purpose, but it was not. We know it was not because he was *moved* by trouble. When we get to the place of fulfilled purpose, *nothing* will be able to move us—no matter *who* tries, or *how hard* they try.

If trouble has moved you from a place or a position, it only means that was just the place of *preparation for purpose*—not the place of *fulfilled purpose*. Even if the move appears to be a backward move, again, something in the God-allowed regressions of life will launch you forward to fulfill your purpose in life.

"But it happened about this time, when Joseph went to the house to do his work, and none of the men of the house was inside, that she caught him by his garment, saying, 'Lie with me.' But he left his garment in her hand, and fled and ran outside."
Genesis 39:11, 12

"So she kept his garment with her until his master came home. Then she spoke to him with words like others, saying, 'The Hebrew servant whom you brought to us came in to me to mock Me; so it happened, as I lifted my voice and cried out, that he left his garment with me and fled outside.' So it was, when his master heard the words which his wife spoke to him, saying, 'Your servant did to me after this manner,' that his anger was aroused. Then Joseph's master took him and put him into the prison, a place where the king's prisoners were confined, and he was there in the prison."
Genesis 39:16-20

Joseph must have been heartbroken! It's one thing to experience trouble in the ordinary, uninfluenced flow of life, but to encounter it at the hands of another's dishonesty is a tough pill to swallow! But God is powerful! And as "Lord of all," He is Lord also over lies and causes even them to work together for our good. Remember, things that are intended to *do us in* are used by God and made to *do us good* by the authority of His lordship!

"But the LORD was with Joseph and showed him mercy, and He gave him favor in the sight of the keeper of the prison."
Genesis 39:21

"It came to pass after these things that the butler and the baker of the king of Egypt offended their lord, the king of Egypt. 2 And Pharaoh was

angry with his two officers the chief butler and the
chief baker. 3 So he put them in custody in the
house of the captain of the guard, in the prison, the
place where Joseph was confined. 4 And the
captain of the guard charged Joseph with them,
and he served them; so they were in custody for a
while. 5 Then the butler and the baker…had a
dream, both of them, each man's dream in one
night and each man's dream with
its own interpretation."
Genesis 40:1-5

"Then the chief butler told his dream to
Joseph, and said to him, 'Behold, in my dream
a vine was before me, 10 and in the vine were three
branches; it was as though it budded, its blossoms shot
forth, and it clusters brought forth ripe grapes. 11 Then
Pharaoh's cup was in my hand and I took the grapes and
pressed them into Pharaoh's cup, and placed the cup in
Pharaoh's hand.' 12 And Joseph said to him, 'This is the
interpretation of it: The three branches are three days.
13 Now within three days pharaoh will lift up your head
and restore you to your place, and you will put Pharaoh's
cup in his hand according to the former manner, when
you were his butler. 14 But remember me when it is well
with you and please show kindness to me; make mention
of me to Pharaoh, and get me out of this house.' "
Genesis 40:9-14

"Now it came to pass on the third day,
which was Pharaoh's birthday, that he made a feast
for all his servants, and he lifted up the head of the chief
butler and of the chief baker among his servants.
The he restored the chief butler to his butlership again,
and he place the cup in Pharaoh's hand."
Genesis 40:20, 21

"Yet the chief butler did not remember Joseph, but forgot him."
Genesis 40:23

Then it came to pass, at the end of two full years, that Pharaoh had a dream."
Genesis 41:1

"Then the chief butler spoke to Pharaoh, saying, 'I remember my faults this day.10 When Pharaoh was angry with his servants and put me in custody in the house of the captain of the guard, both me and the chief baker, 11 we each had a dream in one night, he and I. Each of us dreamed according to the interpretation of his own dream. 12 Now there was young Hebrew man with us there, a servant of the captain of the guard. And we told him, and he interpreted our dreams for us; to each man he interpreted according to his own dream. 13 And it came to pass, just as he interpreted for us, so it happened. He restored me to my office, and he hanged him.' 14 Then Pharaoh sent and called Joseph, and they brought him quickly out of the dungeon; and he shaved, changed his clothing, and came to Pharaoh. 15 And Pharaoh said to Joseph, 'I have a had a dream, and there is no one who can interpret it. But I have heard it said of you that you can understand a dream, to interpret it.' 16 So Joseph answered Pharaoh, saying, 'It is not in me; God will give Pharaoh an answer of peace.' "
Genesis 41:9-16

In verses 17-24 Pharaoh shared with Joseph the two dreams he had that troubled and perplexed him. After Joseph interprets these dreams to Pharaoh's satisfaction in the following verses, Pharaoh promotes Joseph for two reasons:

1) Because of Joseph's ability to interpret his dreams

2) Because of the sound advice Joseph shared on how to sustain the country during the upcoming time of famine foretold of in the dreams.

"Then Pharaoh said to Joseph, 'Inasmuch as God has shown you all of this, there is no one as discerning and wise as you. You shall be over my house, and all my people shall be ruled according to your word; only in regard to the throne will I be greater than you.' And Pharaoh said to Joseph, 'See, I have set you over all the land of Egypt.' "
Genesis 41:39-41

These passages prove the point about trouble positioning the Christian for purpose, promises and fulfilled prophecy. As terrible and traumatic as Joseph being placed in prison must have been, prison *positioned* him to meet the chief butler who ultimately introduced him to Pharaoh, who gave Joseph the job that fulfilled the purpose God had shown him in his dreams.

But without *trouble*, the fulfillment of purpose would not have been possible because it was *trouble* that positioned him for the fulfillment purpose.

Movement is often a sign that God is positioning us for a fulfilled purpose.

Trouble positions us for fulfilled purpose; also it sometimes positions us in places and seasons wherein our spiritual gifts, talents and abilities are manifested for cultivation or operation.

It was during Joseph's days in the dampened dungeon that he first realized and utilized his spiritual gift of dream interpretation. Had Joseph never encountered the trouble of prison, the gift of dream interpretation may have never manifested itself to the point where it would make room for him in Pharaoh's presence, and propel him into the fulfillment of his purpose.

**"A man's gift makes room for him,
and brings him before great men."
Proverbs 18:16**

Joseph's gift of dream interpretation brought him before Pharaoh, but it was trouble that positioned him in a place where that gift was first made known. Had he not encountered the trouble that positioned him in prison, his gift would have never brought him before Pharaoh.

In Genesis 41:39 Pharaoh commended Joseph for being "discerning and wise." The *discernment* had to do with his ability to interpret Pharaoh's dream, but the *wisdom* was a product of what Joseph learned while positioned by trouble in Potiphar's house.

Twice God used trouble to *position* Joseph:

The first time God positioned Joseph to cultivate his God-given ability to manage people, property and produce in Potiphar's house. This was a God-given ability because Joseph didn't have any prior experience at managing anything before he ended up in Potiphar's place.

The second time God used trouble to position Joseph was to activate his gift of dream interpretation. Before he interpreted the dreams of the butler and the baker, the Bible has no record of Joseph's interpreting dreams. He wasn't even quite sure of what his own dreams meant in the years prior.

But notice also that Joseph's God-given gifts and abilities were *first* used on a smaller scale before they were used on a much larger, more meaningful scale. By the time Joseph made it to Pharaoh's palace and was put in charge of all of the people, property and produce, he was ready to manage that on such a large scale because that ability had already been cultivated when he had been given the same responsibility only on a smaller scale.

And the dream he interpreted for the butler while positioned in prison by trouble found him favor with the butler who eventually (at the right time) remembered him before Pharaoh. However, the dream he would interpret for Pharaoh would find Joseph on a much larger scale, and Joseph would see his purpose of being second of command of all of Egypt fulfilled.

What can be clearly seen is *trouble* playing a tremendously important role in being used by God to *position* Joseph in the places in which God knew he needed to be in order for his God-given abilities to be cultivated and realized, for his God-given gifts to bring him before great men, and for the great purpose and plan for his life to be fulfilled.

How we find God using trouble in the life of Joseph (and others) is the *exact* same way that God will use any and all trouble that you or I encounter. God allows trouble because He uses it to bring to pass His good, acceptable and perfect will for the Christian's life.

The Leading Into Trouble

The place where promises are fulfilled is rarely, if ever, bordered by the place where the promise was given. There is almost always a space in between the two places that is occupied by time spent in the preparation chamber of trouble.

We find this truth in the history of the children of Israel and the promise given to them about the land of Canaan—the Promised Land. That promise was given to them in Egypt, but when they left Egypt because of the promise, they did not enter directly into Canaan. Egypt, the place of promise given, did not border Canaan, the place of promise fulfillment. Egypt and Canaan did not border because they were separated by a space—a desert land called the wilderness of Zin.

If you have ever read that story, you know that the wilderness was a place purposed to prepare them for the Promised Land living. A place of humility, teaching, learned trust, and dependence on the Lord, the wilderness of Zin was also a place of great trouble.

God hardly ever takes us from where we are directly into promise, purpose or fulfilled prophecy. There is seemingly always that wilderness—that in between, transitional place or period.

Joseph didn't awaken from the prophetic dreams of his father's house and go straightway into Pharaoh's house. No, there was a space—a spiritual wilderness between the place of prophetic dream and the place of prophetic fulfillment. The space was not only occupied by the geography between the two, or even time. Joseph's wilderness was also occupied by the trouble of betrayal, abandonment and mistreatment, as well as teaching, the creation of patience and overall preparation for purpose.

I can recall when the Lord began to deal with me about stepping back from pastoring the church I had started 11 years earlier. I knew I needed to step back for the sake of fulfilling the prophecy that was given to me twice, twelve years apart.

The first was in 1996 during the Brownsville revival in Pensacola, Florida. The first night of that week's revival was a Tuesday and had been designated as prayer night. Thousands who had come from literally all over the world were to pray for the various things stated on banners that were positioned all throughout the sanctuary. After spending 10 to 15 minutes praying at one banner, everyone was to shift to another banner and pray for whatever or whoever was stated on that banner, e.g. family, pastor, church, government, nations, etc.

After everyone had spent time praying at the various banners, the instruction was to return to the area of our seating and begin to pray with and for the people who were seated near us. I had the pleasure of being seated near a wonderful brother and sister couple from Mississippi. The three of us had waited near the very front of the line for approximately 12 hours before the doors opened at 6:00 p.m., one hour before the prayer service began.

After the three of us had prayed for one another, a fellow who seemingly had been standing by waiting for us to finish praying, reached out to shake my hand, and said to me, "How you doin', Preacher?" That greeting took me by surprise because I had never before been to Florida, and I didn't know anyone there. I had not told anyone I was a minister—not even the couple with whom I had spent 12 hours in line. And I certainly was not dressed like anyone's preacher by the image many have when they envision the appearance of a *preacher*. I had on a pair of Michael Jordan basketball shoes, blue jeans, a denim jacket with the collar up (that's the cool way, you know?), and my Chicago Bulls championship t-shirt! So, it obviously wasn't my attire that tipped him off to my being a preacher.

While thinking, "Who is this guy and how in the world does he know I am a preacher?" he said, "Did you know the Lord was going to use you to be a great evangelist, and you're going to be a blessing to thousands and thousands all around the world?"

I remember saying, "Glory" with my mouth, but in my heart, to be honest, I didn't believe him. I didn't believe him because I knew the Lord had already placed pastoring in my heart, and what this fellow was saying, in my estimation, was contrary to that. As supernatural as that encounter felt, it took me a long time to come to grips with it. The memory of our conversation remained in the back of my mind.

The second prophecy came 12 years later while I was ministering a couple of nights on Holy Spirit baptism at a church in the state of New York. As was the case with Florida,

I had never before been to New York, and I only knew the buddy who had invited me to minister and his family.

After having taught on the second night and given the invitation for people to come forth and be filled with the Holy Spirit, nearly everyone came forth and was filled. A gentleman whom I did not know and had never before seen came to me and said, "Brother, the Lord is going to use you to write many books…."

I am typically skeptical about people who prophesy because Jesus says, **"…many false prophets will rise up and deceive many,"** and because 1 John 4:1 says, **"Beloved, do not believe every spirit, but test the spirits, whether they are on God; because many false prophets have gone out into the world."** The fact that Jesus makes His statement to disciples, and that John issues his warning to the "beloved" teaches us that false prophets are not only assigned to deceive the world but Christians as well. For this reason—though I believe strongly in the gift of prophecy—I am not quick to embrace those who claim to carry a prophetic word.

When the gentleman approached me with the mention of "writing many books," right away this comment got my attention because I knew the Lord had those plans for me. In fact, unbeknownst to him, I had brought with me the book proposal for this book for my friend to take a look at. One of the pages contained a list of 12 books I was planning to write. But this gentleman could not have known that.

Specific prophecy gets my attention. I must admit that I am leery about general prophecies. I believe true prophets can share specifics that no one else knows. Statements like, "Oh my brother/sister, the Lord is going to bless you!" are more of a proclamation of what we already know that God is going to do than a prophetic word from the Lord. Specifics help to legitimize that which is said to be prophetic. For example,

"Thursday at 10:32 a.m., someone will call you for a spur-of-the-moment interview for a job for which you applied three weeks ago. They told you that they had filled the position with someone else, but that candidate will fall through, and they will want you. Get your hair cut and get your gray suit cleaned because Mr. Matthews didn't particularly care for the black one you wore to the first interview. Before you go, relax! Don't be so nervous like you were before when you tied your shoestrings together and almost fell on your face before you even left the house. When your salary is discussed, ask for $12,000 more per year and tell them you would need a company car and a parking spot. They will look at you funny, but just keep silent and look serious. They will give you what you ask for."

Now, *that's* an example of a prophetic word! Okay, granted, they don't all have to be *that* specific or detailed, but they should have some degree of specifics, and supernatural knowledge (1 Samuel 9:6, 10:2-10). Accurate specifics without having been made privy to the information about what is, or what is to come—is one way I ***"test the spirits."***

The fellow who mentioned "*the many books*" went on to state, almost verbatim, what the gentleman had prophesied to me 12 years prior, *"The Lord is going to use you to be a blessing to thousands and thousands all around the world."*

I believed this prophetic declaration for two reasons:

1) Because it was preceded by a word that I knew was true concerning me writing many books.

2) Because it was consistent, and confirming of a word I had received 12 years earlier in a city that was over 1,200 miles away.

However, when I finally stepped back from pastoring two years later because the Spirit of God spoke to me and said to me, "You can't get there (the place of prophecy) from here (the place of pastoring)," I expected to step from pastoring right into fulfilled prophecy. Boy, was I ever wrong!

Stepping back from pastoring did not border stepping into fulfilled prophecy. It bordered the wilderness—the place of testing, teaching, humbling, abandonment, betrayal, bewilderment, financial struggle, preparation and positioning—and there was a little of trouble during that time as well.

Often, purpose, fulfilled promises and prophecies are bordered by the wilderness because the wilderness prepares us for these times. God will make known to us His plans, purposes and promises for our life, but He will lead us into the wilderness because the wilderness is on the way to fulfilled plans, purposes and promises. We find the Lord operating in this manner with His people all throughout the Bible. Such was even the case with Jesus before He began to operate in the plan and purpose of the Father for His coming to Earth.

"Then Jesus was led up by the Spirit into the wilderness to be tempted by the devil."
Matthew 4:1

"Immediately the Spirit drove Him into the wilderness. And He was there in the wilderness forty days, tempted by Satan, and was with the wild beasts; and the angels ministered to Him."
Mark 1:12, 13

Although Jesus had come for a specific purpose—mainly to die for our sins and to be resurrected for our right-standing with God—the fulfillment of that prophecy, that plan, and that specific purpose went *through* the wilderness. The wilderness was the place of tempting and trying times where even the Savior needed the help of the angels.

It was after Jesus' wilderness experience that He was propelled—full-throttle—into His purpose of teaching, healing, doing the miraculous, and saving many souls. But He went through the wilderness because the wilderness possessed a purpose of its own—a purpose that is meaningful and necessary for every child of God who is called to make an impact in the kingdom of God!

The Lord may lead us into the wilderness when it is purposefully on the way to fulfilled plans and promises.

Chapter 5
Where in the World Is God When I Am in Trouble?

"Why do You stand afar off, O Lord?
Why do You hide in times of trouble?"
(Psalm 10:1)

If you have ever experienced any sort of serious, prolonged trouble, you have undoubtedly asked this question—at least in your mind. I most certainly have! I may not have literally asked the fifteenth-century version: **"Why standest Thou afar off…?"** but I have definitely wondered in twenty-first century fashion, *"Lord, where in the world are You? And, why aren't You helping me?!"*

Many of us have heard the saying, *"God is never late; He's right on time."* Whereas this expression may be true, I have learned that *"on time"* is not always *on my time.* God is God, and He is on His own schedule as it pertains to His plans to use us and bless our life. And that's okay because His track record proves that He is trustworthy and that His timing is impeccable, though not always understood or agreed with.

It's good to know that God's time is *on time* and be reminded of it through the lives of people like Joseph, David, the three Hebrew boys, and others because the reality is that sometimes it seems like we are the furthest thing from God's mind. And this is probably why David asked, **"Why do You stand afar off, O Lord?"**

In Psalm 13:1 David once asked of God, "**How long, O Lord? Will you forget me forever?"** Seemingly, David had rationalized that God had forgotten him because God had not yet delivered him. Not only had God not delivered David, God seemingly wasn't responding to his questions either.

So in the natural, negative progression of a heart that feels ignored, David's next question was, "*Lord, are You ever going to remember me, and the trouble I'm in*?" I have been there, and I have felt that way. Maybe you have too.

And then there are times when our thoughts graduate from thinking God has forgotten us to thinking He has flat-out forsaken us!

"My God, my God, why have You forsaken me? Why are You so far from helping me, and from the words of my groaning? O my God, I cry in the daytime, but You do not hear; and in the night season, I am not silent."
Psalm 22:1, 2

Psalm 22 is considered one of the Messianic psalms that prophesy about the events involving the life of Jesus. In fact, the words "**My God, My God, why have You forsaken Me**?" were uttered by our Christ from the cross. But I believed these words of David were his own in that he also felt forsaken by his God during his time of trouble—as have I and even you perhaps.

Having even a basic understanding of who David was and Who Jesus is frees us from a feeling of embarrassment or immaturity when we wonder if we have been forsaken by God. If the mighty King David encountered times when he felt forsaken, and the mighty King of kings felt the same, it's not a stretch, a surprise or reason to feel ashamed or spiritually immature when we have such a feeling, or question the whereabouts of our God during our time of serious trouble.

The Israelites were in trouble and had a promise of God for deliverance. And after the time they felt He should have already shown up to deliver them, they began to think that God had forgotten and even forsaken them. But check out God's response to them and understand that since God's Word is the *living* Word, His Word to them back then is also His Word to you and to me—now.

"But Zion said, 'The Lord has forsaken me,
and my Lord has forgotten me.' "
Isaiah 49:14

Listen to what the Lord says in response to how His people were feeling:

"Can a woman forget her nursing child,
And not have compassion on the son of her womb?
Surely <u>they</u> may forget, yet <u>I will not forget you.</u>
See, I have inscribed you in the palms of My hands."
Isaiah 49:15

This verse is an extremely powerful and reassuring confirmation to the fact that the Lord has *not* forgotten, nor forsaken us; and *why* He hasn't forgotten or forsaken us—because the scars from the nails in the palms of Jesus remind Him of His covenant and commitment to us. In the scars of Jesus is spelled out the name of every one of us who believe in Him as Savior, and trust Him as Lord!

Here and now, God wants you to know, and to be *absolutely certain* that He has neither forgotten nor forsaken you. The reality is that when we are in trouble, God is right there with us—*in* our trouble—though it doesn't always seem, or feel like it. Look at what David (who may have been the trouble champion of the entire Bible) wrote after the Lord had delivered him from a number of troublesome circumstances:

"God is our refuge and strength,
A very present help <u>in</u> trouble."
Psalm 46:1

Notice that David said God was "present" with him while he was "in trouble" meaning that not only was God *with* David *while* he was in trouble, God was in David's trouble with him. If there is anyone who knows *where* God is during times of trouble, it's David!

Like David, I too have felt as if God was "afar off," playing golf or something while I was drowning in the pit of despair. However, also like David, I noticed that the Lord was indeed present in my trouble with me.

The purpose of God's presence during our time of trouble is not to be a spectator, but to participate by helping us during our time of trouble and ultimately by helping us out of our time of trouble. It is *extremely* important to understand that before God helps us *out of* our time of trouble, He is helping us *during* our time of trouble. *(Please read that last sentence again.)*

"But the salvation of the righteous is from the
Lord; He is their strength <u>in</u> the time of trouble.
And the Lord shall help them and deliver them;
He shall deliver them from the wicked, and
save them because they trust in Him."
(Psalm 37:39-40)

Notice two points in this Davidic psalm:

1) As he stated in Psalm 46, David reveals here that the Lord doesn't forsake us in trouble; instead, He is with us to **"strengthen"** us **"in the time of trouble."**

2) Notice also that before the Lord delivers us *out of trouble*, He helps us *during our trouble*. We can know this because the verse says God, "**is their strength <u>*in*</u> the time of**

trouble." Any time God *strengthens* us, He is *helping* us. But we also know that God helps us *before* He delivers us because the structure and order of the verse reveals this truth.

Verse 40 says, "...**the Lord shall help them <u>and</u> deliver them....**"

If you remember learning about conjunctions in school, you may remember that a conjunction is a word that links together two separate thoughts, ideas or possibilities. Well, the word "and" is the conjunction that links the two different promises of *help* and *deliverance.*

Help in the time of trouble is one thing, while *deliverance from* the time of trouble is something completely different. And notice that *before* God brings *deliverance,* He provides *help.*

I realize that deliverance is the ultimate help, and the one thing we want more than anything else when we are in trouble; but there is *help* from God that greatly benefits us *before* He delivers us.

Consider this: before God delivered Shadrach, Meshach and Abednego *out of* the burning fiery furnace, He helped them while they were yet *in* the burning fiery furnace. How else does one explain the fact that "*...the fire had no power [over them], nor was a hair of the head singed, neither were their coats changed, nor had the smell of fire passed on them,*" if God did not help them while they were yet *in* trouble?

If that verse doesn't convince you that God was a present help *in* their trouble, how about these words from King Nebuchadnezzar:

"Did we not cast three men bound in to
The midst of the fire?
Daniel 3:24b

Look! I see <u>four</u> men
Loose, walking in the middle of the fire;
And they are not hurt, and the form of the
Fourth (here it is) <u>is like the Son of God.</u>"
Daniel 3:25

If Christ was in the fire with Shadrach, Meshach, and Abednego, wouldn't you agree that God is a "*very present help <u>in</u> trouble*"? And since God changes not, and is neither a respecter of persons, b*ecause* He was "*a present help*" during *their* time of trouble, God is a present help in *your* time of trouble too!

Before the Lord helps us *out of* trouble, He helps us *in,* or *during* our time of trouble. But often this help from God goes undetected by us.

We know that King Nebuchadnezzar saw "the Son of God" in the fire with Shadrach, Meshach and Abednego, but there is no indication that they saw Him. Surely they knew it was the Lord Who protected them *from* the fire and ultimately delivered them *out* of the fire, but they may not have actually *seen* Him at work.

During his time of trouble, Job shares an observation that sheds light on the dealings of God:

"When He works on the left hand,
I cannot behold Him;
When He turns to the right hand,
I cannot see Him."
Job 23:9

Despite his difficulties, Job knew God was at work in his situation even though he could not, "see Him" working. Such is the case with us and our situations; we don't always see God working when He is working. Neither does He announce the fact that He is working (although we wish He would! Just a little, *"Hey, I'm here now, and I'm working it out! Don't worry!"*

would be helpful. After all, the cable man, the plumber, and the electrician all announce when they show up to work. Come on, God!).

God wants us to have faith that He is working on our behalf—even when we don't see Him doing so or when it doesn't *seem* like He's doing so. Remember, **"...faith is the substance of things hoped for, the evidence of things not seen."**

We cannot base what we believe about God helping us on what we *see* Him doing because the "invisible God" works in invisible ways—ways that are not only invisible to our eyes but also to our mind. Whether or not we know it, God is working to help us in our time of trouble and *out of* our time of trouble.

The invisible God works in places that are invisible to our eyes and in ways that are invisible to our mind.

Job goes on to say in chapter 23: **"He knows the way that I take, when He has tried me I shall come forth as gold."** If you know the story of Job, you also know that Job was right, he "came forth as gold," having received double of all he lost during his time of trouble.

Job's declaration about his future was made while he was in the middle of his trouble. He did not know a great deal about his situation, but he knew two things:

1) God was working even though he could not *see* Him working.

2) His trouble would end, and he would be better than he was *before* trouble visited his life.

It is powerful and important to note that everyone we have discussed who experienced times of trouble came out *better* than they were *before* trouble. They all "came forth as gold," and so will you!

There is a great deal to like about God helping, and ultimately delivering the Hebrew boys from the furnace, but I also like what took place with them *after* the Lord helped and delivered them. God was glorified, and they "came forth as gold"!

"Nebuchadnezzar spoke saying, 'Blessed be the God of Shadrach, Meshach and Abed-nego, who sent His Angel and delivered His servants who trusted in Him, and they have frustrated the king's word, and yielded their bodies, that they should not serve nor worship any god except their own God. Therefore, I make a decree that any people, nation, or language which speaks anything amiss against the God of Shadrach, Meshach and Abed-nego shall be cut in pieces and their houses shall be made an ash heap; because there is no other God who can deliver like this. Then the king <u>promoted</u> Shadrach, Meshach and Abed-nego in the province of Babylon."
Daniel 3:28-30

Understandably, we pray and ask God to help us avoid trouble. But the reality is that God doesn't always help us to avoid trouble; however, He will help us during our time of trouble before He finally delivers us from trouble. And after He delivers us from trouble, a promotion awaits us—a promotion that would not have taken place had the Lord not allowed the trouble.

Trouble often precedes promotions. And sometimes, trouble is purposed to produce promotions. The point is, before the Lord delivers us *out of* our time of trouble He is with us, helping us, *during* our time of trouble.

Such was also the situation with Joseph while he was in prison:

"Then Joseph's master took him and
put him into the prison, a place where
the king's prisoners were confined.
and he was there in prison.
[I love this next part!]
But the Lord was <u>with Joseph</u> and showed
him mercy, and He gave him favor
in the sight of the keeper of the prison."
Genesis 39:20, 21

The first thing to notice is the fact that God "was with Joseph," which means the Lord was "present" *during* Joseph's time of trouble. When Psalm 139 talks about the omnipresence of God, it means that God is everywhere, even, and including *with us* in our time of trouble.

"Where can I go from Your Spirit?
Or where can I flee from Your presence?
If I ascend into heaven, behold, You are there.
If I make my bed in hell, behold, You are there.
If I take the wings of the morning, and dwell
In the uttermost parts of the sea,
<u>Even there</u> Your hand shall lead me,
And Your right hand shall hold me."
Psalm 139:7-10

In this passage, David expresses his understanding of the fact that God is everywhere he is, including his time and place of trouble. "*Even there*" does His right hand hold us up and helps us *in* trouble—before He leads us *out* of trouble.

In the same way God was with David He had already been with Joseph—which acts as evidence that God changes not. He does not stand on the outside while we are *in* trouble; God is right there in the thick of trouble with us.

The Lord said to Jeremiah (23:23) that He is **"...a God near at hand...and not a God afar off..."** further indicating that He is with us in trouble. God also feels what we are feeling during the season of malady, **"For we have <u>not</u> a High Priest which cannot not be touched with the feelings of our infirmities…" Hebrews 4:15**

Of Jesus, Isaiah (53:3) prophesied that, **"He is a Man of sorrows, and acquainted with grief."** So the Lord is not only right there with us during our time of trouble, He shares in what we feel.

**"God is our refuge and strength. A very present help in trouble. Therefore we will not fear…."
Psalm 46:1,2a**

Before the Lord delivered Joseph *out of* his trouble, He was with him to help him *in* his trouble by causing him to find "favor in the sight of the keeper of the prison."

That may not sound like a big deal in comparison with what Joseph believed God for (which, of course, was deliverance), but it is important not to overlook the small things God does *during* our times of trouble while looking only for the big thing—complete deliverance.

It is during our trouble, before God delivers us that He does small things that help us and remind us that He is yet with us and has not forgotten or forsaken us. He does small things like, moving someone to bless us, or revealing something positive to us in His Word about our situation—something He causes us to know in Him speaking directly to us about the good that is yet to come.

I know from personal experience that small things in the "time of trouble" go a *looong* way toward reminding us, reviving us, and encouraging us to hang in there because God is with us. He is a "present help in trouble"—even before He delivers us *from* trouble.

This truth is extremely important to understand because there is a tendency to think that if God isn't delivering us *out of* trouble He isn't helping us—but that's not true. Before God helps us by delivering us *out of* trouble, He's helping us even while we are yet *in* our trouble. He's helping us endure so that the trouble He allowed can accomplish what He purposes for it to accomplish.

Trouble often precedes promotions. And sometimes, trouble is purposed to produce promotions.

As was the case with Shadrach, Meshach and Abed-nego being promoted after their time of trouble, such was the case with Joseph who was led from prison to Pharaoh where he begin living the life of which he had once dreamed. But had it not been for *trouble,* Joseph would have never seen the promotion the Lord had planned for him. God was not only with Joseph in his trouble, helping him, God also was using Joseph's trouble to promote him.

I'm blessed and encouraged by these examples, and I hope you are too, because they reveal to us that God is not a purposeless God Who just stands idly by and watches us suffer during our days of difficulty. Instead these illustrations reveal that God is a God Who doesn't forsake us, but helps us before He delivers us! And when He delivers us, He does so into the promotion that is awaiting our arrival! Glory!

Chapter 6

Trouble, Brokenness, and the Spirit of Suicide

**"My spirit is broken,
my days are extinguished,
the grave is ready for me."
Job 17:1**

The types, degrees, terms, and reasons for trouble vary from believer to believer. Trouble shows up in the form of lost loved ones, physical ailments, sickness, depression, financial struggles, challenges with people, and in other ways. Some troubles having varying degrees. For example, some sicknesses can be healed with medicine, another requires surgery, and yet other types require a miracle from God. Terms and reasons for trouble vary as well. Some troubles are short-lived while others live longer. Some troubles are products of disobedience; others are *no-fault* troubles.

Two examples of differing reasons and terms of trouble can be found in the lives of Joseph and Jonah. Because of disobedience, Jonah found himself in trouble in the sea and ended up in the belly of a big guppy. But his trouble only lasted three days, and when he decided to obey God and minister the Word of repentance to the people of Nineveh, his trouble ended.

Joseph's trouble, the result of no wrongdoing, but some *right* doing on his part, lasted 13 years and was designed to prepare and position him for purpose. These two examples reveal at least three truths:

1) There are different reasons for trouble.

2) The term of trouble can vary from days to years.

3) Sometimes the *term* of a person's trouble is in the hands of his compliance with God. But other times trouble must run its course in accomplishing its purpose.

Outside of the trouble of disobedience, which we can control, another factor in the type, depth and term of trouble God allows is what we can handle. Because the internal makeup, level of maturity and purpose in life differ from person to person, the type, degree and term of our trouble will differ as well. Not everyone can handle heavy, deep, long-term trouble. And some light, short-lived trouble will not be enough to prepare a person for the great plan God has in place for him. What Joseph endured may have been too heavy for James, and the three days of trouble Jonah experienced would not have prepared Joseph to become the governor of Egypt.

Although there are varying types, degrees, terms, and reasons for trouble, there is also a trouble that is so deep, long and disturbing that it causes brokenness. It was this type of trouble in which Job found himself that made him say, "**My spirit is broken**."

To be *broken* means "to be disheartened to the point of despair." Brokenness, which is far beyond disappointment and frustration, is where depression, hopelessness and misery meet and feed us the cocktail feelings of failure and forlorn. Brokenness is a state of numbness wherein we exist without enthusiasm or expectation of better than what we have been beaten down by. It is where we are imprisoned after having been so trampled by trouble that our hope and spirit seem incapable of recovering—even if we wanted it to recover.

Brokenness is a state of being with which the average person cannot identify. It is also one to which those who are close to us may not be able to relate. A point came in his time of trouble when Job was broken. And understandably so after having encountered the type of trouble he encountered—and in such a short period of time. The flaw in his friends addressed in an earlier chapter was their misconception that Job's trouble was the result of his transgression, and it was not. The problem with the error of their estimation (aside from its being errant) was that their faulty thinking failed to allow them to *see* their friend's brokenness and thus they failed to encourage him in it and through it.

After listening to a lengthy monologue of mistaken accusations by his friend Eliphaz, (a long list of nonsense that Job deserved a medal of endurance and humility for listening to), Job finally responds to all his friends in chapter 16 with, **"Miserable comforters are you all!"** They were incapable of comforting Job, not only because they didn't know the real reason for his troubles, but also because they could not identify with the brokenness he was experiencing.

People who misjudge *why* you are going through *what* you are going through are not capable of being a source of encouragement. I wish we all were friends of people who have experienced the type of trouble that bleeds sympathy. For then the scar that remains from the wounds caused by trouble past would remind them of their troubling times and enable them to be an encouragement. However, people cannot draw encouragement from a dry well that has never been filled with the rain waters of adversity.

Although they may mean well, people like the friends of Job can sometimes do more harm than good. The lack of understanding, support, and encouragement from Job's friends may have contributed to his brokenness. I say this because Job expresses his brokenness in chapter 17—after two chapters of being accused of sin by Eliphaz and his saying that Job was being punished by God; a chapter by Bildad urging him to come clean and repent; a chapter by Zophar urging him to repent, saying essentially, "Even the Lord knows you're not being honest"; and another chapter from Eliphaz accusing Job of lying to God about not being in sin. All of the words of discouragement from his friends was more than enough to drive Job deeper into despair.

"Then Job answered and said:
'How long will you torment my soul,
and break me in pieces with words?
These ten times you have reproached me;
you are not ashamed that you
have wronged me.' "
Job 19:2, 3

I don't think Job's friends meant to wrong him, but they certainly were of no help to him. The unfortunate reality is that humans—even family members and good friends—can sometimes be a source of discouragement by not believing you, believing *in* you, or by not sticking by you. Job's story resonates with us because he felt what we feel.

"My relatives have failed me,
And my close friends have forgotten me."
Job 19:14

We should most certainly embrace encouragement when it comes, and by all means, treasure those through which that encouragement comes. But **Psalm 118:8** says, **"It is better to trust in the Lord than to put confidence in man."** This is also why we have a High Priest Who can sympathize with our brokenness, and One Who invites us to"**...come boldly to the throne of grace, that we may obtain mercy and find grace to help in the time of need." Hebrews 4:16**

Those who have been broken minister most effectively to those who are broken. In fact, God calls people to brokenness that He may *mend them* and *send them* to minister to others who are broken. The apostle Paul, writer of most of the New Testament, was more insightful and encouraging than the other apostles *because* he had encountered and endured far more difficulty than they had. Take a read of Paul's resume of adversity as he made the case for the authenticity of his apostleship to the church at Corinth after others had attempted to undermine his ministry:

"Are they ministers of Christ?—I speak
as a fool—I am more: in labors more abundant;
in stripes above measure,
in prisons more frequently, in deaths
often. 24 From the Jews five times I received
forty stripes minus one. 25 Three times I was
beaten with rods; once I was stoned;
three times I was shipwrecked; a night and
a day I have been in the deep; 26 in journeys
often, in perils of waters, in perils
of robbers, in perils of my own countrymen,
in perils of the Gentiles, in perils in the city;
in perils in the wilderness, in perils in the sea,
in perils among false brethren; 27 in weariness
and toil, in sleeplessness often, in hunger
and thirst, in fastings often, in cold and
Nakedness—28 besides the other things,
what comes upon me daily; my deep
concern for all the churches."
2 Corinthians 11:23-28

Because of the depth of trouble Paul experienced, when he ministers he is able to encourage and inspire *because* he can identify. Such will be the case with all who experience the type of trouble that causes brokenness. God has allowed people to be broken in the past because their past brokenness allows the valuable lessons of trouble to leak from them. And the *leak* leads us to people, or draws them to us so that they can drink from the encouragement, and the experience that leaks from us.

The broken body of our Lord and King leaked the blood that purchased our redemption. And it was not by accident that the spikes that nailed the hands of Jesus to the cross created a wound and left a scar. The wound signified the trouble He endured for our transgressions, and the scar allows us to know He can identify with our troubles. Christ told Thomas to touch the scar as proof of His resurrection. Though the resurrection power healed the wound, the scar remained as a reminder that the skin of His hands was broken so that with those same hands He could remember our brokenness and would heal our broken spirit!

No one can comfort and encourage broken people like people who have once been broken. This is why support groups of people who have been through similar traumatic experiences are formed and are extremely helpful. The people who create and comprise such groups have been where the newcomers are, and they have experienced what they are experiencing. And they are able to help *because* they can relate.

Broken things in the world are of little to no worth. But in body of Christ, people who have been broken are priceless! Job may have never known why he was broken. We know he was tested to prove his loyalty to the Lord in the face of adversity. But he was *broken* so that the story of his brokenness—and repair—could minister to us in our brokenness as we prepare for repair. Even through the brokenness your trouble has caused you, know that the King of kings has great use for you in the kingdom of His Christ!

Broken people who are repaired by the Potter are of greater value than they were in their pre-broken state.

It is important that we recognize the value of our brokenness. It is important because it in the abyss of despair that the devil lurks, "**...seeking whom he may devour.**" If we do not realize that our brokenness is not the end of us, but that we can be repaired to a *better than before,* more helpful state of being, the enemy will more than likely have his way with us—a way that holds no good for us. Jesus teaches, "**The thief [devil] does not come except to steal, to kill, and to destroy" (John 10:10).** The progressive pattern of harmful intent allows us to know that Satan is not simply satisfied with stealing our peace, joy, and our substance during our time of trouble; he is also interested in taking our life during that time—and using us to do so!

When God gave Satan permission to trouble Job, the Lord placed the life of Job off-limits to him. However, that didn't mean Satan would stop entertaining the idea of Job dying; he just had to figure out another way to get it done. After all, death is what the devil *comes* to bring, and he probably receives greater satisfaction by causing the child of God to end his own life than by dying any other way.

Thoughts of suicide are not uncommon with Christians. Some thoughts are fleeting and are quickly dismissed. Some are given consideration. Some are so harassing they force serious consideration. And unfortunately, some thoughts of suicide give birth and become the actual act. This situation can be found with a number of people in the Scriptures. Most, if not all of them, had some level of relationship with the Lord:

- King Saul (1 Samuel 31:4, 5)
- Ahithophel, counselor and advisor to King David and later his son Absalom (2 Samuel 17:23)
- Zimri, king over Israel (1 Kings 16:18);
- Judas, one of the original 12 apostles (Matthew 27:5).
- Samson, judge of Israel (Judges 16:25-30).
  Some would say that Samson committed suicide when he lost his life in the process of killing the Philistines.

Aside from the children of God who actually committed suicide, others undoubtedly entertained the idea. Job cursed the day of his birth and talked about his death so much it would be hard to believe that he didn't think about taking his own life. Although he and others like him didn't take their lives because of the brokenness caused by their troubles, because they did not commit suicide does not mean that wasn't the devil's objective in sowing the idea of suicide.

It is extremely important to realize that the thoughts and ideas of suicide are demonic in nature. Not every idea of suicide is from clinical depression; many result from demonic oppression. The devil and his unclean angels operate in us by placing ideas on our mind. Ideas, when entertained too long, can mature and become the actual action of the suggestion. The sole assignment of the unclean spirits of suicide is to place thoughts, ideas and suggestions of suicide in the mind of people—even people of God—and surely people God wants to use.

Before I address two good reasons *why* people should refrain from suicide and *how* to do so, consider the following passages as evidence for the case against Satan being guilty of instilling the idea of suicide, and the existence of unclean spirits of suicide.

"Then the devil took Jesus up into the holy city, set Him on the pinnacle of the temple, and said to Him, 'If You are the Son of God, throw Yourself down. For it is written: 'He shall give His angels charge over you, in their Hands they shall bear you up, lest You dash your foot against a stone.'" Matthew 4:5, 6

In this Scripture, Satan, the *chief* of all unclean spirits, places the idea of suicide on the mind of Jesus when he said to Him **"...throw Yourself down."** Anytime anyone *says* something to us, their words become thoughts in our mind to consider, or *ideas* for us to carry out. Therefore, when Satan **"said"** to Jesus, "**throw Yourself down**," he was depositing the thought or the idea of suicide in the mind of Jesus in the hopes that his words would become the act of Jesus.

The fact that Satan operates in the arena of suicidal thoughts serves as evidence for the case that unclean spirits also sow thoughts of suicide into the mind of people. And because devil did so with the Christ, it is not unreasonable to conclude the devil's angels do so with Christians and people in general. The devil doesn't only hate Christians and desire their premature death by way of suicide; he hates and desires the same for all people because he is incapable of loving. The following passage provides proof that there are unclean spirits of suicide.

"Then they sailed to the country of the Gadarenes, which is opposite Galilee. 27 And when He stepped out on the land, there met Him a certain man from the city who had demons for a long time. And he wore no clothes, nor did he live in a house but in the tombs. 28 When he saw Jesus, he cried out, fell down

before Him and with a loud voice said,
'What have I to do with You, Jesus, Son
of the Most High God? I beg You, do not
torment me!' 29 For He had commanded the
unclean spirit to come out of the man.
For it had often seized him, and he was
kept under guard, bound with chains
and shackles; and he broke the bonds
and was driven by the demons
into the wilderness.

30 Jesus asked him, saying, 'What
is your name?' And he said, 'Legion,'
because many demons had entered him.
31 And they begged Him that He would not
command them to go out into the abyss.
32 Now a herd of many swine was feeding
there on the mountain. So they begged
Him that He would permit them to enter
them. And He permitted them. 33 Then
the demons went out of the man and
entered the swine, and the herd ran
violently down the steep place into
the lake and drowned."
Luke 8:26-33

The first evidence of demonic influence was, "**no clothes**." You don't have to agree with me, but people who walk around in public with "no clothes" are under the influence of something—be it drugs, alcohol, demons or all three! The second indication of demonic influence, and the *first* sign of the *type* of demon with whom he was dealing is the word "tombs." Tombs are for the dead, so clearly these were demons of death, and specifically, death by suicide.

We are allowed to know this by what these demons did after Jesus commanded them to leave the man. They, "... **entered the swine, and the herd ran violently down the**

steep place into the lake and drowned." The fact that the unclean spirits caused the swine to drown themselves indicates that these were unclean spirits of suicide. Though they preferred the suicide of the person, they settled for the suicide of the swine. But the point is, what they influenced the swine to do reveals the purpose of their particular assignment—to cause suicide.

The demonic attack of suicidal thoughts are rarely successful with the first few "deposits" of the idea. Such a weapon is typically at work in the minds of people for months or even years before these thoughts cause a person to actually follow through with a suicide attempt. This is why the man who lived in the tombs had not already killed himself by the time Jesus arrived though he had "...**had demons for a long time."**

But how should the unclean spirits of suicide be handled? I believe the first key is to acknowledge their existence. If their existence is not acknowledged, we won't seek to defend ourselves against them because we typically do not defend against things we don't think exist or present a threat to us. The next key is to follow the examples of Jesus in dealing with the devil and his unclean demon spirits.

The first example is seen in Matthew chapter four when Satan deposited the idea of suicide into the mind of Jesus. We see Jesus' overcoming the suicidal thoughts of the devil with the life-giving Word of God. The valuable lesson to be learned here is that when the idea of suicide crosses our mind, we should simply speak the Word of God that is contrary to the deposited thoughts of the devil.

I say, "*Simply speak the Word of God*" because it's easy to do, and it is powerful when done! **"For the Word of God is living and powerful, and sharper than any two-edged sword..."** any enemy would employ against us. When the enemy sows the seed of suicide into our mind, from our mouth we should declare, **"I shall not die, but live and**

declare the works of the Lord!" That life giving Word about living is enough to instantly render ineffective *every* word from the enemy about suicide.

When we use the Word of God to resist and render powerless the demonic deposits of suicide, we may have to use His Word over and over again. Why? Because when demons and their thoughts are rebuked, they may return. We learn this fact in the rebuke of Satan by Jesus. Luke's account of this story says, "**And when the devil had ended all the temptation, he departed from Him for a season." (Luke 4:13)** This verse indicates that after being rebuked by the Word of God, the devil or his unclean spirits may return to *try it again* at another time. And that's fine because, if the Word of God worked to rebuke them before, guess what? The Word of God will rebuke them again! It doesn't matter if they go back to the drawing board, regroup, or get help, there is *nothing* they can create, conjure, or come up with that is stronger than the *Word* of the Lord our God! Nothing! So when the enemy goes and comes back with a new version of their old tricks, we simply whip out the same old eternally powerful Word of God and beat them back again... and again, and again, and again!

The second example set by Jesus when it comes to dealing with the spirit of suicide operating in other people is casting it out. Sometimes the spirits of suicide can only place the idea of suicide in the minds of people, but there are instances when unclean spirits are more aggressive in their control of the actions of people—actions that are intended to be harmful and even suicidal.

"Then one of the crowd answered and said,
'Teacher, I brought You my son, who has
a mute spirit.'"
Mark 9:17

Before I go further, notice in this verse how this unclean spirit is identified by his assignment or his ability to cause a certain type of problem. This particular demon was hindering the man's son from being able to speak as well as causing him other problems. But notice how Jesus dealt with this spirit:

"...He rebuked the unclean spirit, saying to it: 'Deaf and dumb spirit, I command you, come out of him and enter him no more!' Then the spirit cried out, convulsed him greatly, and came out of him."
Mark 9:25, 26

This type of unclean spirit not only had the ability to keep people from speaking, it could also hinder their hearing. In casting out the unclean spirit, Jesus corrected the boy's condition because the unclean spirit was the *cause* of his condition, proving that some maladies are spiritual in nature. In these cases, no amount of medical attention can help. This isn't the case 100 percent of the time; sometimes identical conditions can be physical in nature and not spiritual in nature.

"Then they brought to [Jesus] one who was deaf and had an impediment in his speech, and the begged Him to put His hand on him. And Jesus took him aside from the multitude, and put His fingers in his ears, and He spat and touched his tongue. Then, looking up to Heaven, He sighed, and said to him, 'Ephphatha,' that is, 'Be opened.' Immediately his ears were opened, and the impediment of his tongue was loosed, and he spoke plainly."
Mark 7:32-34

In this passage, Jesus healed someone from a deaf and mute condition, and there is no mention of unclean spirits. Though the condition was identical to that of the boy in Mark chapter nine, the *cause* was different. One was natural while the other was spiritual in nature. For the spiritual, Jesus cast out the unclean spirit that caused the condition, while He simply prayed and healed the other's natural condition. Although the identical conditions were by two separate things, Jesus used spiritual power and authority to correct them both. He has provided this same power and authority to the body of Christ so that we can do the same. We must do the same whether it is healing sickness and/or disease that arises naturally or casting out unclean spirits who cause sickness, disease, malady and even suicide.

In Mark chapter 9, the Scripture lists additional problems the **"deaf and dumb spirit"** caused the man's son.

"Then one of the crowd answered and said, 'Teacher, I brought You my son, who has a mute spirit. And wherever it seizes him, it throws him down; he foams at the mouth, gnashes his teeth, and becomes rigid....'"
Mark 9:17,18

"Then they brought him to Jesus. And when He saw Jesus, immediately the [unclean] spirit convulsed him, and he fell to the ground and allowed, foaming at the mouth. So Jesus asked his father, 'How long has this been happening to him?' and he said, 'From childhood. And often [the unclean spirit] has thrown him both into the fire and into the water to destroy him. But if You can do anything, have compassion On us and help us.'"
Mark 9:20-22

In verses 25 and 26 Jesus cast this demon out of the boy, but notice that not only was this unclean, "**deaf and dumb spirit**" able to keep his victim from speaking (and possibly hearing as well), it was also trying to kill him by causing him to throw himself into *fire and water*—fire to burn to death, and water to drown. Just like jumping from cliffs, buildings, and bridges, both fire and water are additional methods of suicide used by people.

When the unclean spirits of suicide in **Luke 8** were cast out of the man in the tombs, they caused the death of the swine when **"...the herd ran violently down the steep place into the lake and drowned."** Again, the suicide that occurred with the swine that was intended for the human indicates the presence of demons (unclean spirits of suicide) that are often behind the suicidal tendencies of people, including Christians. At least *some* of what the medical world considers mental illness or psychosomatic in nature is actually spiritual and demonic in nature. Today, people who cry without cause, cut themselves or fall into fire and water are termed mentally unhealthy. But the Bible reveals such a person to be under demonic attack. We, as Christians, must not ignore this truth, but acknowledge it and take the appropriate action of casting out unclean spirits with the power and authority Jesus has given us.

"And when He had called His twelve disciples to Him, He gave them power over unclean spirits, to cast them out, and to heal all kinds of sickness and all kinds of disease."
Matthew 10:1

"Behold, I give you the authority to trample on serpents and scorpions, and over all the power of the enemy, and nothing shall by any means hurt you."
Luke 10:19

It is an unfortunate reality that many believers in the body of Christ do not seek to operate with the power and authority we have been given. Many have never practiced or have gotten away from the practice of casting out demons, praying and laying hands on the sick. There are a few reasons for this:

1) Some don't *really* believe they have the power and authority to cast out demons and to heal the sick.

2) Some are false apostles, prophets, pastors and teachers who don't really care about what hinders people.

3) Fear is a strong reason. Some are afraid of unclean spirits, and they shouldn't be. The office of the apostle, prophet, evangelist, pastor and teacher is no place for pansies. Jesus has given His children power and authority—not the *spirit of fear.* We must therefore operate in the Spirit of power and authority—not in fear.

Others are afraid of how they will look to people if they try to lay hands on the sick, and they *are not* healed. We cannot be concerned about that aspect of healing. When we live holy, the power and authority of the Holy Christ operates through us, and when people are not healed when we pray and lay hands on them, it's not a reflection on us. Rather, there is often something going on with them. Sometimes there is sin in their life, an unforgiving spirit, or some other form of disobedience. We cannot refuse to pray for the many because we have prayed for a few who have not been healed. Those who are not healed, are not healed because of God's inability to heal, or because God isn't still using us to heal, but because they have something present in their life that is preventing God's healing power from healing *them*.

Even if we pray for 15 people and none of them receives healing, we cannot be concerned with looking impotent to people to the point where we stop praying for healing. A little bit of both pride and fear are at work when that happens. If none of the 15 gets healed this week, *still* pray *and believe* God for the ones for whom you pray next week. If we keep praying and no one *ever* gets healed, then we, as apostles, prophets, evangelists, pastors and teachers, must examine ourselves to make certain there isn't anything keeping the power and authority of God from flowing *to us* or *through us*.

I also believe Christians have shied away from casting out demons because we are concerned that the world would think us extreme or lunatic. But we cannot be concerned about what the world (and even some in the church) think because the consequence of our concern with criticism is the allowance of all sorts of unclean spirits to operate in the lives of people—people who have been entrusted to us to help.

I'm fairly sure that in His day Jesus was considered crazy, outrageous, foolish, and some other *not-so-nice* descriptions, but He did not concern Himself with His critics. Neither was He intimidated by their words or thoughts of Him. He was only concerned about the souls and the well-being of the people He was empowered to impact.

Let's pray that the spirit of boldness that operated in Christ would be revived again to operate unapologetically in His church and through His people. Though we may be mocked by the world, such boldness would be helpful to the people of God who rely on His power to be healed, made whole, and set free from the spirit of suicide.

Some of what we consider physical or mental illness is spiritual and demonic in nature. We must exercise the power and authority Jesus has given us to bring about the healing and deliverance He desires for us.

Choose to Live; You'll be Glad You Did!

"What strength do I have, that I should hope? And what is my end, that I should prolong my life?"
Job 6:11

These questions from the broken spirit of God's faithful servant reveal that he, at this point, did not have the confidence to believe that life would get better or that he had a reason to live. These questions are created from the lies that are sown into our heart while we're visiting *the abyss of brokenness.* These were questions Job asked out of the demonic ideas that said to him, "*Things are never going to be better. You'd be better off dead! Besides, no one loves you, no one cares for you and no one needs you. So there's point in prolonging your life.*" Of course, we know the devil and his host of demons are all liars and are incapable of telling the truth. In fact, the ideas of the devil tip the hand of God. When the devil deposits thoughts of our worthlessness, it *must* mean that we're valuable because the devil is the father of lies. Lies are the opposite of that which is true. When the devil says *"No one loves, cares or needs us,"* that statement automatically means that people *do* love us, do care for us and do need us to live.

We may not always *feel* this or *know* this, but we know it's true if for no other reason than it is the opposite of what the devil, the liar, says.

People loved and cared for Job, and he had reasons to live! For one, it turned out that his after-trouble life was better than his before-trouble life. Also, in his living and not taking his own life, he helped other people! He gave birth to more kids, recovered financially, and helped people and their family with jobs. Just as importantly, his life was used by God to be a testimony to millions and millions of people enduring trouble and being blessed in the end! It's the same for every child of

God. There is a great life remaining to be lived, and there are lives we will touch when we do!

A story in the book of Acts tells about a fellow who considered suicide. Because he changed his mind, the eternal destiny of his family was changed. This story takes place after the apostle Paul and Silas, his companion in ministry, had gone to the city of Thyatira to share the Word of God. While in prayer on one occasion, they encountered a young lady who was **"… possessed with a spirit of divination"** (which is one of the unclean spirits behind the work of fortune telling, psychic readings, tarot cards, the summoning of the dead, astrology, etc.). After casting the unclean spirit out of the woman, Paul and Silas were jailed—mainly because the **"much profit"** the spirit brought her masters would be no more. *(People often become irate when their revenue is interrupted.)*

"And when they had laid
many stripes on them,
[we're not talking body paint or tattoos here]
they threw them into prison,
commanding the jailer to keep
them securely. 24 Having received such
a charge, he put them into the inner prison
and fastened their feet in the stocks. 25 But at
midnight Paul and Silas were praying and
singing hymns to God [praise in trouble], **and**
the prisoners were listening to them. 26
Suddenly there was a great earthquake,
so that the foundations of the prison
were shaken; and immediately all the doors
were opened and everyone's chains were
loosed. 27 And the keeper of the prison,
awaking from sleep and seeing the prison doors
open, supposing the prisoners had fled,
drew his sword and was about to kill himself.
28 But Paul called with a loud voice, saying,

'<u>Do yourself no harm</u>, for we are all here.'
29 Then he called for a light, ran in, and fell
down trembling before Paul and Silas.
30 And he brought them out and said, 'Sirs,
what must I do to be saved?' 31 So they said,
'Believe on the Lord Jesus Christ, and
you will be saved, you and your household.'
32 Then they spoke the Word of the Lord to him
And to all who were in his them the same
hour house. 33 And he took of the night and
washed their stripes. And immediately
he and all his family were baptized. 34 Now when
he had brought them into his house,
he set food before them; and <u>he rejoiced</u>,
having believed in God with
all his household."
Acts 16:23-34

Wow, what a story! The jailer went from considering suicide to rejoicing over the salvation of his household! He thought there was no hope and what his future held would be too torturous to endure, and ending his life would be best. Boy was he ever wrong! Had he killed himself, the family that he led to salvation may have ended up perishing. But because he chose to live, it was Heaven and not Hell for them. His choice *not to* end his own life was directly responsible for their *eternal life*!

Not only does this Scripture passage reveal the value of our life to others, it also proves that situations we think are too difficult to overcome can indeed be overcome, and we can go on to live a joyful life in the Lord. We see this revealed in the lives of the jailer and Job. Remember, Job's latter days, after his desire for death, were more blessed than the days before his trouble. I am certain that both Job and the jailer were happy they hung in there!

Now the Lord blessed the latter days of Job More than his beginning... Job 42:12

I thought I was finished with this chapter, but as I was rereading it, a personal story came to mind. This personal story reveals how my own life benefited from a *failed* suicide attempt—an attempt by my very own mother.

I didn't initially think to include this story in this book, perhaps because I was unconsciously reluctant to revisit this time in my life. I should not have been hesitant because I have long recognized the benefit her life being graciously extended by God has had on my life as well as on that of my siblings and others from the church she faithfully attended for years before relocating to Heaven.

In the summer between my first and second year of high school, I recall being at a neighborhood friend's home playing cards with three other buddies. As the cards were being dealt for the next hand and small talk and laughs were being exchanged, I faintly heard a report over the radio of a woman being rescued after "she fell" onto the public transportation train tracks. I didn't give the news story a second thought because reports of accidents, crime, and tragedies of all sorts were a common occurrence on Chicago radio and television stations.

Maybe an hour or so passed before I left and walked back across the street to my house. Moms was at work, my older brother was working out of state, and my younger sister was somewhere in the neighborhood playing with her friends. So the house was empty when I returned to eat lunch, which was pretty much the only thing 14-year-old kids did in the house during the summertime back then—eat, fuel up, and head back outside to play—be it cards, baseball, football, or *"the dozens"* which was when we made up jokes about one another's family members.

Before I could make my way back to the great outdoors, the telephone rang. "Hello." The unfamiliar, uncommon professional voice on the other end said, "*Hi. Is this the home of Adrienne F. Bailey?*" "*Yes…* " I said. "*Who is this?*"

The business-toned man replied, "*This is Officer (whatever his name was). Is there an adult there I can speak with?*"

Instantly, I knew something was wrong! "*What's wrong with my Moms?*" I asked, already on the brink of tears. The gentleman wouldn't give me any information, which only exacerbated my anxiety, causing me to imagine the worst. The tears uncontrollably flooded my eyes and fled down my face. "*Where is my Mom?!*" I asked repeatedly, frantically.

I have never been able to remember what took place from there. I don't even think I've ever tried to. I don't know if the authorities eventually called an alternate number or if the officer was able to get me to calm down and take his number for someone else to return his call. The latter seems unlikely. I cannot imagine composing myself enough to find a pen and paper to write down a phone number, considering how extremely unnerved I was by the ideas that tormented my mind. Maybe I did. I don't remember much of anything from that day after that call.

I wouldn't learn until years later that my mother had attempted to commit suicide by *throwing herself down* onto those train tracks because she felt as if she was in a *time of trouble* that was too great to overcome and/or too embarrassing to address. She had somehow lost the best job she had ever had, and she may have thought that everything she had worked so hard to provide for us as a single parent would be lost. As it turned out, what she feared wasn't the case—even after losing her job and nearly her life.

I thank God for His mercy that allowed my mother to escape that suicide attempt and live. But she wouldn't escape serious injuries that hospitalized her for over six months and restricted her to her bed at home upon her release with daily nurse visits for what may have been another year or so. She was disabled for life having lost the ability to use her right hand, and the use of her left hand being limited by skin grafting work and the amputation of her baby finger. But as tragic as all of that was, I believe the greatest things in life came from it—her salvation and that of her children.

I committed my life to Christ on October 23, 1988, two and a half years before Moms went to be with the Lord, and fifteen years or so after her attempt to take her own life. Before I committed my life to Christ, she would talk to me about spiritual matters that, either I could not appreciate, or didn't believe—like the vision the Lord gave her of me. News of that vision came near the end of one of our phone conversations in response to my request that she *"not worry about me."*

She matter-of-factly stated, *"Boy, I've stopped worrying about you…."* For a moment that reply bothered me because my understanding was that mothers would *always* worry about their children. After all, I had always thought that worrying was a part of caring. But she quickly explained why as she continued, *"The Lord gave me a vision of you in the pulpit, so I know you're going to be okay!"* I remember thinking, *"Wow, Moms has gone from wanting me to go to church to wanting me to be in the pulpit of a church!"*

I don't remember exactly when it was, but I do remember her telling me sometime after her accident that she *"had been playing church."* She hadn't been serious about God, and she had only been going through the motions, talking the talk but not walking the walk. When my mother was taken to the hospital and her possessions were processed, in her purse was a Bible—a Bible she had been carrying but had not committed to living by. I think she thought that her *living on the fence* contributed to her suicide attempt. The *fence* is the place between complete commitment to Christ, and continued participation in sin and the world.

Living on the fence is a dangerous place to be because that person does not have the full power or protection of God he or she would have when living in complete commitment to God. Thus, the person living on the fence becomes very vulnerable to the enemy. The enemy targets people who are on the fence because he is trying to keep and discourage them from becoming completely committed to Christ. He believes he can afflict them, cause them to blame God in their mind, and thereby alienate them from God. And without the power to rebuke and recognize him at work, they often fall prey to his lies.

The *fence* is a dangerous place to be also because the hypocrisy of *the fence* provides a *place* for the devil to operate in our mind that would otherwise not be accessible to him. (Ephesians 4:27) It is this *place* where the devil wreaks havoc and bombards the mind with thoughts of hopelessness that contributes to the brokenness that inspires suicide.

I praise God that His grace allowed my mother to live so that she could be saved and so that her prayers would be heard in His ears and cause His hand of protection to be upon my siblings and me. Because God allowed my mother to live, we would also be saved and be used to touch the lives of others. These victories are only made possible *because* she didn't lose her life at her own hands.

The point is, when life gets tough and seems unbearable and there doesn't appear to be any hope for better days or reasons to continue living, there is! There is hope, there is help, and there are reasons to live. Christian, whatever you are facing, you are strong enough to handle it because God will help you overcome whatever it is. There are reasons to continue to live, and there better days on the other side of your trouble.

I don't know if life can get any worse than what Job experienced—losing all of his children to death, losing his source of income from the loss of all that he owned, being distanced from his wife while the remainder of his family gave up on him, and losing the support and understanding of his friends. Despite all of these incredible losses, Job was able to fight off the idea of ending his life. Because he hung in there and trusted God, he was able to see a time when he was not only restored, but when things were better than they had *ever* been. Because he chose to live, he has also been a blessing to untold thousands and thousands! The great thing is, the same God, the same Holy Spirit and the same ability that helped and enabled Job to hang in there is available to you, to me, and to all of God's children.

Like Job, the jailer, and my mother who lived to help and lead their family and others to eternal life in Heaven, if you are reading this book, it is because God has a plan to use you as well. Yes, *you!* You are extremely valuable to God, and He has a plan to bless you and use you to positively impact the lives and destiny of others. So, hang in there, please. Despite your trouble, your brokenness and everything else you're feeling right now, the best of your life is in the rest of your life!

Chapter 7
The Importance of the Word in the Time of Trouble

**"Unless Your law had been my delight,
I would then have perished in my affliction."
Psalm 119:92**

The words *laws, commandments, ordinances, precepts, statutes, testimonies, judgments, decrees or ways* are all references to God's Word. For example, a *law* is found in one of the first five books of the Bible and was given by God to Moses to give to the people on the *do's and don'ts* of life. A *commandment* was a specific order from God (as in the Ten Commandments). An *ordinance* had to do with instructions on conduct, behavior, etc. Individually or collectively, these words are all considered as synonyms for the *Word of God.*

There are a number of reasons why the Word of God is particularly important to those who are hurting during their time of trouble. There are so many in fact, that I will probably only scratch the surface of the Bible's helpfulness to us as Christians when things are not going well.

One of the things I love about the Word of God is how it grants us access into the hearts, minds and lives of the children of God who lived before us. *Their* trouble allows us to know that *our* trouble is not an uncommon experience, and neither is what we feel during our times of trouble—disappointment, abandonment, failure, frustration, perhaps thoughts of giving up on God, and even giving up on life.

I also love how the Bible allows us to see how those before us handled their hard times, were sustained in their trials, and eventually triumphed over their troubles. In making these examples visible, the Word of God provides a blueprint for us to do the same.

When it comes to looking into the hearts, minds and lives of the Josephs, the Davids, the Jobs and the Pauls of the Bible, my favorite verse is **Romans 15:4**, which says,

"For whatsoever things were written of before were written for our learning, so that we through the patience and comfort of the Scriptures might have hope."

I absolutely love this verse because it teaches us that we can learn from those who have traveled the path of trouble on which we find ourselves! We, through the patience and comfort provided by the Word of God, can have a confident expectation of God bringing us through the trial and bringing us to the victory as He did for them!

It doesn't matter that those mentioned in the Bible were Jews, kings, governors, rich, poor, or apostles because God doesn't see and deal with them any differently than He deals with us.

"For the Lord your God is God of gods
and Lord of lords, the great God,
mighty and awesome,
who shows no partiality…."
Deuteronomy 10:17

This Scripture means that when it comes to His people, God doesn't show preferential treatment based on who we are, where we live, our heritage, our economical status or our social standing. He deals with all of us in the same way as we live in reverence and righteousness before Him.

Therefore, whatever worked in the Word for the widow of Zarephath and the widow with the unjust judge will work for us. Whatever moved the hand of God on Jehoshaphat's behalf will move His hand for us as well. However God responded to Enoch, Esther and Ezekiel for doing what they did, He will respond to us in the same way if we do the same thing. Whatever caused the Lord to show up in the fire with Shadrach, Meshach and Abednego and send an angel to aid Daniel in the lions' den will cause God to do like things for us as we live before Him as they lived before Him.

"In truth I perceive that God shows no partiality. But in every nation whoever fears Him and works righteousness is accepted by Him."
Acts 10:34, 35

The lives and experiences of others are for our learning.

In the opening verse of this chapter, the Word of God permits us to peer into the past of one of its psalmists. From the words of this particular psalmist we are taught that even true worshipers of God are not exempt from experiencing times so tough they are worthy of tears.

Psalm 119 is dedicated entirely to the Word of God and its benefits. In verse 92 the Psalmist writes in reflection of a troublesome time he had experienced; he credits his relationship to the Word of God with helping him survive and not be overwhelmed. He even said that God's Word, "*...had been my delight*" or something that brought him pleasure or relief.

If you have ever been through dark and difficult days, or are experiencing them at the present, you know that *relief* and *pleasure* can be hard to come by. But in looking back, the psalmist realized it was the Word of God that brought him *"delight"* during his darkest days.

The *delight* the psalmist received from the Word of God was in the form of encouragement through reading and hearing teachings from the older books of the Bible, namely the Pentateuch (the first five books of the Bible) and probably the book of Job.

We partake of and spend time with that which we "delight" in. As we delight in, partake of, and spend time with the Word of God, our troubles—no matter what type or how intense—cannot overwhelm us to the point of harming ourselves or losing our mind.

The psalmist said, had it not been for God's Word he ***"... would have perished in his affliction."*** The Hebrew word for *affliction* also means "trouble," while the word *perish* in this context means "to lose oneself (mind)", or "to break (snap) under pressure." These definitions say to us that, even for children of God, trouble can be mentally disturbing to the point where it causes one to "snap" or "lose his mind," *unless* the Word of God is that person's *delight* and thereby allowed to play a preventative role.

This truth is taught by the writer of Psalm 119:92. He was saying his trouble was so taxing that he would have lost himself had it not been for the Word of God. Listen to what he goes on to say in the following verse:

"I will never forget Your precepts,
For by Them You have quickened me."
Psalm 119:93

The word *quickened* used here means "to: keep, revive, nourish up, recover and repair or, to restore to life." The psalmist was not talking about being restored to physical life. We know this because he was already physically living. Instead, he was talking about God's Word reviving, restoring and recovering him emotionally from the mental attack of his trouble.

The fact that this son of God was "quickened" or revived emotionally is powerful because his trouble had already gotten the best of him; however, the Word of God encouraged him so greatly that it restored him emotionally and psychologically! Emotional and psychological restoration is intangible change that cannot be seen, but can be felt. It's a change that aids us inwardly until a change comes outwardly in our circumstances.

All throughout Psalm 119, we find talk about how God's Word encouraged, strengthened, comforted and uplifted the heart and head of the child of God who had been assaulted by affliction.

"My soul clings to the dust;
revive me according to Your Word."
Psalm 119:25

"My soul melts from heaviness,
strengthen me accord to Your Word."
Psalm 119:29

"Remember the word to Your servant,
upon which You have cause me to hope.
This is my comfort in my trouble,
for Your Word has given me life."
Psalm 119:49-50

"I remembered Your judgments of old,
O Lord, and have comforted myself."
Psalm 119:52

"Trouble and anguish have overtaken me,
yet Your commandments are my delights."
Psalm 119:143

**"Great peace have those who love Your law,
and nothing causes them to stumble."
Psalm 119:165**

Each of these verses speaks of being encouraged by the Word of God during times of trouble. And whereas encouragement indeed accompanies the reading and hearing of God's Word, tangible, external blessings and benefits are also produced by our *living* according to the Word of God.

Many Christians turn off at the talk of living by or obeying the Word of God, as if it is a burdensome task to do. But in all honesty, it is not at all too tough to do for the child of God who *truly* loves God.

In 1 **John 5:3,** the apostle wrote, "**For this is the love of God, that we keep His commandments. And His commandments are not burdensome."**

Talk of living in trustful obedience to God's Word is worthy of our attention because when we walk in God's Word we experience different types of *good* from God that are not attainable aside from following His Word. Amongst these *goods,* God's Word anchors us and causes us to be emotionally immovable by the storms of life. This is exactly what Jesus teaches as it pertains to obeying the Word of God.

**"Therefore, whoever hears these
sayings of Mine [the Word of God],
and does them, I will liken him
to a wise man who built his house
on the rock; and the rain descended,
the floods came, and the winds
blew and beat on that house; and it did not
fall <u>because</u> it was founded on the rock."
Matthew 7:24, 25**

The rain, the floods and the winds represent varying degrees or types of trouble. In this particular instance Jesus seems to be speaking from the perspective of each of these taking place at the same time, representing the immensity of the trouble.

The point the Master makes in this verse is that no matter the massiveness, type, or the terribleness of the trouble, if we live life on the rock of God's Word, trouble will not be able to move us from the place of emotional stability. Trouble may rock us, sway us or cause us to lose our balance momentarily, but it won't break our foundation of trust in God. Yes, the storms may break some branches, cause us to lose some leaves and spoil some fruit, but it won't uproot us. Trouble won't break our foundation or uproot us because the Word of God is working *in us* to strengthen us against the annihilating aim of the storms of life.

Listen to what the apostle Paul taught about living by the Word of God in his letter to the church in Thessalonica:

"For this reason we also thank God without ceasing, because when you <u>received the Word of God</u> which you heard from us, you welcomed it not as the word of men, but as it is in truth, the Word of God, which also <u>effectively works in you</u> who believe."
1 Thessalonians 2:13

When Paul says they *"received the Word of God,"* he's not just talking about them having received it in that it was given by him; he is also saying they received it in that they *embraced* and *believed* what was given by him.

Nothing reveals our *embrace* and *belief* in the Word like our obedience to the Word. When we believe the Word to the point of being "doers of the Word," the Word *works effectively in us*. It works effectively in us to strengthen and stabilize us which will enable us to stay the course until the storm stops, and our time of trouble yields to triumph!

The Word strengthens us by reminding us of God's faithfulness and the fact that He promises not to forsake us in our time of trouble. As the living Word of God, the Bible will also speak things to us that will encourage us and help us overcome our season of obstacles. This is why the psalmist said,

"Unless Your law [Word] had been my delight,
I would then have perished in my affliction."
Psalm 119:92

Let me take you back to the beginning—the book of Genesis—to show you how the applied Word of God accomplishes good and brings us *delight* even in our seasons of challenge.

"In the beginning God created the heavens and the earth. The earth was without form, and void; and darkness was on the face of the deep. And the Spirit of God was hovering over the face of the waters.
Genesis 1:2

"Then God said…."

Let me pause here and say that any time we see the phrase, *"God said"* in the Bible, it means His Word went forth because to *say* is "to speak" or "to project words." This definition may sound elementary, but understanding it will help make the point about the *good* the Word brings.

"Then God said, "Let there be light"; and there was light. And God saw the light, that it was good."
Genesis 1:3

In this verse we find the very first recording of Words spoken by God. In this same verse we also discover the result and outcome of the Words spoken by Him. When God, "…

said, 'Let there be light;'" the *result* is that there was light; the *outcome* is that "it was **good**"!

What we see here is a direct association between **"good"** and God's Word, or what He **"said."** In other words, whenever what God *says* is done, the outcome will be *good.* Let's look further:

"Then God said, 'Let the waters under the heavens be gathered together into one place, and let the dry land appear,' and it was so. And God called the dry land Earth, and the gathering of the waters He called Seas. And God saw that it was good."
Genesis 1:9, 10

Here again is another example of result and outcome: "**God said**" (or His Word went forth) "**it was so**" meaning that what He said was done (or applied), and the outcome is that "**it was good**."

Not yet convinced? Okay watch this:

"Then God said, 'Let the earth bring forth grass, the herb that yields seed, and the fruit tree that yields fruit according to its kind, whose seed is in itself, on the Earth"; and it was so. And the earth brought forth grass, the herb that yields seed according to its kind, and the tree that yields fruit, whose seed is in itself according to its kind. And God saw that it was good."
Genesis 1:11, 12

In yet another instance, "**God said…it was so [done]…it was good"!** Still not convinced? Okaaaay!

"Then <u>God said</u>, 'Let there be lights in the firmament of the heavens to divide the day from the night; and let them be for signs and seasons, and for days and years; and let them be for lights in the firmament of the heavens to give light on the earth'; and <u>it was so</u>. Then God made two great lights, the greater light to rule the day, and the lesser light to rule the night. He made the stars also. God set them in the firmament of the heavens to give light on the earth and to rule over the day and over the night, and to divide the light from darkness. And God saw that <u>it was good.</u>"
Genesis 1:14-18

Okaaay, there it is again: "**God said…it was so** (or what He said was done, and)…**it was good"!** We find the same in verses 20 and 21 where when what "God said" was done, the outcome "was good."

"Then <u>God said</u>, 'Let the earth bring forth the living creature according to its kind: cattle and creeping thing and beast of the earth, each according to its kind'; and <u>it was so</u>. And God made the beast of the earth according to its kind, cattle according to its kind, and everything that creeps on the earth according to its kind. And God saw that <u>it was good</u>."
Genesis 1:24, 25

"**God said…it was so…it was good"!** Seven times in Genesis chapter one, concluding in verses 26 and 31, the outcome of God's Word being *done* was *good*. This record not only gives us revelation of what happened during Creation, it also established a pattern of what is produced when what God *says* is applied to our life.

Creation is a product of the Word of God having its way. In keeping with that pattern, *whenever* the Word of God has its way in the lives of His people—His born-again, new creations—the result will also be "good."

Our times of trouble cannot break this pattern; they can only provide opportunity for proof that God's Word can cause good even when things are *not so good*. In fact, the writer of Psalm 119:92 said if it had not been for the Word of God (law), his time of trouble would have destroyed him! He attributes the Word of God with literally saving his life!

If the Word of God was powerful enough to save his life, which is the ultimate in "good," surely the Word of God can accomplish "goods" that would be lesser in comparison!

Throughout history whenever the people of God followed the Word of God, the outcome was "good." Let's look at just a few instances of this truth:

> **"And now, Israel, what does the Lord your God require of you, but to fear the Lord your God, to walk in all His ways and to love Him, to serve the Lord your God with all your heart and with all your soul, and to keep the commandments of the Lord and His statues which I command you today for your good?"**
> **Deuteronomy 10:12, 13**

The instruction to "keep the commandments of the Lord" simply means to allow what "**God said**" to "**be so**." Notice the promised benefit of their doing so: "**for your good."** Notice also that the pattern established in Genesis is still being followed hundreds of years later.

It is also worth mentioning that this Word was given to the children of Israel during their time of trouble—when they were in the wilderness. This says to us that God's Word can bring good while we're yet in the wilderness, waiting to possess the promise.

Here's another example to consider:

"But this is what I commanded them, saying, "Obey My voice, and I will be your God, and you shall be My people. And walk in all the ways that I have commanded you, that it may be well with you."
Jeremiah 7:23

In every era of history, the pattern established in Genesis chapter one is honored—even during the difficult times God's people encountered. There is a good that is accomplished from walking in the Word while other things in life are not so good.

The reality is that there may be some things in which God is requiring us to walk in that may not *feel* good! But even the things that do not feel good will bring about a good that will make us glad we trusted in God's Word!

As was the case with the previous passage, the children of Israel found themselves in trouble because of sin. But God gave the prophet Jeremiah a Word to give to the people that gave them an opportunity to experience God's goodness—if they would walk in His Word.

"So they said to Jeremiah, 'Let the Lord be a true and faithful witness between us, if we do not do according to everything which the Lord your God sends us by you. Whether it is pleasing or displeasing, we will obey the voice of the Lord our God

to whom we send you, that it may be well with us when we obey the voice of the Lord our God."
Jeremiah 42:5, 6

The children of God understood and believed in the pattern that was established at the time of Creation as it pertained to the "good" that accompanies doing what *"God said."* They also understood that sometimes doing what *"God said"* is not always easy or pleasing, but it was "good" in that it would always ultimately cause things to be "well with them."

As it turned out, they did not obey "the voice of the Lord"—even though they believed doing so would be to their benefit. *(Well, well, well...doesn't that sounds just like us?)* But in times when we not only *believe,* but also *trust* God's Word enough to do it (even when doing it is difficult or displeasing), we will always find the "good" that is a part of the pattern.

The book of First Kings contains two stories of trusting God, doing what He said, and experiencing the "good" He purposes His Word to accomplish. Let's look first at a season of trouble for Elijah, a prophet who loved and trusted God, but like us, he experienced times of trouble.

In chapter 17, Elijah found himself in the midst of a famine, which is the modern equivalent to a recession or an economic crisis. During this time, Elijah was completely dependent on the Lord to provide his needs. And God did provide Elijah's needs, but only as the prophet did what "God said."

And Elijah the Tishbite, of the inhabitants of Gilead, said to (King) Ahab, "As the Lord God of Israel lives, before Who I stand, there shall not be dew nor rain these years, except at my word."
1 Kings 17:1

"Then the <u>Word of the Lord</u> came to him
saying, "Get away from here and turn
eastward, and hide by the Brook Cherith,
which flows into the Jordan. And it will be
that you shall drink from the brook, and
I have commanded the ravens to feed
you there. So, he went and stayed by
the Brook Cherith, which flows into the Jordan.
The ravens brought him
bread and meat in the morning,
and bread and meat in the evening,
And he drank from the brook."
1 Kings 17:2-6

There was only one reason Elijah experienced the *good* of the bread and meat brought by the raven, and it wasn't simply because he was a child of God. It was because, as a child of God trusted in what *God said* enough to let it *be so* by doing it. In other words, **"God said…it was so…(and)it was good."**

If Elijah had not followed God's Word and gone to the brook, he would have missed the "good" God intended because the raven God had commanded was going to the brook with the bread and meat and nowhere else. There are times, even during our times of trouble, when we miss certain blessings because we didn't allow what "God said" to "be so" and lead us to the place where "good" was commissioned to meet us.

In those times, it isn't necessarily our heart's intent to be rebellious in not obeying; we are often distrusting or unable to understand *how* obeying a certain something "God said" is going to bring a "good" we need. But don't wait to understand God before you trust Him and follow His Word. In fact, *true* trust is obeying God—even when we do not understand Him.

In **Proverbs 3:5** Solomon said, **"Trust in the Lord with all your heart and lean not to your understanding."** We cannot delay or refuse to trust God because we don't understand Him. Since **"{His} thoughts are not our thoughts, nor are {our} ways, {His} ways," (Isaiah 55:8)**, we will not always understand how God will use our obedience to bring about our blessing. We simply have to trust Him.

**"Then the Word of the Lord came to Elijah,
saying, 'Arise, go to Zarephath,
which belongs to Sidon, and dwell there.
See, I have commanded a widow
there to provide for you.' So he arose
and went to Zarephath.
And when he came to the gate of the city,
indeed, a widow was there gathering
sticks. And he called to her and said,
'Please bring me a little water in a cup, that
I may drink.' And as she was going to get it,
[since that seemed to be working out well...]
he called to her and said, 'Please, bring me
a morsel of bread in your hand.' "
1 Kings 17:8-10**

There are a few noteworthy points in this story:

1) Again, Elijah did what God said, and his obedience led him to the place where he would be fed when his provisions were no longer meeting him at the brook of Cherith. Understand that just because provision stops coming from one source or place, it doesn't mean that provision will stop coming altogether. Places and people are just vessels of provision; they are not our provider. As we follow what "God said," it will *always* lead us to the next place or person of provision.

2) Because there was a famine in the land, the widow to whom God sent Elijah was experiencing trouble as well. And what "God said" to her was intended not only to be a blessing for Elijah, but to bring "good" to her and her family as well—but only if she would trust what "God said" to the point of doing it.

"So she said, 'As the Lord your God lives, I do not have bread, only a handful of flour in a bin, and a little oil in a jar, and see, I am gathering a couple of sticks that I may go in and prepare it for myself and my son, that we may eat it, and die.' And Elijah said to her, 'Do not fear; go and do as you have said, but make me a small cake from it first, and bring it to me; and afterward make some for yourself and your son. For thus says the Lord God of Israel: "The bin of flour shall not be used up, not shall the jar of oil run dry, until the day the Lord sends rain on the earth." ' So she went away and did according to the word of Elijah; and she and he and her household ate for many days. The bin of flour was not used up, nor did the jar of oil run dry, according to the Word of the Lord which He spoke by Elijah."
1 Kings 17:12-16

The widow trusted the Lord by allowing what He said to be so, and she received the *good* that accompanied doing so.

There is no question about the fact that the idea of doing so must have been extremely "displeasing" and difficult because she probably could not understand *how* the flour bin would not be used up or how the jar of oil would not run dry. But she did not allow her inability to understand to keep her from trusting. She trusted, she obeyed, and she got blessed!

3) Another amazing fact about this story is that this widow was not an Israelite; therefore, she had no covenant relationship with God at the time He spoke to her. But because she followed His Word, He delivered her from what distressed her.

If that isn't amazing enough, consider this passage:

"Fools, because of their transgression, and because of their iniquities, were afflicted. Their soul abhorred all manner of food and they drew near to the gates of death. Then they cried out to the Lord in their trouble, and He saved them out of their distresses."
Psalm 107:17-19

(How?)
"He sent His Word and healed them, and delivered them from their destructions."
Psalm 107:20

Now, if God, by His Word, saved a widow with no covenant relationship with Him and some **"fools"** from their troubles and distresses, shall He not do the same for us—His blood-bought children—when *we* trust and follow His Word? Surely He will!

When we walk in God's Word, we experience God's good—even during the trying times of life when we most need it.

As with the psalmist, the widow would have perished in her trouble had it not been for the Word of God. But because she trusted and followed what the Lord had "commanded" her, she was sustained *during* her time of trouble, and she was delivered *from* her time of trouble.

Remember, **"For whatsoever things were written of before were written for our learning, so that we through the patience and comfort of the Scriptures might have hope." (Romans 15:4)**

Throughout history the pattern holds true: when we allow the Word of God be "so" by doing what the Bible says, the results will be "good"—even during our times of trouble!

Chapter 8
The Importance of Prayer in the Time of Trouble

"Then Jesus spoke a parable to them, that Men always ought to pray and not lose heart...."
Luke 18:1

Because we find people like David, Daniel, Paul, Silas and others praying in the Bible during their time of trouble, there is an easy tendency to think that prayer comes effortlessly or that it is a natural occurrence during difficult times. But the fact that Jesus encourages us to *"pray always and not lose heart"* ("faint" or "give up on prayer"), reveals to us that there is a trouble that seeks to outlive our prayer life. It is a trouble that is long-lasting and so tough that it can distract us *in* prayer and distance us *from* prayer!

Jesus encourages us not to abandon our prayer life, not because doing so places us at odds with God or causes Him to be angry with us, but because Jesus knows the benefit of praying even when it *seems* as if prayer is not benefitting us or bettering our situation.

Before I share the importance of prayer and how it does indeed benefit us during our times of trouble (even when it doesn't appear to be doing so), I want to address what I believe is a misunderstanding concerning prayer—a misinterpretation that once hindered the effectiveness of my prayer life.

There is absolutely no question about the fact that prayer in and of itself is a great and helpful tool for Christians. The Lord knows the good behind His encouragement for us to pray and even to "...**pray without ceasing." (1 Thessalonians 5:17**) Prayer has been a vital part of the life of every notable Bible character from Abraham in Genesis to the apostle John in the book of Revelation.

Prayer is a source of help—help out of trouble as well as sustaining help during the season of trouble. Prayer is also an anchor that keeps us steady during the struggles of life, and a lifeline that keeps us from being lost and overwhelmed by the unfavorable and unexpected occurrences that look to overcome us. Prayer is a wonderful, helpful and powerful part of the "...**whole armor of God**"(Ephesians 6:11) with which we should don ourselves on a daily basis.

However, in agreeing with and affirming these undeniable realities, I have learned that there can be a hindering element concerning prayer. Of course, it is not prayer itself; rather, it is the idea that one *must* spend a certain amount of time in prayer in order for prayer to work, or in order to have a legitimate, or an accomplishing prayer life.

Maybe you haven't struggled with this element in prayer. If not, praise God! But I believe that many others, like me, have at some point. Even now some are secretly struggling with the notion that if they do not spend a certain amount of time in prayer that their prayer is purposeless, and will probably be fruitless.

Many of us have heard teachings and/or read books from well-meaning Christians about prayer and how much time we *should* spend in prayer. Some teach that we need to spend at least an hour in prayer a day, while others talk about saints who spend five hours a day in prayer, or Jesus Who, "... **continued all night in prayer" (Luke 6:12).**

There isn't anything wrong with any of these views. And it certainly would not hurt to spend an hour or an entire night in prayer. In fact, I am sure it could be very helpful. However, nowhere in the Bible do we find instructions on how long to pray. We know that Jesus prayed for an hour in the Garden of Gethsemane before His arrest and subsequent death, burial and resurrection, and it is from this reference that many draw the inference that Jesus is teaching us to spend one hour in prayer a day.

In that story in Mark 14, when Jesus found Peter, James and John asleep while He prayed, Jesus asked them "*...could you not **watch** with Me one hour?*" Jesus didn't ask, "*Could you not **pray** with Me one hour*"; He said, "*watch,*" or "be on the lookout, you sleepyheads!"

While it is true that in the very next verse He says, "**Watch and pray, that you enter not into temptation**," that was a general statement—not an instruction for them (or us) to pray for an hour every time we pray. If that were the case, we would find other instances in the Bible that support a time prescription for prayer, but we do not.

Not only do we not find prescriptions for time in prayer anywhere in the Word of God, when teaching the disciples how to pray (**Matthew 6:5-15**) Jesus makes no mention of time. Surely if a certain amount of time was required in prayer, Jesus would have revealed it while teaching on prayer.

If we are to take the fact that Jesus prayed for an hour, or all night as designated lengths of time we should spend in prayer, then we must also take the amount of time He spent fasting as the designated length of time we should fast, i.e., 40 days. But of course we know that we can fast less than forty days (or even the three days mentioned in the book of Esther) and benefit from fasting. And in the same way that Jesus' forty day fast, or the three day fast of Esther and Mordecai are not instructions for us to fast those lengths of time, neither is Jesus' spending an hour in prayer an instruction for us to spend an hour in prayer.

Again, spending an hour in prayer a day could be helpful, as could fasting for forty, or even three days. But those are options—not requirements—unless specifically instructed by God.

The element of *time* in prayer can become a hindrance because there is a natural (and sometimes even a super-natural enemy-aided) tendency to think that if we do not spend a certain amount of *time* in prayer that our prayers will not possess power or will not be heard and answered. I am fairly certain that no right-hearted person who teaches the need to spend a certain amount of time in prayer intends for this to be the case, but for many, it is.

What is *far more important* than our *time* in prayer is our *faith* in prayer. Look at what Jesus teaches about prayer on another occasion:

> **"*Now in the morning, as t*hey passed by, they saw the fig tree dried up from the roots. And Peter, remembering, said to Him, 'Rabbi, look! The fig tree which You cursed has withered away.' So Jesus answered and said to them, 'Have faith in God. For assuredly, I say to you, whoever says to this mountain, 'Be removed and be cast into the sea,' and does not doubt in his heart, but believes that those things he says will be done, he will have whatever he says. Therefore, I say to you, whatever things you ask when you pray, believe that you receive them, and you will have them."**
>
> **Mark 11:20-24**

Here again, in another teaching about prayer Jesus makes no reference to time; however, there is a reference to faith—"**… when you pray, <u>believe</u>.…**" The emphasis in this verse is on *believing*—not on *time.*

There have been times in my walk when I've struggled to "believe" because I wondered if I had spent enough *time* in prayer. Consequently, my lack of faith in prayer hindered me and the productivity of my prayers more than my lack of spending an hour in prayer.

We can spend five days in prayer, but if we don't "**believe we will receive**," we've just wasted five days. On the other hand, we can spend five minutes in prayer *believing we will receive,* and that five minutes of prayer will be more rewarding and productive than five days of faithless prayer! Some may disagree only because they place more of an emphasis on *time* in prayer than fa*ith* in prayer. But Jesus did not misplace the emphasis, and neither should we.

Again, again, again, there isn't anything wrong with spending long periods of time in prayer. If the time spent in prayer is also spent "believing" that you will "receive," it will undoubtedly be tremendously beneficial! And if the Lord leads you into long times of prayer, by all means, go! Go without hesitation! But go *believing* that He will reward your *faith in prayer* and not your *time in prayer.*

But as it pertains to your ordinary everyday prayer life, if you have struggled with the hindering element of *time* in prayer, I have prayed that this portion of the book would free you and allow you to go forth knowing that God is more concerned about your *trusting Him* to hear and answer your prayer than He is about your meeting a time quota in prayer. Now, don't get me wrong! I am not suggesting that you should only spend five minutes in prayer, but I am suggesting that you not allow time of any measure to be the focal point of your prayers.

We should indeed have a daily period of prayer with God. A period that consists of thanksgiving, worship (maybe a song, maybe words of praise and adoration, or maybe both), intercession (praying for others, including family, friends, government, other believers, co-workers, enemies [who sometimes double as family members, other believers, or co-workers—grrrr!], or whoever the Holy Spirit places on our heart) and certainly praying for ourselves.

However long it takes to do this, so be it. One day it may take 10 minutes; another day it may take 110 minutes. God does not view the prayers of those times differently because He is not concerned with the amount of *time* we spend in prayer; rather, He is concerned about our going to Him in prayer and *believing Him* in prayer.

"Therefore, I say to you, whatever things you ask when you pray, <u>believe</u> that you receive them, and You will have them."
(Mark 11:24)

<u>The Invisible Aid of Prayer</u>

Just as **"...faith is the substance of things hoped for, the evidence of things not seen" (Hebrews 11:1),** there is a benefit of prayer that goes unseen. Not everything that God does to benefit or help us is visible to the eye.

There is a tendency to think that because we don't *see* God doing anything outwardly with our circumstances, it means that He is not doing anything in response to our prayers. This thinking can eventually lead us to the point where we lose heart and give up on praying.

The reality is, before God begins to move on our behalf *outwardly*, He is helping us *inwardly*, in the invisible places, through our times of prayer. A good example of this inward, invisible help can be seen in a seed that has been sown. A seed is sown for the sake of seeing, and ultimately benefitting from the fruit it is purposed to produce. However, before the seed produces fruit we *can* see, it's working underground in the place we *cannot* see. It is producing roots we cannot see, but are a vital part of the fruit-bearing process. No root, no fruit!

Prayer is the sown seed, and just because the fruit of prayer cannot be seen in a certain amount of time, it does not mean that the seed of prayer hasn't taken root in a place that is invisible to our eyes or to our understanding. Just as the seed invisibly works to produce a root we cannot see *before* it produces fruit we *can* see, prayer is also working to produce things *in us* that is out of our sight. Our prayer is working in ways to which we are oblivious.

A better, Biblical example of prayer working in the invisible places, and in ways we cannot see before it works in places we can see, is found in two verses from the apostle Paul's letter to the believers at Philippi:

"Be careful for nothing, but in everything by prayer and supplication, with thanksgiving let your requests be made known to God; and the peace of God, which surpasses all understanding, will guard your hearts and minds through Christ Jesus."
Philippians 4:6, 7

The Greek word for *careful* is a word that also means, *"to be troubled with cares."* The idea of being *troubled with cares* indicates that something on the *outside* of us is affecting the *inside* of us. In other words, Paul is speaking about experiencing some sort of trouble.

Paul's Holy Spirit inspired instruction was for them to pray. And what he said next didn't provide a promise for prayer bringing an *outward* change to the *problem,* but an *inward* change to *us, through* prayer.

"...and the peace of God...will guard your hearts and minds through Christ Jesus."

The *peace* and the *heart* have two things in common:
1) They are both inward.
2) They are both invisible.

This promised *peace* is God's work on *our* heart because of our prayer. It's the inward root in the invisible place that precedes the outward fruit in the visible places—proving that before prayer makes things better *outwardly*, it first betters us *inwardly!*

It is also important to take note of the *role* of peace according to this verse. Paul said God's peace would "*guard*" our hearts and minds. Guards have both a protecting and a preserving responsibility; they don't allow *out* things that are supposed to remain *in*, and they don't allow *in* things that are supposed to remain *out*.

To have the peace of God guarding our hearts and minds during our times of trouble is extremely helpful because it keeps faith, trust, confidence and commitment from *exiting* our heart and mind, while keeping worry, stress, doubt and fear from *entering* our heart and mind.

People, who through worry and stress over their outward circumstances, have been sickened inwardly (physically and/or emotionally) because they didn't have the peace produced by prayer safeguarding their heart and mind. And when their outward circumstances changed and got better, the inward sickness still remained, having caused its own, separate troubles that must yet be addressed and overcome. However, this could have been and can be prevented by prayer that provides internal protection from the anxiety that can accompany external problems.

God's peace doesn't permit things to enter our heart and mind that should remain out; and it doesn't allow things to exit our heart and mind that should remain in.

Noteworthy also is the fact that the apostle Paul penned this passage from prison. I have long said that I was interested in hearing what someone who was imprisoned had to say to free people about peace because ordinarily when a person is incarcerated there are many things on their mind that naturally, and understandably prevent them from having peace.

It is encouraging to me that while Paul himself was in trouble he was able to encourage others about the power of prayer in the time of trouble. It sounds to me like the importance of prayer during the time of trouble was something Paul had learned firsthand.

**"I thank my God upon every remembrance of you, always in every prayer of mine making request for you all with joy."
Philippians 1:3, 4**

Amazing! Here we find the imprisoned apostle Paul praying for folks who were outwardly in a better predicament than he was. It is also amazing that people can be better off inwardly when things outwardly are not good, and be better off inwardly than people who don't have it as bad outwardly.

I would have thought that they should have been writing to encourage Paul about praying, peace, and joy since *he* was the one who was locked up. Instead, he was writing and encouraging them! Externally, his situation was worse, but internally his soul was better!

Things don't have to change outwardly before we can feel better inwardly.

Another internal, invisible benefit that blessed Paul because of his prayer life in times of trouble was that of joy. Verse four says he prayed for them with *"joy."*

Certainly, Paul could not have prayed for them with joy if he didn't have any joy. From where did he get joy during his time of trouble? The same place he received peace—from the Lord. Peace and joy are both internal, invisible blessings that come from God.

The phrases **"...the peace <u>of</u> God,"** and, **"the joy <u>of</u> the Lord"** reveal that God is Owner, Master and the One Who controls and bestows peace and joy upon whomever He wills. God did so for Paul, and He brought that peace and joy through the two-way funnel of prayer. When we pray to God, the same vessel that carries our prayers *up* carries peace and joy back down to us.

We know peace is important because it *guards* our heart and mind, but joy is also important because it strengthens us and provides a source of protection, as peace does.

Listen to the words of Ezra as he encouraged the people of God who were encountering trouble while God was restoring the life He promised them:

"...Do not be sorry, for the joy of the Lord is your strength."
Nehemiah 8:10

The word *strength* in this verse does not only mean "power, force, or might." The Hebrew word for *strength* also means "stronghold; a place of safety and human protection." Just as the peace that belongs to God provides a level of protection for us, so also does His joy.

Peace and joy are the invisible, internal blessings that are produced by prayer—even before we begin to see any external benefits of prayer. Peace and joy protect, strengthen and stabilize us inwardly until our change comes outwardly.

Psalm 55 reveals that David, the king of trouble, also understood the strengthening and sustaining power of prayer.

**"Give ear to my prayer, O God,
and do not hide Yourself from
my supplication; attend to me,
and hear me; I am restless in my complaint,
and moan noisily, because of the voice
of the enemy, because of the oppression
of the wicked; for they bring down
trouble upon me, and in wrath
they hate me."
Psalm 55:1-3**

**"As for me, I will call upon God,
and the Lord shall save me.
Evening and morning and at noon
I will pray, and cry aloud, and He
shall hear my voice. He has redeemed
my soul in peace from the battle that
was against me, for there were
many against me."
Psalm 55:16-18**

**"Cast your burden on the Lord,
and He shall sustain you;
He shall never permit the
righteous to be moved."
Psalm 55:22**

Allow me to share two important points:

1) Before the Lord "saved" or "delivered" David from the trouble his enemies created for him, God strengthened him by restoring his peace through his prayer life—his consistent,

non-fainting prayer life. It may not have been a prayer life that prayed three times a day every day and perhaps not even every day. However, David's prayer life, which was described by the terms "*restless complaint*" and "*moaned noisily,*" prove he didn't abandon or give up on prayer even when it didn't appear as if God was moving through his prayers. God was moving; but He moved inwardly to help David before He moved outward to deliver him.

2) When David said, *"Cast your burden on the Lord,"* he was being inspired to encourage *us* out of what had proven to work for him. David through prayer had cast the burden of his trouble on God, and God strengthened him not to move away or give up because of his troubles, but to hang in there. God wanted David to continue to believe Him for the outward change and the better days that await the arrival of the righteous, though we be challenged now.

The overall point is that before prayer changes our situations or circumstances outwardly, it changes *us* inwardly. It changes us by infusing us with peace and joy that enable us to hang in there until the tool of trouble has built whatever God is using it to build. Prayer changes us by ridding us of that which worries and overwhelms us, and prayer imparts to us that which leaves us peaceful, patience and trusting in the Lord.

Peace and joy are the invisible blessings produced by prayer even before we begin to see the external benefits of prayer.

Not only does prayer bring about inward, invisible blessings and benefits, it also works invisibly in places and in people.

In Luke 18 we find Jesus encouraging us not to faint or give up on praying. We also find Him making a case for trustful persistence in prayer by telling a story about a woman who had been wronged, but was unyielding in her pursuit of justice. Consider this passage:

**"Then He spoke a parable to them, that men always ought to pray and not lose heart,
2 saying: 'There was in a certain city a judge who did not fear God nor regard man.
3 Now there was a widow In that city; and she came to him, saying, "Get justice for me from my adversary." ' "**

(Someone had obviously caused her trouble.)

**4 "And he would not for a while; but afterward he said within himself, 'Though I do not fear God nor regard man,
5 yet because this widow troubles me I will avenge her, lest by her continual coming she weary me.' "
6 Then the Lord said, 'Hear what the unjust judge said.
7 And shall God not avenge His own elect who cry out day and night to Him, though He bears long with them?' "
Luke 18:1-7**

This is unquestionably a parable that is purposed to encourage us to be persistent in praying about things, situations, and even people who trouble us. This story illustrates the fact that God, for different reasons, doesn't always answer our prayers for vindication or deliverance immediately. Sometimes it takes a while, but He will eventually move favorably on our behalf.

A closer look at this situation also allows us to see how God works invisibly in others through our prayers. The widow going repeatedly to the judge is the symbolic equivalent of our persistently going to God in prayer. And although she couldn't literally see it, her persistence in going to the judge was working invisibly inside of him, moving him to the point where he changed his mind and provided her with what she sought from him.

If she had stopped going to him (praying), the invisible movement inside him would have also stopped; she would not have received that to which she was entitled. Her persistence paid off as it worked in ways she could not visibly see. Such is the case with our persistence in praying. God is using it to work in people in ways we cannot see, and it's working in God Himself in ways we cannot see!

Just as the widow's persistence paid off with the unjust judge, our persistence in prayer will pay off with a just God because a just God will not be outdone by some ol' wicked, unjust judge who can't even put his robe on the right way!

Our persistent prayers also work invisibly in other people.

Our prayers not only work in other people in ways we cannot see, they are also working invisibly in places we cannot see.

Sometime after Daniel had been delivered from the trouble of the lions' den, no doubt through prayer, he found himself in prayer to God again. Upon hearing his prayer, God sent forth an angel in direct response to Daniel's prayer.

"Suddenly, a hand touched me which made me tremble on my knees and on the palms of my hands. And he said to me, 'O Daniel, man greatly beloved, understand the words that I speak to you, and stand upright, for I have now been sent to you.' While he was speaking this word to me I stood trembling. Then he said to me, 'Do not fear,

Daniel, for from the first day that you set your heart to understand, and to humble yourself before your God, <u>your words were heard</u>....' "
Daniel 10:10-12

The phrase *"your words"* offered by the angel was a reference to Daniel's prayer. When Daniel *first* began to pray, God began to move in response to his prayer. However, the movement of God was invisible to the eyes and the understanding of Daniel. Things were happening because of Daniel's prayer, but they were happening in places Daniel could not see.

Listen to what the angel (possibly Gabriel) went on to say:

"...and I have come because of <u>your words</u>. But the prince [demonic angel] of the kingdom of Persia withstood me twenty-one days; and behold, Michael, one of the chief princes [angels], came to help me, for I had been left alone there with the kings of Persia.
Daniel 10:12, 13

After Daniel prayed, the answer to his prayer was postponed, but not because God was twiddling His thumbs. Rather, the postponement was due to the angel—who had been commissioned to carry out his prayer request—being delayed by demonic opposition.

There are times when the answer to prayer comes quickly—like when Daniel was in the lions' den, as well as in this experience in Daniel chapter nine:

"Now while I was speaking, praying, and confessing my sin and the sin of my people Israel, and presenting my supplication before the Lord my God for the holy mountain of my God, Yes, while I was speaking in prayer, the man Gabriel, whom I had seen in the

vision at the beginning, being caused to fly swiftly, reached me about the time of the evening offering."
Daniel 9:20, 21

Gabriel the angel showed up in response to Daniel's prayer request even before Daniel had finished praying, indicating that there are times when response to prayer happens "swiftly." But on the occasion of chapter ten, the angel was delayed because he was engaged in a confrontation.

As Christians, I think we sometimes forget that we are engaged in spiritual warfare where there is literal opposition to many, if not all of what we're trying to obtain and accomplish spiritually. Sometimes this opposition is through the devil's use of other people, but sometimes it's through the devil's use of his fallen angels who are on satanic assignment to hinder us and to keep our prayer requests from being fulfilled.

"For we do not wrestle against flesh and blood, but against principalities, against powers, against the rulers of the darkness of this age, against spiritual hosts of wickedness in the heavenly places."
Ephesians 6:12

The *principalities, powers, rulers of the darkness,* and the *spiritual hosts of wickedness* speak of the various ranks and orders of the fallen angels who were expelled from Heaven with Lucifer, the devil. "The heavenly places" is a reference to places that are invisible to the natural eyes—places where the angels of the Lord are doing battle and defeating the angels of the devil (Matthew 25:41).

The battles and the battlegrounds of these angelic confrontations are invisible to us, but they are not any less real than we are. And sometimes the delay of visible fulfillment of our prayer requests are due to things that are taking place in the invisible realm.

Be that as it may, Jesus says, "…**men ought always to pray and not lose heart**" (or not give up on praying and believing) just because when and what we have prayed for has yet to happen during the period of our prescribed timeline.

I have learned that there are occasions when the Lord never answers a particular request. Still, He is remains worthy of my trust because God is too great to hang the entirety of my trust in Him on one unanswered prayer request. **Psalm 84:11** says,

"No good thing will He withhold from them who walk uprightly."

I have one or two ways of thinking as it pertains to this verse:

1) If I pray and it hasn't happened yet but it's still possible, there may be a spiritual holdup or it's simply not time. But I keep praying and believing.

2) If I pray and it didn't happen, it's not the "good thing" I thought it was; and God has something better in store. In this I have noticed that the *real "good thing"*—God's "*good thing*"—takes place after the door on *our "good thing"* has been closed.

God's *"good thing"* takes place after the door on *our "good thing"* has been closed.

As it pertains to the practice of being persistent in prayer during troublesome times, we see believers all throughout the Bible being urged to continue praying—even when the outward change of their circumstances didn't come as soon as they would have liked.

The apostle Paul wrote and encouraged the Christians in Rome always to be:

"…rejoicing in hope, patient in tribulation, continuing steadfastly in prayer…."
Romans 12:12

To the church in Ephesus he wrote:
"...praying always with all prayer
and supplication in the Spirit...."
Ephesians 6:18

To the Colosse Christians he wrote:

"Continue earnestly in prayer,
being vigilant in prayer with thanksgiving...."
Colossians 4:2

And to the church of the Thessalonians again, he simple instructed them to:

"...pray without ceasing...."
2 Thessalonians 5:17

The Holy Spirit would not have inspired Paul to encourage Christians to be persistent in prayer if persistence in prayer wouldn't pay off.

It is important to know that although prayer may not be changing things outwardly right away, prayer is not idle in that it isn't accomplishing anything. It is true that before prayer brings about outward change in *things*, it is working at accomplishing inward change in *us*. These changes not only help us inwardly, but they also prepare us for the outward changes and blessings which we have persistently been in prayer about.

"Men always ought to pray and not lose heart...."
—Jesus

What are you waiting for? Go pray! God is waiting to hear from you, one of His favorite children!

Chapter 9

The Importance of Praise in the Time of Trouble

"Now it happened, as we went to prayer, that a
certain slave girl possessed with a spirit of
divination met us, who brought her masters much
profit by fortune-telling. 17 This girl followed Paul and
us, and cried out, saying, 'These men are the servants
of the Most High God, who proclaim to us the way of
salvation.' 18 And this she did for many days.
But Paul, greatly annoyed, turned and said to the spirit,
'I command you in the name of Jesus Christ to come
out of her.' And he came out that very hour. 19 But
when her masters saw that their hope of profit was gone,
they seized Paul and Silas and dragged them into the
marketplace to the authorities.
20And they brought them to the magistrates, and said,
'These men, being Jews, exceedingly trouble our city;
21 and they teach customs which are not lawful for
us, being Romans, to receive or observe.' 22 Then
the multitude rose up together against them; and the
magistrates tore off their clothes and commanded them
to be beaten with rods. 23 And when they had laid
many stripes on them, they threw them into prison,
commanding the jailer to keep them securely. 24 Having
received such a charge, he put them into the

inner prison and fastened their feet in the stocks. 25 But at midnight Paul and Silas were praying and singing hymns to God, and the prisoners were listening to them. 26 Suddenly there was a great earthquake, so that the foundations of the prison were shaken; and immediately all of the doors were opened and everyone's chains were loosed."
Acts 16:16-26

With Paul and Silas we also find faithful, purpose-fulfilling believers in trouble. They had been beaten and imprisoned by the authorities of the city of Philippi. The very fact that they were *in prison* is an indication that they were *in trouble.* For them prison was purposed to be a prelude to their execution. Had there not been a divine interruption, and the case against Paul and Silas made it to trial, there is little doubt that the socially influenced guilty verdict of the Philippian authorities would have resulted in a sentence of death. However, it did not because God intervened.

The point is that although their trouble was designed to lead to something worse, the worse did not occur despite the occurrence of trouble. This further indicates to us that there is a difference between trouble and what trouble seeks to accomplish. God permitted the imprisonment but not the death sentence to which the imprisonment was purposed to lead.

What Paul and Silas did in their time of trouble that helped them to be delivered is an example of what we should do in our time of trouble. Paul and Silas "**prayed, and praised**" God—even after having been badly beaten and tossed into prison.

In the middle of physical affliction and emotional distress, Paul and Silas prayed and praised God because they understood He was *still* worthy of their praise. They also believed prayer and praise would be instrumental in them getting out of trouble. And they were right!

As Christians, many of us have learned about the helpful importance of prayer during our times of trouble; however, many of us are unaware of how equally important and helpful *praise* is during these times.

A number of David's psalms of prayer, praise and worship were penned during his many times of trouble. Some were written before he became king, and some were written after he became king—revealing the lesson that status or positions do not exempt anyone from trouble and therefore should not change our dependence on prayer and praise.

David's commitment to prayer and praise *during* his times of trouble serves as an excellent example for all Christians. It may have been from the writings of David and other Old Testament characters that Paul and Silas learned about the power of prayer and praise during trying times.

Remember Romans 15:4, which says, **"Whatsoever things were written of aforetime were written for our learning..."** Paul and Silas learned from what had been written and applied it to their life, and it worked for them. Because that truth worked for *them* when *they* applied it, the same truth will also work for *us* when *we* apply it.

Consider these few passages of praise written by David during his time of trouble, and you'll see that he did not permit trouble to deplete his praise. Instead, trouble compelled David to praise God even more! Maybe it was because David understood the importance and power of praise and how beneficial it was to him during those times in his life. Or maybe he just rightfully recognized that regardless of what he was going through, God was still worthy to be praised. Or it could have been both. In any instance, let's take a look at David's mindset toward praise during his days of difficulty.

**"Deliver me from my enemies, O my God;
defend me from those who rise up against me.
Deliver me from the workers of iniquity, And save me
from bloodthirsty men. For look, they lie in wait
for my life; the mighty gather against me, not for
my transgression nor for my sin, O Lord."
Psalm 59:1-3**

In this situation, David was clearly in trouble. Anytime we find ourselves in a den of lions, a fiery furnace, a dingy dungeon, or around bloodthirsty enemies who are setting ambushes for us, we are in *trouble*!

David was obviously in trouble, but while he was *in* trouble he was also *in* prayer asking God to protect him from the ultimate objective of the trouble. While we see David *praying* in trouble, this psalm reveals David *praising* God in trouble as well.

Anytime we are *in praise* to God, we are also *in prayer* to Him because, like prayer, praise is communication with the Lord. We are communicating our knowledge, our understanding and our agreement with how great, gracious, wonderful, strong, mighty, holy and awesome He is!

**"But I will sing of Your power;
Yes, I will sing aloud of
your mercy in the morning;
for You have been my defense and refuge
<u>in the day of my trouble</u>. To You,
O my strength, <u>I will sing praises</u>;
for God is my defense, My God of mercy."
Psalm 59:16, 17**

In this Scripture, God was being a Protector *during* David's days of difficulty days—even though He had allowed the trouble to come. God did not protect David *from* the trouble, but He did indeed protect him from the tragedy that accompanied trouble. But the point here is that David continued to praise God—even "**in the day of (his) trouble.**"

We know his praise was helpful to him because even though David was in trouble, trouble never completely had its way with him. David went on to fulfill God's purpose for him in the earth.

Consider the words of this particular psalmist (possibly David) as he reveals his trouble and reminds himself of the importance of praise *during* his troublesome season:

"My tears have been my food day and night,
while they continually say to me,
'Where is your God?' "
Psalm 42:3

Before I go further, let me pause to acknowledge that our troubles can bring tears, and that our tears have a way a quietly questioning the whereabouts of our God during our time of trouble. Tears are not only produced by our pain, they are also products of feeling forgotten or forsaken by God. Tears are the bleedings of a heavy heart—heavy with disappointment and despair. However, our praise has the power to silence our tears and stop the bleeding of our heart.

To *praise* God means "to lift up our hands unto Him, give thanks and to make confessions of Who and what we know Him to be." An example of praise would be our coming before the Lord with our hands outstretched, saying something to the effect of:

"*Lord, I thank You for Your goodness, Your kindness and Your mercies that are made new every morning. And I thank You for Your compassions toward me that never fail. I thank You for blessing me, helping me, leading me, guiding me and protecting me. Lord, You are holy and wonderful! You are a great God and a great King above all gods. There isn't anyone like You. You are the only true and living God. You are the Creator of all that is.*

You are He that has all wisdom, knowledge and power. You can do anything because nothing is too hard or impossible for You. You are holy, wonderful and faithful. Great is Your faithfulness, O God. And great is Your loving kindness."

Anytime we are *in praise* to God,
we are also *in prayer* to God.

We can praise God through our words of confession, or of course, we can sing praises to God. Either way, our praise is tremendously helpful to us during our time of trouble.

Listen to what the psalmist goes on to say in Psalm 42:

"Why are you cast down, O my soul?
And why are you disquieted within me?
Hope in God, for I shall yet praise Him
for the help of His countenance."
Psalm 42:5

In this verse we find the songwriter linking praise to help. "...**I shall praise Him for** the **help** of His countenance."

The word *countenance* takes on at least two meanings that are relevant to our being helped by praise in our time of trouble.

1) Firstly, the word *countenance* as it is used in Psalm 42:5 has to do with "appearance." However, this definition is not the appearance of how one *looks,* but in a person "showing up, or making an appearance." When we praise God He shows up or He makes an appearance because of our praise. He may not make a visible, physical appearance, but our praise paves the way for the spiritual presence of God to visit us.

In Psalm 22:3 David said the Lord, "**...inhabits the praises of Israel**"—His people. To *inhabit* means "to live, reside or to dwell in." Each of these definitions is tied to God being present. When we praise God, He is not only present to make an appearance because of our praise; He occupies, takes up residence, dwells and makes His home in our praise.

In 2 Chronicles chapter 5 after Solomon had finished building the house of the Lord, the singers and musicians began to play and sing praises to God; and upon doing so, God made an *appearance.*

"Indeed it came to pass, when the trumpeters and singers were as one, to make one sound to be heard in praising and thinking the Lord, and when they lifted up their voice with the trumpets and cymbals and instruments of music, and praised the Lord, saying: 'For He is good, For His mercy endures forever,' that the house, the house of the Lord, was filled with a cloud, so that the priests could not continue ministering because of the cloud, for the glory of the Lord filled the house of God.
2 Chronicles 5:13, 14

The *"glory of the Lord"* that *"filled the house of God"* was nothing less than the presence of God. God appears *because* of our praise. Praise honors God, and when God is being praised He shows up as the *Guest of honor*! When God shows up or makes an appearance, what accompanies His presence is all that makes Him God.

2) This explanation takes us to the second meaning of "*countenance*" in Psalm 42:5. The "*countenance*" is also an *outward* expression of *inward* emotions or existences. Whatever emotions that exist *inside of us* are almost always expressed *outside of us* either through our words, actions or facial expressions.

The troubled child of God said, "...**I shall yet praise Him [God] for the help of His countenance**," meaning that there was something *inside* of God that would be helpful to him once it was unlocked by praise.

Acts 17:28 says, "**In Him we live and move and have our being.**"

What is it that is *in* God that can help us during our time of trouble? Everything! Everything we need to *live* through our season of trial and *move* from "strength to strength," "faith to faith," and from one level to a higher level is *"in"* God. Everything we need to make it through our troublesome times and become the person God is molding us to be, is *in Him.* Everything we need not to grow weary in well doing and possess what awaits us on the other side of this time of tribulation is "*in Him.*" For these reasons we should praise God during times of trouble. Praise taps into that which is *in God* and what is *in Him* helps us by getting into us. Praise initiates a spiritual infusion.

Let's take a look at a couple of the intangibles that are *in* God that will be helpful to a person during his time of trouble:

David wrote in Psalm 16:11, **"In Your presence there is fullness of joy...."** This "*fullness of joy*" is a product of "*the joy of the Lord.*" The joy *of* the Lord exists *inside* Him, and it shows up whenever He shows up. When God is present, or when He makes an appearance, He brings His joy for us to partake of during our times of trouble. When our pity party becomes a praise party, God shows up and brings His joy to the party!

This knowledge and understanding of joy is extremely helpful because Nehemiah 8:10 says, **"...the joy of the Lord is your strength**." The strengthening ability of God's joy enables us to endure our days of difficulty. And this is one reason why our praise during our trouble is so vitally important.

When our pity party becomes a praise party, God shows up and brings His joy to the party!

When God makes an appearance with His presence because of our praise, what also accompanies Him is His peace. In **John 14:27** Jesus says, **"...My peace I give to you...."** The word "my" is a possessive pronoun that speaks of ownership. As the Prince of Peace, Jesus is also the Owner of peace, and as its Owner He has the authority to *give* peace as He pleases.

God's peace also always accompanies His presence. Therefore He is never without His peace, and there is never a curl in the brow of God's countenance. He is always at peace inwardly and He brings that inward peace to the place of praise and allows those who are engaged in praise to partake of His peace in their time of trouble. Through our praise of God comes an impartation of His peace to us.

Remember also that, as a *guard*, peace keeps the good stuff in and keeps the bad stuff out. Peace keeps *in* the joy of the Lord that strengthens us, and simultaneously keeps *out* the worry that stresses us.

In Psalm 42:5 the songwriter sums it up for us when he goes on to say:

"Why are you cast down, O my soul?
and why are you disquieted within me?
Hope in God; for <u>I shall yet praise Him</u>,
<u>the help of my countenance</u> and my God.

When we "praise God for the help of His countenance" (or for the help of what's *in* Him), it helps *our* countenance, or it helps what is *in* us. Inwardly, God is *always* confident, strong, joyful, peaceful and full of faith. And when we praise Him, what's *in Him* gets *in us!*

When we lift our hands in the midst of all that is going wrong and thank Him for all that is yet right, the joy of the Lord will find its way *into* us, strengthening us and overwhelming worry. During our days of difficulty, when we dedicate ourselves to declaring how holy, awesome, wonderful, faithful and powerful God is, that which is *in* Him is withdrawn and deposited into us!

The peace and joy of the Lord accompany His presence. When He shows up in response to praise, they arrive with Him.

Our praise and our enemy

In John 10:10 when Jesus says, "**The thief does not come except to steal, kill and to destroy**," Jesus doesn't specify exactly *what* the devil seeks to steal because he seeks to steal any and everything God gives or makes available to His children. Yes, the devil is in the business of stealing material things, but he is just as interested in stealing immaterial things like time, joy, peace, prayer, and...praise!

Unlike human thieves, the devil does not steal things from us so that *he* can benefit from having them. Instead, he steals things from us so that *we cannot* benefit from having them. In the time of trouble, the enemy seeks to steal our praise of God because he knows how helpful and healthy our praise is during difficult times.

The devil seeks to steal our praise by bombarding our mind with doubt, fear and feelings of hopelessness. He seeks to steal our praise because he knows our praise of God will help us to weather the storm of the troublesome season.

Let's be careful not to allow the enemy to steal our praise or to accidently leave praise out of our prayer. Individually, both prayer and praise are good, but prayer and praise as a team possess the power to produce a *mighty* move of God! This is exactly what happened in the life of David, Solomon, Paul and Silas.

Unlike human thieves, the devil doesn't steal things from us because *he* can benefit from having them. Instead, he steals things from us so that <u>*we* cannot</u> benefit from having them.

It was probably from David and other Old Testament giants of faith that Paul and Silas learned about the power of prayer and praise while in trouble. In fact, it was the apostle Paul who wrote in Romans 15:4, **"Whatsoever things were written of aforetime were written for our learning...."** Obviously Paul understood that the experiences of God's people in the past were intended by God to be examples and lessons for all of His children who would follow.

Paul and Silas learned from what was written from the lives of the Old Testament saints, applied it to their lives, and it worked for them. Their praise during their time of imprisonment (trouble) invited God into their ordeal—an ordeal from which the praise-dwelling presence of God delivered them.

Praise is important because whenever God makes an appearance or wherever He shows up, His peace and joy accompany His presence, and the peace and joy of the Lord are <u>*tremendously*</u> helpful to us during our time of trouble.

Our praise to God glorifies Him, but it edifies, strengthens and encourages us. In order to understand this truth, we must understand the power of our words. In being created to be "like God," one of the ways we resemble Him is that our words have power just as His Words have power.

We know God's Word has power because His Word created everything that is. In the first chapter of Genesis, "God said" and what His Word "said," "was so." In much the same way, our words have power—not world-creating power (that's been taken care of already), but power to create that which edifies, strengthens and encourages us during our times of trouble.

Here's how it works: **Proverbs 18:21** says, **"Death and life are in the power of the tongue, and those who love it will eat its fruit."** This verse reveals the power of our words (tongue), but it also reveals that our words will either be to our detriment or to our betterment.

When from our tongue we offer up praise during our time of trouble, those words work to our betterment and benefit because, again, our words of praise speak of the wonder and power of God. As those words come from our mouth, they are re-deposited through our hearing and help remind us of how awesome, strong and mighty our God is and how great is His faithfulness!

Having our praise making that sort of deposit into our hearts on a regular basis strengthens, edifies, encourages and enables us to go forth in our time of trouble with a renewed spirit as well as a healthy and hopeful outlook.

While David was on the run from King Saul, he paused to pen his commitment to praise even during his days of difficulty:

"I will bless the Lord <u>at all times</u>;
His praise shall continually be in my mouth."
Psalm 34:1

To *"bless the Lord"* means "to speak well of Him." It also means "to state words of praise that tell of God's grandeur, grace, mercy and magnificence"! David was committed to blessing God—even in troubling times—because God was still worthy of such blessings, and because praising God helped David!

Many of us think that praise is what we do *after* God has blessed, or delivered us. And most certainly we are to praise

God during those times. However, we should also praise Him in the not-so-good times. Doing so helps our hope.

"O God, do not be far from me;
O my God, make haste to help me!
Let them be confounded and consumed
who are adversaries of my life;
let them be covered with reproach
and dishonor who seek my hurt.
But I will hope continually, and
<u>I will praise You yet more and more</u>."
Psalm 71:12-14

Again we find David being committed to praise during his difficult days. In fact, when he said, **"I will praise You yet more and more,"** David was not only revealing his commitment to praise in crisis, but he was vowing to *increase* his praise in his time crisis! David's praise helped get him through his difficult days.

Our praise makes a deposit into our heart—a deposit that encourages us, strengthens us, and revives our hope.

Among other meanings in the Bible, the word *"hope"* in Psalm 71 means "confident expectation." Despite his trouble David never wavered in his *confident expectation* of God's help *during* trouble, and God ultimately delivering him *from* trouble.

David was able to "*hope continually*" in Psalm 71 because he "*praised continually*" in Psalm 34—revealing the connection between hope and praise. In fact, from these passages, it is apparent that praise gives birth or rebirth to hope.

Although his circumstances had not changed, David maintained a healthy, internal hope that they would. It is an amazing fact that praise brings about an inward change while things on the outside remain the same—proving that our situation or circumstances don't have to change *outwardly* in order for us to feel better *inwardly*. Praise possesses the power to make that change!

(I realize that outward change to our troublesome situations is what we want. But if it isn't time for that outward change to occur, the next best thing is inward change that strengthens, encourages and enables us to cope until the outward change comes. I also realize that inward change may not be an answer to your prayer, but it is an answer to the prayer of our Christ and King Who lives forever to make intercession for us. It is an answer to the intercession the Holy Spirit makes for us when praying for help with our weaknesses—which include our internal, invisible, emotional ones. Praise helps to accomplish what Jesus and the Holy Spirit are praying for on our behalf.)

This is why it is important to sing and to express words of praise to the Lord even during our times of trouble. When we praise God in our time of trouble, He makes an appearance. What accompanies His presence are all of the helpful things we need to weather the storm and reap the harvest the rainy season *always* leaves behind!

If we learn and apply what is written in the Scriptures particularly about praise, those examples and lessons will work for us as well.

Continual praise births continual hope.

If you are experiencing a time of trouble, let me encourage you to begin to praise God on a regular, daily basis. You can take any amount of time you want or have to praise Him. When you are in church, sing to the Lord—not just from your mouth, but from your heart. Do this by being mindful of what you are saying when you are singing.

Of course you can sing praises to the Lord when you're all alone, or you can speak praises to Him. Either way, God will occupy your praise and impart to you that which will bless and encourage you.

This is the end of the chapter and a great place to take a praise break! Even if you cannot lift your hands or vocally express your praise at this moment, begin to do so in your heart. Just for a moment, close the book, close your eyes and just begin to thank God for all of His goodness. Begin to say to Him whatever you know Him to be (i.e., great, mighty, holy, loving, kind, saving, healing, providing, protecting, etc.) Instantly you will begin to feel *His* countenance helping *your* countenance. You will feel a spiritual infusion as God funnels peace, strength and encouragement to your heart. Go ahead! Praise Him now!

Chapter 10
The Importance of Church Attendance in the Time of Trouble

**"May the Lord answer you in the day of trouble;
may the name of the God of Jacob defend you;
may He send you help from the sanctuary,
and strengthen you out of Zion...."
Psalm 20:1, 2**

This psalm, like many of the others, is probably a product of David's personal experience from which he withdrew to enlighten and to encourage people who would also tread the trail of trouble. David's use of the word *"you"* indicates that these Spirit-inspired words of song are also Spirit-inspired words of prayer for anyone who is trusting God to lead him through days darkened with difficulty.

In these words of song and prayer, we also find words of wisdom from the king of trouble. Among other things we are allowed to know that during trying times there is help for us in the sanctuary of our God. When we talk about the sanctuary, we are also talking about the chapel, the temple, the church, the house of God, or any place of gathering wherein a family of Christians worships God.

During our time of challenge, there is help for us *in* the sanctuary. This is evident in that the Lord could not send us help *from* the sanctuary unless there was help *in* the sanctuary to begin with. For example, if I promise to send you money *from* my bank account, it automatically means there is money *in* my bank account from which I can draw. It is the same with the Lord sending us help *from* the sanctuary. Because there is help *in* the sanctuary, our presence there will allow us to benefit from this help firsthand. It's good to know that God will "send" us help from the sanctuary, but it is also good to know that we can also go to the house of the Lord and receive this same help.

The type of help that comes from the sanctuary includes peace, joy, wisdom, guidance, instruction and encouragement. And there are additional helps that I will address shortly, but they all contribute to the importance of our attending church on a regular basis, *especially* during troublesome times.

The devil's aim is to keep Christians out of church as much as possible during these times. In John 10:10, Jesus says that the devil *"comes to kill, steal and destroy."* Aside from our praise, another thing the enemy seeks to steal is our desire to go to church. He steals this desire by depositing thoughts of why we shouldn't attend church. One of his desire-stealing deposits is the thought of, *"Church doesn't really help," or "If church was so helpful, why are you in trouble?" or "God understands what you're going through right now. He knows you need a little time away from church."* It's easy to identify these thoughts as being from the enemy because they stand in opposition to the Word of God. The Word of God is true, and anything that opposes it is a lie. All lies originate with the devil because he is the "father of lies." God's Word says that there is help in the sanctuary, and when we have thoughts that are contrary to that the Word of God, we can automatically know it's the enemy trying to steal our desire to go to church. Satan tries to keep us from attending worship services because he knows how helpful they are in strengthening and inspiring us to hang in there as God prepares us for plans and promises.

We know that the church building or place of gathering is where children of God assemble to praise, worship, pray, and corporately receive the Word of God. The helpfulness of these things has already been addressed in previous chapters, but primarily as they pertain to our private practice of them and not necessarily in the church setting. Again, these elements are important because they are helpful. But as we participate in them in the house of God, an added helpfulness accompanies them.

Many people whom the Holy Spirit inspired to write about attending church understood the importance of church attendance. I will speak to some other things David wrote about the benefits of church attendance, but first consider the words of the apostle Paul who encourages getting together with the church congregation, and the powerful (but often overlooked) and invisible benefits of doing so.

"And let us consider one another in order to stir up love and good works; not forsaking the assembling of ourselves together, as is the manner of some, but exhorting one another, and so much the more as you see the day approaching."
Hebrews 10:24, 25

"Not forsaking the assembling of ourselves together" is an encouragement to come together—not just for a potluck (which has a helpful place during the time of trouble)—but for the purpose of praying, worshiping and praising God together as a church family. Also, hidden in the words of these two verses are some very good reasons why we *should not forsake the assembling of ourselves together.*

Notice first that Paul says the church is a place where we are *considered* by one another. The Greek word for *consider* also means "to behold," "to perceive," "to discover," "to observe," "to understand," "to fix one's eye on," and "to consider attentively." The idea communicated by each of these definitions is to notice, recognize, or *spiritually discern* the concern carried by another brother or sister who is experiencing trouble.

We all have a level of discernment when it comes to being able to detect that something is amiss with someone else. Sometimes we are tipped off by the standoffishness of someone who is ordinarily jovial or sociable, or by some facial expression, or by an expression of emotion. But God also supernaturally enables certain Christians to perceive when something isn't quite right with one of our brothers or sisters in Christ when there is no evidence of such. This supernatural ability is the spiritual gift of ***"discerning of spirits,"*** mentioned in 1 Corinthian 12:10 by the apostle Paul.

Some people only understand this gift to operate in discerning truth from fallacy, or the works of God from those works that are demonic in nature. Whereas the gift of discerning of spirits most certainly does recognize the works (and people) of opposition to the work of God, this gift does not *only* recognize such works.

Jesus was endowed with every spiritual gift, including the gift of discernment, and He used this gift in a number of different ways. On one occasion after Jesus healed a man and forgave his sins, **Matthew 9:3** says, **"…at once some of the scribes said within themselves, 'This Man blasphemes!' "** Verse four goes on to say, **"But Jesus, knowing their thoughts, said, 'Why do you think evil in your hearts?' "** Although the scribes did not verbally state their sentiments, through the gift of discerning of spirits, Jesus understood their thoughts as if they were spoken words. He was able to do that because those who have this gift are able to sense what is not expressed—whether evil thoughts, motives or intentions, feelings of worry, doubt, fear; or other issues that signify the presence of trouble in a person's life.

What people know about us through the gift of discernment is because of what God knows because of His omniscience. **Psalm 139:2** says that the Lord, **"...knows [our] thoughts afar off."** Solomon would echo the words of his father, saying of God in **1 Kings 8:39**, **"...You alone know the hearts of all the sons of men."** And the Bible says that God, Who is His Word, "...**is a discerner of the thoughts and the intents of the heart. And there is no creature hidden from His sight, but all things are naked and open in the eyes of Him to whom we must give an account." (Hebrews 4:12b, 13)**

The point is that, out of *the everything* God knows about our lives, circumstances and thoughts, He imparts portions of that knowledge to someone in our church to whom His Spirit has given the gift of discernment. It is through this supernatural impartation of knowledge that healthy and helpful dialogue begins—dialogue that always leads to encouragement, and often leads to our exit out of our trouble. However, if we do not attend church or don't continue to do so, we will not place ourselves in the proximity of people whom God has equipped to help and bless us.

"...let us consider one another in order to stir up love and good works, not forsaking the assembling of ourselves...."

The term *stir up* in this verse means "to provoke." When we regularly attend church during our time of trouble, the Lord not only allows someone to know that we are struggling, but He also *provokes* them to show us love and to perform some *"good work"* that will help us, and remind us of God's faithfulness toward us.

God enabling people in the church fellowship to know that something is troubling us is nothing short of caring, amazing and miraculous! Despite our best efforts to mask our problems with makeup and masculinity, the Lord has a way of allowing people to see beyond the mascara, the male bravado, and the "*everything-is-fine*" persona we project, and recognize that something is *not quite right* with us. I am happy He does so because it alerts people to fact that we are in need of prayer; and it *stirs them up* to show us God's love during our time of difficulty.

God grants people discernment to see behind the makeup, and beyond our masculinity. He stirs their heart to help us.

In a previous chapter I wrote about the importance of praise. Church attendance is important also because of our participation in praise while we are in God's house.

"Then they cry out to the Lord in their trouble,
and He brings them out of their distresses.
He calms the storm, so that it waves are still.
Then they are glad because they are quiet;
so He guides them to their desired haven.
Oh, that men would give thanks to the Lord
for His goodness, and for His wonderful
works to the children of men! Let them
exalt Him in the assembly of the people,
and praise Him in the company of the elders.
Psalm 107:28-32

In this passage the psalmist is writing about trouble, deliverance, thanksgiving, and praising God as a part of a church body. Thanksgiving is a form of praise. One of the hardest things to do during the time of trouble is to thank God for His goodness. It's difficult to thank God for *good* when everything is going *bad!* However, we must remember that praise—particularly the praise of thanksgiving—helps to sustain us because it reminds us of God's past goodness. This is a blessing because it makes us to know that if God gave us reason to be thankful in times past, and He changes not, He shall again give us reason to be thankful as He helps and delivers us from our troubles!

So the praise of thanksgiving is extremely helpful when life appears to be opposing us. But the word "also" in verse 32 indicates that not only are we to praise God in the privacy of our homes or in our own company, but also "in the assembly of the people" as well. Or in other words, in *church*!

It is not a coincidence that this passage opens with trouble and closes with encouragement to praise the Lord in the presence of other people. Even during the time of trouble, we must make time to praise God in His house and in the company of other Christians.

David made it a practice to praise God in the company of others—even in the middle of his trouble. I like using David's life as an example because if anyone knows about what to do to be helped during trouble, David does! Look at the words he paused to pen to God while he was on the run from those who sought to take his life:

"Lord how long will You look on?
rescue me from their destructions,
my precious life from the lions."
Psalm 35:17

"I will give You thanks in the great assembly;
I will praise You among many people."
Psalm 35:18

"Let them not rejoice over me who
are wrongfully my enemies;
nor let them wink with the eye
who hate me without a cause."
Psalm 35:19

In verses 17 and 19 David makes it plain that he is speaking from one of the difficult seasons of his life. But notice that in between verses 17 and 19 (verses of trouble), David in verse 18 promises to praise God in "the great assembly" or in church. It is not a coincidence that a verse of praise would be in the middle of verses that speak of trouble. This structure provides a picture of how we should praise God in church—even though we are in the *middle* of challenging times.

David praised God in the presence of others even while he was in the midst of trouble because he had seemingly learned the benefits of doing so. Again, there are most certainly blessings and benefits in offering God personal praise in private settings—be it from the confines of our home, walks in the park, or while riding in our car—but there is also a spiritually healthy and helpful connection between trouble and the praise we offer to the Lord in church.

When we are present with other saints who are singing and expressing to God His worthiness, goodness, kindness, mercy, graciousness, power and faithfulness—hearing these words of praise from them imparts affirmation to us that reminds us of God's goodness and causes us to be encouraged.

In this prophetic, Messianic psalm, consider this printed commitment made by David during another time of trouble:

"I will declare Your name to My brothers;
in the midst of the assembly I will praise You."
Psalm 22:22

While we are declaring (through praise) God's name to our brothers and sisters in Christ, they are declaring His name to us through their praise. The praises of others to God in church are declarations to *us* of the goodness of God for which they are praising Him. As we repeatedly hear the praise of God from others, our soul is strengthened with confidence in God's ability, willingness, and commitment to helping us during that tumultuous time in our life.

It may sound odd, but congregational praise is spiritual therapy for our soul. As we attend church services, we are not only helped by our offerings of praise to God in His sanctuary, but we are also blessed by the praise of God from others who may have no idea that their praise is helping our heart and healing our hurt.

Praise is therapeutic.
Congregational praise is
a higher level of therapy.

We know that trouble found David like kids find cookies in the cabinet. However, David found his own treasure—praising God in the church setting when he was in trouble. Notice what else he says in this Psalm 22:

"My praise shall be of You
in the great assembly;
I will pay my vows before
those who fear Him."
Psalm 22:25

Despite his trouble, David's vow was to praise God in the assembly of other saints because he understood the value of praise in the house of God during the problem periods of his life.

Consider these other passages that encourage and promise God praise in His house:

"Behold, bless the Lord, all you servant
of the Lord, who by night stand in
the house of the Lord! Lift up
your hands in the sanctuary,
and bless the Lord."
Psalm 134:1, 2

"Praise the Lord!
Sing to the Lord a new song, and His praise
In the assembly of saints."
Psalm 149:1

"I will praise the Lord with my whole heart,
in the assembly of the upright and
in the congregation."
Psalm 111:1

The Bible repeatedly encourages us to attend church during our time of testing simply because doing so helps us immensely!

David found his own treasure when he was in trouble, praise in the house of his God.

"May the Lord answer you in the day of trouble;
may the name of the God of Jacob defend you;
may He send you help from the sanctuary,
and strengthen you out of Zion;
may He remember all your offerings,
and accept your burnt sacrifices."
Psalm 20:1-3

It makes sense that the Holy Spirit would inspire David to write about offerings in the verse that follows talk about the sanctuary because we typically give offerings when we go to the sanctuary.

However, it can be difficult to embrace the idea of financial offerings if our time of trouble is financial in nature. Just as it can be difficult to give thanks to God for His goodness when times are bad, it can be equally as difficult to give offerings to God when we are trying to make ends meet, and we only have one end with which to work.

It's not always that we don't believe in giving or that we are selfish or rebellious and refuse to give. Sometimes it's just tough to trust God in giving because things are tough and financially tight. But it is when things are tough that we can prove our trust.

I've come to realize that even as Christians we don't always see giving in the right light or in the entirety of its purpose and process. We can see how our giving *to* the church helps the church, but miss how our giving to the church helps us. We often only view giving as immediate subtraction while ignoring or not knowing about the delayed addition that completes the cycle. We sometimes see giving only as a subtraction that removes from the here and now, leaving us completely without. However, we don't always realize that what we give in the here and now is stored by God and used to help us later.

This is what we saw with the widow of 1 Kings 17. The Lord "commanded" her to give the little flour and oil she had remaining—not so that she could forever be without and starve—but so that He could apply the principle of sowing and reaping to what she gave and help her thereby until her situation changed. When she trusted God and gave, He blessed her by supernaturally making certain that she always had what she needed.

The point is that we should view giving in tough times in this light; the light that reveals that God is not trying to take something *from us* as much as He is trying to get something *to us* by way of trust.

This is the farmer's view of seed sowing. Farmers know that parting with seed in the here and now guarantees them a greater return on the seed later. They understand that the ground never forgets the seed sown but brings forth fruit from it to help at some point in the future.

Just as the ground never forgets the seed sown by the farmer, the Lord never forgets the offerings we give to Him. Instead, He stores them and causes them to bring forth fruit at a later time of need. This is one of the things David had in mind when he wrote, "May [the Lord] remember all your offerings."

The word "*remember*", not only means "not to forever forget," or "to recall," it also means "to record for the sake of revisiting." The Lord records our offerings, and He revisits them for the sake of rewarding them.

A great picture of this latter meaning of "remember" is seen in the story of Esther. If you have never read the story of Esther in the book of Esther, make time to do so. This wonderful story illustrates how God fulfills His purpose in the lives of those who follow Him, how He is with us through adversity, how He delivers us from evil, and how He shows us favor. Every time I read that story, I learn something new, and the story never gets old!

The following portion of this story helps make the point about how God *remembers* our offerings, and during our time of trouble, helps us because of it.

"That night the king could not sleep. So one was commanded to bring the book of the records of the chronicles; and they were read before the king. 2 And it was found written that Mordecai had told of Bigthana and Teresh, two of the king's eunuchs, the doorkeepers who had sought to do harm to King Ahasuerus. 3 Then the king said, "What honor or dignity has been bestowed on Mordecai for this?" and the king's servants who attended him said, "Nothing has been done for him." 4 So the king said, "Who is in the court?" Now Haman had just entered

the outer court of the king's palace to suggest that the king hang Mordecai on the gallows that he had prepared for him. 5 The king's servants said to him, "Haman is there, standing the court." And the king said, "Let him come in." 6 So Haman came in, and the king asked him, "What shall be done for the man who the king delights to honor?" 7 Now Haman thought in his heart, "Whom would the king delight to honor more than me?" and Haman answered the king, "For the man whom the king delights to honor, 8 let a royal robe be brought which the king has worn, and a horse on which the king has ridden, which has a royal crest placed on its head. 9 Then let this robe and horse be delivered to the hand of the one of the king's most noble princes, that he may array the man whom the king delights to honor. Then parade him on horseback through the city square, and proclaim before him: 'Thus shall it be done to the man who the king delights to honor!'" 10 Then the king said to Haman, "Hurry, take the robe and the horse, as you have suggested, and do so for Mordecai the Jew who sits within the king's gate! Leave nothing undone of all that you have spoken."
(Esther 6:1-10)

Mordecai was the older cousin and guardian of Esther, who became the queen of King Ahasuerus with Mordecai's help. Despite the fact that his cousin was the queen, Mordecai found himself in trouble with Haman because he refused to bow down at his presence. This perceived lack of respect outraged Haman and he vowed to hang Mordecai for what he considered blatant dishonor.

But it was during this time of Mordecai's trouble that the Lord caused the king to *remember*—through **"the book of**

the records"—the good that Mordecai had done. In the king remembering Mordecai's past good, the king rewarded him during his time of trouble.

The king *remembering* the past good of Mordecai was inspired by God's own nature and tendency to do the same. We also see this nature and tendency of God in the life of Hezekiah when he was troubled by sickness.

"Then Hezekiah turned his face toward the wall, and prayed to the Lord, and said, 'Remember now [in my time of trouble], O Lord, I pray, how I have walked before You in truth and with a loyal heart, and have done what is good in Your sight.' And Hezekiah wept bitterly. And the word of the Lord came to Isaiah, saying, 'Go and tell Hezekiah, "Thus says the Lord...I have heard your prayer, I have seen your tears; surely I will add to your days fifteen years."'
Isaiah 38:1-5

What we see in God *remembering* Hezekiah's past good and rewarding him during his time of trouble is exactly what we see King Ahasuerus doing for Mordecai in his time of trouble. This remembering of Ahasuerus, and his rewarding of Mordecai is not a surprise because Proverbs 21:1 says, **"The king's heart is in the hand of the Lord...the Lord turns it wherever He wishes."** God turned the heart of King Ahasuerus so that it was in alignment with His own character, and God caused him to remember Mordecai's past good during his present time of trouble.

So when Psalm 20:3 talks about the Lord *remembering* our offerings, the verse is saying that God will reward our past giving during our time of trouble. And the story of the widow in 1 Kings 17 proves He will also reward our right now—*in the time of trouble*—giving.

I understand that because we live in a *right now* time of technology, we expect not only a rapid return on our taxes, but also on our tithes and offerings. But it is important to know that some of our Spirit-inspired seed offerings are not intended to bring forth fruit in the season of sowing, but in a later season of need, or trouble.

Psalm 1:3 talks about how "planted" things **"bring forth fruit in its season...."** *"Its"* indicates that some sown things have specific seasons wherein they are purposed to bring forth fruit. Such is the case with some of the offerings we have sown in times past. We don't always see immediate results with our giving for at least two reasons:

1) Some of the things our giving does is inward and invisible to the eye.

2) Because our giving is purposed to bring forth fruit in a later season when the need is greater.

It is not uncommon for God to call us to give in the present with our future in mind. After all, farmers don't sow seeds in the present for fruit in the present; they sow seeds in the present for fruit in the future.

In addition to the Lord remembering our past offerings, He will also accept and honor our present offerings—especially our sacrificial offerings. This is good because you may have not been a giver, or a faithful giver in the past; therefore you may be thinking God has nothing from you to "remember." But the Lord is faithful in His grace and mercy in that, just as He *remembers* the good of the past, He also *forgets* the *not-so-good* of the past. He gives us new mercies and new opportunities to start afresh every day.

While you are in church, begin to trust God in the area of giving; He will move upon your tithes and your offerings, and He will help you in your time of trouble!

It is when things are tough that we prove our trust.

Another important reason to attend church during troublesome times is because God's house is where we hear God's voice of encouragement and instruction. While it is absolutely true that God can speak to us anywhere and at anytime, it is also true that there are some things that God will speak to us in *His* house that we won't hear from Him in *our* house.

"...the tabernacle of meeting...where I will meet you to speak to you. And there I will meet with the children of Israel, and the tabernacle shall be sanctified by My glory."
Exodus 29:42a, 43

In these verses the Lord tells Moses that He will **"meet"** and **"speak"** to him in "the tabernacle of meeting." This obviously meant that there were some things the Lord wanted to communicate to Moses while he was in God's house that the Lord would *not* speak to Moses outside of Moses' being in His house. Therefore, when God goes on to say, **"And there** [in His house] **I will meet with the children of Israel,"** it also means that there were some things the Lord was planning to speak to the Israelites inside of the tabernacle that He would not speak to them outside of the tabernacle.

This Scripture would most certainly apply to the message God has given the minister to share with the congregation, but also to a message God may want to speak directly into your heart. As it pertains to the message from the minister, I realize we live in a time when we can get the message on CD, DVD, MP3, ABC, LMNOP, or the Internet; but there is nothing like receiving the Word of God in an anointed atmosphere that has been bathed in prayer and praise!

Praise and worship in the house of God places us in a special presence of God wherein our heart is tilled by the Spirit of God. Once our heart has been prepared by God, it is ready to receive the good seed of His Word and bring forth the good fruit God desires! Don't make the mistake of assuming that hearing the message secondhand is just as good as hearing it in the sanctuary because it is not. It's like choosing to go to a Gospel concert live, or simply having someone bring you a recorded version of that concert.

There is nothing like the words we receive from God when we are assembled together with His saints. In fact, whether it was through the gift of prophecy, (which, along with the other gifts of the Spirit, operate pretty much exclusively when saints are assembled), or the Lord speaking directly to me—every destiny-revealing, destiny-defining, and destiny-directing word I have ever received from God came when I was in His house.

There are some things God will speak to us in His house that we will not hear from Him in our house.

Over the years I have both heard and overheard people who were experiencing trouble of some sort say, "I need to get back into church!" They said this because they recognize that getting off track with church can lead to getting *on track* with trouble, the prolonging of trouble, or our inability to live in peace during trouble. They make this statement also because they realize that when we are in trouble, there is help of all sorts for us in church. David understood this truth about church and trouble. (Actually, I think David understood *everything* about trouble and *anything*! David knew about trouble and church, trouble and bears, lions and giants, trouble and enemies, trouble and family, trouble and God's law, trouble and outlaws, and, trouble and in-laws!) These words from

Psalm 20 communicate to us David's understanding about trouble and the house of God:

"May the Lord answer you in the day of trouble;
may the name of the God of Jacob defend you;
may He send you help from the sanctuary,
and strengthen you out of Zion."
Psalm 20:1, 2

Here we find another passage of Scripture that links help in troublesome times with the place of worship. This verse makes it plain that there is help for us in the house of God "**in the day of trouble**" because if the Lord can send us **"help *from* the sanctuary",** it means that there is help *in* the sanctuary to begin with. We can benefit from this help when we visit the sanctuary on a regular basis and participate in what takes place there.

"When I thought how to understand this,
It was too painful for me—
until I went into the sanctuary of God;
Then I understood their end."
Psalm 73:16, 17

In the earlier verses of Psalm 73, we are taught that David was in a time of trouble and he was struggling with why *he*—a person who loved and worshiped God—was in trouble while the wicked seemingly didn't suffer at all. Aside from whatever else was troubling David, he was wrestling in his heart with what he felt was an injustice. He was experiencing what he felt ungodly people should experience while they were experiencing the blessings of life he felt belonged to him.

I understand how David felt, and you may too. But what we must also understand is that the feeling that God is dealing with us unjustly presents a problem of its own. Aside from the difficulties of life with which we are dealing, the idea that the God we are faithfully serving isn't dealing with us fairly is not only a hard pill to swallow, it's one that troubles our heart.

This is because deep within the recesses of our heart, we know we don't have anyone like God on whom we can count. And the thought that *He* is wronging us makes it hard for us to continue to trust and expect good from Him. I imagine that this erroneous idea caused an internal struggle for David as well. That is, **"...until [he] went into the sanctuary of God."**

It was in the sanctuary of God where David assembled himself with other people who were praying and praising God—and where the Spirit inspired Word of God was going forth—that David received an understanding that freed his heart from what was further troubling him. The freedom that was keyed by the understanding he received in the house of God allowed him to get his heart back on track with trusting God.

After gaining understanding from the Word he received in the sanctuary, listen to what David said of the condition of his heart before and after receiving that understanding:

(Before he went to the sanctuary)
"...my heart was grieved, and I was vexed in my mind. I was so foolish and ignorant; I was like a beast before You."
Psalm 73:21, 22

(After receiving understanding in the sanctuary)
"...I am continually with You; You hold me by my right hand. You will guide me with Your counsel, and afterward receive Me to glory. Whom have I in heaven but You? And there is none upon earth that I desire besides You. My flesh and My heart fail; but God is the strength of my heart and my portion forever."
Psalm 73:23-26

This passage is powerful! Notice that before David went to the house of the Lord, his heart and mind was troubled because of something he did not understand. But in going to God's house, there awaited a Word from the Lord that brought him understanding and restored his confidence in the fact that God was still with him, favored him, and loved him—despite the fact that he was being troubled by life.

But think about the flip side of the coin, if David had not gone to the sanctuary of God, he would not have received the revelation that gave him the understanding that freed his heart from being held hostage by unhealthy thoughts. It wasn't what David heard from God in *his* house, it was what David heard from God's house that gave him the helpful understanding that delivered him from the unhealthy thoughts that hindered his focus and his faith.

It can be difficult, but it is extremely important to attend church during our days of challenge. It blesses and benefits us to participate in the praise and worship and to listen attentively to the Word that's being shared. The Lord knows what we need to hear to help us and get us back on track to overcoming our time of trouble! And a large part of what we need, we find in the house of the Lord.

What we hear in the house of God helps to get our heart back on track with trusting God.

Consistently attending church when life is difficult is important not only because it encourages and strengthens us—enabling us to endure our trouble—but also because it is a factor in our fruitfulness and the blessings of our future.

"Those who are planted in the house of the Lord shall flourish in the courts of our God."
Psalm 92:13

To be *planted* means "to be grounded and rooted in God's house." It means to be *fixed* in our determination to go to church—even when things are tough and we don't feel like it.

Being *planted* is important because only things that are "planted" begin to take root. Not only do roots strengthen and stabilize what has been planted, they also cause what has been planted to bring forth fruit. Where there is no commitment to church attendance, there is no planting. And when there is no planting, no rooting can take place. And where there is no root, there can be no fruit—nor any of the benefits that help us overcome our adversity.

The word "*courts*" used in this verse speaks not only of the place that is immediately outside of the sanctuary (house of God); it speaks also of "one's town or dwelling place." In essence this verse is also saying that when we are planted by regular attendance in *God's house*—even in a time of trouble—things will go better for us in *our house*.

With this thought in mind, it is important to know that things can *go* better before they *get* better. Even before our trouble comes to an end, our ability to endure and deal with trouble and live in peace until it passes can *get* better. The next best thing to trouble's passing is living in peace while trouble is present. The peace that comes from attending God's house helps us to better cope with trouble when we're in our house.

I have seen husbands and wives go through trouble and abandon going to God's house; not long thereafter things went from bad to worse in their house. Unfortunately, such relationships often end in divorce. But I have also seen trouble visit homes where husbands and wives continued to attend church; participate in praise, worship and giving; live by the word they receive at church; and their home remain intact through their trouble. Their marriage and lives were blessed after they had weathered the storm.

Whether we are single or married, regular church attendance promises to be a helpful blessing *now*—during our time of trouble and well into the future. This is what this passage goes on to teach us.

"They shall still bear fruit in old age;
they shall be fresh and flourishing,
to declare that the Lord is upright;
He is my Rock, and there is no
unrighteousness in Him."
Psalm 92:14, 15

The reference in verse 14 to *"old age"* speaks of the future. The psalmist is foretelling of the time in life long after trouble has subsided. He is saying that those of us who overcome trouble with the aid of being **"planted in the house of the Lord"** shall **"still bear fruit in old age."** We cannot **"still bear fruit in old age"** unless we first bear fruit in our younger, earlier times of life. This verse teaches us that regular church attendance will help us and bless us both now and later in life.

In conclusion, consider these last two verses as further evidence of the fact that there are blessings and benefits to visiting our God and King in His house and praising Him in His palace.

"Blessed is the man You choose, and cause
to approach You, that he may dwell
in Your courts. We shall be satisfied
with the goodness of Your house,
of Your holy temple."
(Psalm 65:4)

"How precious is Your lovingkindness, O God!
Therefore the children of men put their trust
under the shadow of Your wings. They are abundantly
satisfied with the fullness of your house, and You give
them drink from the rivers of Your pleasures.
(Psalm 36:7, 8)

It pleases God when we worship Him in His house. And out of His pleasure, He pleases us by helping and blessing us! So go to church! Our King is awaiting your arrival!

Chapter 11
The Importance of Patience in the Time of Trouble

"...Rejoicing in hope,
patient in tribulation..."
Romans 12:12

The word "*hope*" means "to have confident expectation." When there is *hope,* there is also the ability to *rejoice* because we are *confident* that what we are expecting we will also experience. The fact that we are in expectation indicates that we do not yet have what we are expecting because we don't hope for what we already have.

During the time of tribulation we are encouraged to have this hope, or this *confident expectation* of experiencing better times. It is also during our time of expectancy that we are to be *"...patient in tribulation."*

The Word of God never encourages us to do anything we are not capable of doing. Therefore, when this verse says for us to be *"...patient in trouble,"* it does so with the understanding that doing so is not beyond us, and that doing so is important and beneficial to us.

In chapter four of this book, we looked at James 1:3 and how God allows trouble because it produces the Christ-like characteristic of patience is us as Christians. In Romans chapter five the apostle Paul echoes this truth first introduced by James.

"And not only so, but we glory in tribulations also; knowing that tribulation works [produces] patience."
Romans 5:3

I remarked previously that God uses our trouble as a tool to work, build or produce attributes in us that cannot be accomplished by any other tool. Just as there are certain tools that are designed to accomplish certain tasks, (i.e., hammers drive nails and wrenches tighten and loosen nuts and bolts) nothing can build patience like the tool of trouble.

The very first accomplishment of the patience that has been created in us by trouble is the ability to weather the trouble that is creating the patience. In fact, the sign that the tool of trouble has completed its task of building or producing patience in us is our ability to be patient for the remaining time of our trouble. When we are impatient in trouble, it is because trouble has not completed its assignment of creating patience in us. So, the work continues as the trouble lives on.

In order for God to use us according to His plans, He first has to create patience in us because patience will be needed for where He wants to take us, how He wants to use us, and how He wants to bless us.

If you can recall, chapter four of this book talks about how patience was a prelude to blessings and fulfilled promises for many people in the Bible. And such is the case with you and me as post-Bible characters. Blessings, fulfilled promises, and purpose will follow patience. This is one of the reasons why patience in the time of trouble is important.

I will share six definitions of *patience* for the sake of communicating the importance of patience:

1) – "To be steadfast despite opposition, difficulty or adversity" **(1 Corinthians 15:58)**
2) – "To endure under strain" **(2 Timothy 2:3)**
3) – "To continue doing right even under duress" **(Galatians 6:10)**
4) – "To exercise staying strength and commitment until change comes" **(Hebrews 10:36)**
5) – "To bear trials without complaining" **(Philippians 2:14; 1 Corinthians 10:10)**
6) – "To wait" **(Psalm 27:14)**

Before I proceed and address the patience of waiting on God, let me focus on the problem with *impatience*. Impatience compounds our outward troubles by causing trouble on the inside of us.

In fact, impatience is a trouble all by itself—a trouble that causes and contributes to the frustration we are already experiencing because impatience is the enemy of peace. In the battle between the two, too much, or a prolonged impatience will conquer our peace, which again is assigned to "guard our hearts and mind through Christ Jesus."

When the *guard* of peace has been conquered by impatience, peace is also removed from its post of purpose in the process. When peace has been overcome, impatience replaces it with worry, a false guard that puts out the good and holds open the door to our heart for stress, fear and doubt to enter in. This is why *impatience* is a problem. And this is also why *patiently waiting* on the Lord is important.

When we *wait* on someone or something, it means that we are anticipating the fulfillment of something. *Waiting* means that we have an expectation, (justifiable or not) of something coming to pass or being accomplished.

The waiting season can be a challenging season simply because we are without that for which we are waiting. The greater, and more important the thing for which we are *waiting* is, the tougher and more taxing the *waiting season* can be.

I thank God, Jesse and his wife for the life of David because it is from David's life that we learn a great deal about trouble. Jesus is the King of kings, but as I have already mentioned, David may be the king of trouble.

Many of David's actions *in* trouble, and reactions *to* trouble have already been referenced and analyzed. We know that David prayed, praised, and cried—and that he was even perplexed by his times of trouble. But now, let's focus on the *patience* David displayed during his times of challenge.

"I waited patiently for the Lord;
and He inclined to me, and heard
my cry. He also brought me up
out of a horrible pit,
out of the miry clay, and set
my feet upon a rock, and
established my goings."
Psalm 40:1, 2

Remember, the fact that David was in a *"horrible pit"* and *"miry clay"* means he was in trouble. Before I proceed about patience, let me speak on the "pit" and "clay" about which David spoke.

Although he travelled through some places and treaded upon terrains where *pits* and *clay* would not have been uncommon, I personally do not believe David was speaking of a literal pit or clay. The *pit* and the *clay* he references are symbolic of situations from which we are powerless to remove, or free ourselves. They can also represent times in our life where we are either making no progress, or slow progress.

In the Bible, pits have three common purposes:

1) Pits were hiding places from enemies.

2) They were used as wells to house rainwater.

3) They were traps for animals and/or enemies, and if one was very fortunate, both were trapped at the same time!

When the hateful brothers of Joseph decided against killing him, electing instead to "**cast him into some pit**," they did so because they knew the pit was a place he could not free himself.

"Then the Midianite traders passed by; so the brothers pulled Joseph up and lifted him out of the pit, and sold him to the Ishmaelites for twenty shekels of silver. And they took Joseph to Egypt."
Genesis 37:28

Allow me to make two points: First, the fact that his brothers "*pulled him up and lifted him out of the pit*" says that Joseph was unable to extricate himself from the pit. For different reasons, sometimes as Christians we go through seasons wherein it doesn't matter what we do, we just cannot seem to get out of the rut or pit until that season has run its course and accomplished its purpose. The "miry clay" presents a similar situation, or season in that the Christian is *stuck* and seemingly can make no progress toward promise, purpose or personal goals!

The fact that Joseph was in the pit says that even upright, God-fearing children of God are not exempt from the pits or the pitfalls of life. (The life of Job serves as further evidence of this fact.) But the fact that Joseph was alone in the pit says that the troublesome, horrible pit and the miry clay season is a season where we may not have the help or support of people who were once close to us.

Don't expect everyone to understand the time of the *horrible pit* or the *miry* clay. Some people have no understanding of such a season because it may not have been appointed for them. And God has a way of separating us from certain people during this time, and not allowing others to be helpful or supportive of us—even questioning the God-ordained path (that sometimes leads to pits) we have committed to follow.

The important thing is for us to avoid the trap of being upset with such people and harboring animosity toward them. Animosity is an anchor that, like the miry clay, keeps us from making progress. The difference is that the miry clay is a tool of God while animosity is a weight and weapon of the devil, "*which so easily ensnares and entangles us*" and keeps us from going forth.

The second point is that although the text says his brothers took Joseph out of the pit, it was God Who used them to do so. Because God is, "Lord of all," even our enemies are under His influence, and He uses them to accomplish His plans and purpose for our trouble.

As bad as the pit was, it was an acceptable alternative to the brothers' original plan of death. Sometimes we consider our situation and wonder why God didn't protect us from it. The reality is that God protected us from something far worse than what we're experiencing! But it's hard to see that reality without knowing that there was something worse or what that "worse" was.

If I were a betting man I would place my money on the notion that Joseph wondered why the Lord allowed him to end up in that pit. But if he had known about Plan A, Joseph would have praised God *for* the pit, while he was *in* the pit.

As bad as your situation is, or seems to be, the enemy had something worse in mind, but the Lord didn't allow it. The Lord only allows what He is planning on using to create patience, and to fulfill purpose. If it doesn't "*…work together for our good…*" God doesn't allow it. If it does—He does.

God used that pit as a holding place in the life of Joseph. But when it was time for his *pit stop* (pun intended) to end, God used Joseph's enemies to raise him up from the pit and place on the path to preparation in Potiphar's house and to fulfilled purpose in the kingdom of Pharaoh.

Pits are the pits! However, they are extremely important because while one is in the pit, patience is brought into being—patience that is a necessity to function effectively in purpose.

Before continuing, I want to share a very important point about pits that is found at the end of Genesis 37:24. There is a portion of this passage that can easily be read over without much thought being given to it, but there are six words that reveal something of value to us about *God-purposed pits.*

"Then they took him and cast him into a pit, and the pit was empty, there was no water in it." Genesis 37:24

As I have already mentioned, pits were typically dug for three purposes. The pit in which Joseph found himself was not a trap for animals, or for enemies. Neither was the trap designed to be a hiding place because it was obviously located in the open where his brothers were able to find it and not in an inconspicuous, off-road location. The pit in which Joseph found himself had been created to be a well.

Although wells are not as common nowadays, we must understand that because they house water, they typically have a depth that may nearly double the height of the average man. "No water in the pit" means that it would have been impossible for Joseph to drown, signifying that God-purposed pits do not have the power to overwhelm us; they can only temporarily detain us until God is ready to lift us out.

As bad, dark and deep as your pit may be, *there is no water in it,* it is therefore incapable of overcoming you. You may feel overburdened or even overwhelmed, but if you continue to trust God and be patient, you will not be overcome because God is with you to deliver you from *whatever* you're going through!

God is our refuge and strength, a very present help in...the pit!

The Bible teaches that plans are important. Often, if not always, when there is an absence of success, it is because there is the absence of a plan or a well-conceived plan. However, sometimes in order to have the success for which we long and that God desires, more than a plan is needed; we need patience.

In fact, in the season when God is *creating* patience, our plans don't work. This is why **Proverbs 19:21** says, **"Man has many plans in his mind, but it is the Lord's purpose for him that will stand."** The patience-producing purpose of God trumps any plans we may have that do not correspond with His present plan.

When God is working His plan to create patience in us our plans have to bow out, or be *back-seated* in respect of His divine plan. Our plan may be a *good plan,* but it may also be an *untimely plan*—a plan that is not on one seasonal accord with His plan to create patience in us.

However, sometimes we'll notice that after the plan of God to create patience in us (or teach us something of significance) has prevailed, our plans—the same *good plans*—will also prevail even after failing initially. The patience created by God's plan makes us more effective at working our plan!

If a plan is going to succeed, patience has to be a part of that plan.

I don't believe Joseph or David would have been as anointed and effective in their purpose had they not spent time in *the pit.* Although David's pit was not a literal one, there he demonstrated, and maybe even learned patience. When we're in a "horrible pit" or "miry clay" and cannot get out or go forward, we only have two choices: give up and forfeit all of the good that is to come (and you've come too far and fought too hard to forfeit now), or to be patient. According to Psalm 40, David chose the latter:

**"I waited patiently for the Lord;
and He inclined to me, and heard
my cry. He also brought me up
out of a horrible pit,
out of the miry clay, and set
my feet upon a rock, and
established my goings.
Psalm 40:1, 2**

David **"...waited patiently for the Lord"** because, not only could he not free *himself* from that particular situation, no one else could either. Maybe this is why **Psalm 146:3** says, ***"Do not put your trust in princes, nor in a son of man, in whom there is no help."*** How important it is that we do not misplace our trust! We misplace our trust when we expect too much from man.

Whether or not we have misplaced our trust is revealed in how we respond or react to people who let us down after expecting them to come through. When we react angrily and/or become bitter, it is simply because we have placed our trust in man; we are disappointed in their letting us down.

However, when it bothers us but doesn't bend us out of Christ-like character, it is because our trust is in the Lord and not them. If God does not use or continue to use them to help us, it's perfectly fine; He has someone else. Not only do the cattle on the thousand hills belong to Him, God also has many rams in many bushes!

In 1 Kings 17 when there was a drought in the days of Elijah, the Lord told him to go to the Brook Cherith and there God would command a raven to bring him food. Elijah did so, and just as God commanded, the raven brought Elijah food. But when the raven stopped bringing him food, Elijah didn't get angry at the raven and call the bird names. He didn't say to the raven, *"You bat! Why did you stop bringing me food?"*

Elijah did not react in this way because his trust wasn't in the raven; his trust was in the Lord of the raven—the One Who commanded the raven to feed him in the first place. He knew that just as the Lord had commanded the raven to feed him, He had someone else lined up to pick up where that ol' bat—I mean where the raven left off. And He did. God had spoken to a widow in the next town, and God worked through her to feed him.

Sometimes people can't help us because they literally cannot; they actually do not have what we need. There are also times when people do not help simply because they are selfish and unconcerned. However, there are other times and other people who cannot help us because the Lord doesn't allow them to help us. That's because it's not time to allow them to help or often simply because He wants our trust, hope and dependence to be on Him. That way, when He comes through (and He always does), He receives all of the glory. God is justifiably glory hungry. For that reason He says, **"…My glory will I not give to another…." (Isaiah 42:8)**

The point is that, as Christians we cannot place our trust in people because people are flawed. Because we are human, we are often undependable, unpredictable and prone to disappoint each other. Our trust and our *wait* must be on the Lord because He is the One Who sees and supplies all of our needs.

"When my father and my mother
forsake me, then the Lord
will take of me."
Psalm 27:10

"Truly my soul silently waits for God;
from Him comes my salvation."
Psalm 62:1

"My soul, wait silently for God alone,
for my expectation is from Him."
Psalm 62:5

In the time of trouble, David chose to *wait patiently for the Lord.* You may be thinking that because he couldn't get out, or go forward he didn't have a choice aside from waiting. You would be correct. David had no other choice *but* to wait. However, he did have a choice of whether or not to wait *patiently*. In waiting, patience is always an option—never an automatic occurrence.

The term *waited patiently* almost sounds like an overstatement because there is a tendency to think that *waiting is* being patient. But that is not necessarily true; it's possible to *impatiently* wait on the Lord. We're impatient while we are waiting on Him because we have no power to bring about the change we desire.

Remember, one of the indications of *impatiently* waiting on the Lord, (and one we must guard ourselves against) is complaining. Complaining not only displeases God but it also contributes to our own discouragement.

The psalmist Asaph wrote:

"In the day of my trouble I sought the Lord; my hand was stretched out in the night without ceasing; my soul refused to be comforted. I remembered God, and was troubled; I complained, and my spirit was overwhelmed."
Psalm 77:2, 3

David was not the only psalmist who experienced a time of trouble. Asaph acknowledges experiencing a trouble that was so difficult that it prevented him from sleeping. He also prayed and sought answers as to why he was going through what he was going through. And when he found no comfort he eventually began to complain. But notice the effect his complaining had on him. His complaining overwhelmed his spirit, burdened him and contributed to his disappointment. Though Asaph was already troubled, couldn't sleep, or be comforted, he wasn't "overwhelmed." The order in which this verse is constructed reveals that he wasn't overwhelmed until *after* his complaining—proving that complaining compounds our trouble—teaching us that it does more to harm than to help.

In fact, the Hebrew word for *overwhelmed* also means "to faint." When we complain, or when we are always talking about what's wrong, and what's not going right, our own words can overwhelm us, can cause us to worry, and can cause us to "faint" spiritually. Then we give up on trusting and waiting on God. Furthermore, complaining digs an emotional pit that traps us and gets deeper and deeper the more we complain. That emotional pit can become so deep that it can forever keep us from going forward and living in the Promised Land.

On the other hand, praise—specifically the praise of thanksgiving—is important because thanksgiving is the opposite of complaining and will therefore have the opposite effect on us. Complaining causes us to "faint" or lose strength and be stagnant, while the praise of thanksgiving increases our spiritual stamina, helps us to look forward with hope, and assists us in hanging in there until our change comes!

No complaining please!
Complaining digs and deepens the pit of despair, deprives us of peace, and keeps us from moving forward.

Two other examples of being in seasons where we are incapable of causing change can be seen in Joseph's time in prison as well as during Job's time of heartache, sickness and despair.

I do not know if Joseph had developed any plans while he was in prison, but I do know that his plans could not have worked *while* he was in prison. Therefore, he was in a season of "no progress"—a season he was powerless to change on his own. That natural reality speaks of a spiritual truth for many who are in a season of trouble. Though we may not be physically incarcerated, we are not yet free to go forth.

Such was the case with Job. He was imprisoned by his situation and powerless to progress until the Lord brought about his change—a change he confidently expected would take place when he said, **"All the days of my appointed time I will wait till my change comes." (Job 14:14)**

Not only did Job *know* a change in his circumstances was forthcoming, the term, **"appointed time"** says that Job was *doing time*, incarcerated by his circumstances, and incapable of bringing about that change on his own.

This is a tough spot in which to be for a number of reasons, including the fact that there is an unquenchable yearning to do more and to be more. It is not a good feeling to know that you are called to do more, but your circumstances prevent you from doing what you are called to do. Such was the case with

Joseph being imprisoned. He knew he was called to do more and he craved doing more, but he was caged and incapable of doing more.

Although neither Joseph nor Job could free themselves from their "appointed time" of imprisonment, their imprisonment was *only* for an "appointed time." The Lord of time had already determined when they would be freed, and the plan of their release was already in place.

After an unspecified amount of time, Job's freedom came in when **"...the Lord restored Job's losses when he prayed for his friends....the Lord gave Job twice as much as he had before." (Job 42:10)**

However, the freedom of Joseph arrived years after he had *patiently waited* while in prison. In prison was where he was found by Pharaoh after the ruler had received a word from his chief butler about having met a fellow who could interpret the ruler's dreams. So Pharaoh sent and had Joseph freed from prison, and Joseph would soon begin to live in the dreams God had shown him, and the life for which his times of trouble had prepared him.

As odd as it may sound, Joseph's time of imprisonment—the time when he was paralyzed from progressing—turned out to be one of the most important times of his life. Not only was his spiritual ability to interpret dreams birthed and sharpened, but when the time came for that ability to bring him before Pharaoh, the prison made certain that Joseph would be found.

Sometimes we experience still or stagnated seasons of no progress because it keeps us in the appointed place where the Lord would have us to be found. Impatience can remove us from this appointed place and cause us not to be present when deliverance comes calling, looking to unlock us.

Obviously, God had the power to free Joseph from prison anytime He wanted, but the Lord allowed him to remain there. God knew about His own plans to give Pharaoh the dreams he would need interpreted, and God alone knew the ability He had given Joseph to interpret those dreams.

It was from the season and place of *no progress* that both Joseph and Job were propelled into the fulfillment of purpose and promise. You may be in such a place right now. But from that place—no matter how dark, difficult or lonely it may be—seek God through prayer and praise, and wait on Him with patience. He will not forever leave you where you are. God is going to come through for you and deliver you into the good He has predestined for you!

"The Lord is good to them that wait for Him, to the soul that seeks Him."
Lamentations 3:25

Chapter 12
Equipped to Endure

"You therefore must endure hardship as a good soldier of Jesus Christ."
2 Timothy 2:3

The second letter from the apostle Paul written to Timothy was written primarily to help his son in the faith during his time of hardship—hardship Paul knew Timothy's office as a pastor did not exempt him from.

In John 16:33, when Jesus says, **"...you shall have tribulation,..."** He no doubt was speaking of all Christians, but He was speaking directly *to* 11 of the 12 apostles He had chosen. This verse thereby reveals that no Christian—no matter his office or area of service—would be immune from troublesome times.

Paul's approach to helping young Pastor Timothy was one of prayer, encouragement, loving instructions, and admonition—all of which were offered from a stance of understanding gathered by Paul from the trouble he himself had experienced and was enduring at the penning of this epistle.

It is important to know and remember that the lessons we learn and the comfort we receive during our season of suffering are not only for us during *that* time—, they are also purposed to help others during their times of struggle. In fact, a part of the reason why God permits us to go through trouble is so we can identify and sympathize with others in their troublesome times. God wants us to offer them encouragement from the knowledge and understanding gained through our own experience with difficulty.

Remember Paul's words to the church at Corinth:

> **"Blessed be the God and Father of our Lord Jesus Christ, the Father of mercies and God of all comfort, Who comforts us in all our tribulation <u>that we may be able to comfort those who are in any trouble</u> with the comfort we ourselves are comforted by God."**
> **2 Corinthians 1:3, 4**

Directly and through others, God helps us so that we can be a help to others as He was to us. And this is exactly what we find Paul doing with Timothy, comforting him with what he himself had received from God, and helping him with what had learned about hardship.

Paul's letter gives insight into just how difficult Timothy's struggle was when he wrote, "**I remember you in my prayers night and day...being mindful of your tears...**" **(2 Timothy 1:3, 4)**. Anytime anything can bring anyone to tears, it means that thing is difficult. Anytime anything can bring a Spirit-filled, holy and upright living pastor to tears, it means that thing is *extremely* difficult.

The first line of help Paul provides is prayer. It is important to be connected with a pastor and other trusted people of God and to be open with them about your challenges so that they can be in prayer for you. Although it is somewhat of a lost relationship, I also think it is important for pastors—particularly young pastors—to be connected to apostles, older pastors, mentors and even other pastors who can play a helpful role in their life as the apostle Paul did in the life of Timothy.

Too many pastors fall victim to trouble because they do not have the prayerful love and guidance of an apostle Paul-like figure in their life.

Secondly, we find Paul helping Timothy by *reminding* and encouraging him to **"stir up the gift of God which is in you through the laying on of my hands" (2 Timothy 1:6).** I do not believe Paul was talking about a spiritual gift, but the gift of the Holy Spirit **(Acts 2:38, 10:45).** I also believe the gift of the Holy Spirit is *stirred up* when He is permitted to pray and make intercession for us through the speaking of tongues.

You may be reading this book and are in opposition to the idea of praying in tongues (which is different from the spiritual gift of tongues) or praying in the Spirit as it is also known in the Bible. But when I consider the role of the Holy Spirit as spelled out in the Scriptures—a Comforter Who consoles us, Who helps us, and Who prays for things for which we don't know to pray, or we don't know how to pray for them, I don't want to limit or restrict Him from operating fully in His role, especially in my time of trouble!

In an earlier chapter I wrote about the importance, and the tremendous benefit of praising God during our season of challenge. In adding to that, it is also important to understand that the Holy Spirit plays a role in our praising God. In fact, in the very first occurrence of tongues in the second chapter of the book of Acts, the Holy Spirit is praising God through the believers who had just been filled with the Holy Spirit.

"And when this sound occurred, the multitude came together, and were confused, because everyone heard them speak in his own language. 7 Then they were all amazed and marveled, saying to one another, 'Look, are not all these who speak Galileans?

8 And how is it that we hear, each in our own language in which we were born?
9 Parthians and Medes and Elamites, those dwelling in Mesoptamia, Judea and Cappadocia, Pontus and Asia,
10 Phrygia and Pamphylia, Egypt and the parts of Libya adjoining Cyrene, visitors from Rome, both Jews and proselytes,
11 Cretans and Arabs—we hear them speaking in our own tongues, the wonderful works of God.' "
Acts 2:6-11

Anytime the **"wonderful works of God"** are being spoken of, the God of the wonderful works is being praised! Because we see this *praise* of God being expressed in tongues by the Holy Spirit through the disciples, we know that the Holy Spirit not only *prays* for us, He also offers *praise* for us in tongues—praise that helps us during our days of difficulty!

I do not know why anyone would be opposed to something that is *clearly* of God and is provided by Him to aid us in our relationship with Him, and in our walk through life! The Holy Spirit helps us *during* our time of trouble, and He can help get us *out of* our time of trouble as well. This explains why the *very first* word of instruction Paul gave Timothy in his time of trouble was to "...**stir up the gift of God"! (2 Timothy 1:6)**

The Holy Spirit not only *prays* for us, He offers *praise for us!*

Paul also encouraged Timothy by allowing him to know that his trouble was not uncommon, and that they *"shared in suffering."* There is nothing like words of encouragement and advice from people who have experienced the type, or the degree of trouble we are experiencing. While it is true the every believer "shall have tribulation," it is not true that every believer shares the same type, length or degree of difficulties.

God only allows people to go through the degree of difficulty they can handle. Not all Christians encounter the same type or the same amount of trouble during their walk with God. This doesn't make them any better or any worse than any other Christian—that is just the fact of the matter. But be careful not to expect too much understanding or support from people who haven't gone through too much trouble. Such people are not capable of relating to where you are; neither have they personally learned anything that can be helpful to your length or type of trouble.

Job may have had some of the worst friends in the history of the world! Yes, they came to visit Job during his time of trouble, but they didn't have anything positive or encouraging to say! Neither did they have any helpful advice from personal experience to offer. Instead, they spent their time trying to convince him to confess and repent from sin—sin of which he was not guilty and had nothing to do with his troublesome times.

Whereas sin can indeed contribute to our times of trouble, our times of trouble are not always the product of sin. We want to be careful not to blame a person's situation on sin when we are not certain that sin is the culprit. Time wasted incorrectly accusing people of sin could be time spent inspiring and encouraging them in their situation.

Job's friends, Eliphaz, Bildad and Zophar, *the three know-it-alls,* could not console or encourage Job because they could not see past their inaccurate assessment of his situation; neither could they relate to what he was experiencing. Some of the worst people to be around when you're going through *something* are those who have been through *nothing*. They have no sympathy, or *same situation comfort* from which to draw. As much as the presence of some friends can help us, we would sometimes prefer to be without the presence of others!

Job 42:10 says, **"And the Lord turned the captivity of Job, when he prayed for his friends...."** Now, the Bible doesn't specifically say what Job's prayer for his friends was, but I would have been praying for their relocation! With friends like that in the time of trouble, who needs "*the fiery darts of the wicked*"?!

The reality is that not all friends are for all seasons. The season of trouble separates fair-weather friends from true, come-what-may friends. Although some friends will change toward you in your time of trouble, the test, and the Christ-like thing to do is not to change toward them *because* of their change toward you.

Having to endure difficult times is not just about the adversity of the times themselves, it's also having to endure the change of people toward us and their distancing themselves from us during these days. Neither is this situation uncharted water. Job said, **"My relatives have failed, and my close friends have forgotten me" (Job 19:14).** No wonder Job had to settle for the company of *those* friends, his "*close friends*" were nowhere to be found!

There are a few reasons family and friends would give for failing and forsaking us. Although we don't think any of them are worth the weight of air, we must continue to treat them as if they have always been there and have been helpful to us. If not, the feelings of betrayal and abandonment will creep into our heart and cause problems that are counterproductive to our struggle to shake our trouble. This is why **Proverbs 4:23** says, **"Guard your heart with all diligence, for out of it comes the issues of life."**

Because of the twisted twins of betrayal and abandonment, we need God's peace to guard our heart and mind. The feelings of betrayal and abandonment give birth to resentment and unforgiveness. Resentment, unforgiveness, and every other offspring of ill feelings are traps—traps that create or compound the emotional challenges of our troublesome times and keep us from going forward toward freedom from our troublesome times.

"Thorns and snares are in the way of the perverse; he who guards his soul will be far from them."
Proverbs 22:5

If we do not protect our heart, we can prolong our residency in the city of trouble because our life will be anchored by animosity and the harboring of resentment.

Nursing ill feelings toward people who have failed, forgotten, or forsaken us is almost always a sign that we have misplaced our hope for help; placing it in people instead of in God. When our expectation of people is too great, we fall long and hard into the pits of despair and disappointment. We can also fall into the trap of ill feelings when people fail to meet, or continue to meet our expectations. There can only be a *great fall* after there is unfulfilled *great expectation. This* is one of the reasons the Word tells us, **"Do not put your trust in princes, nor in a son of men, in whom there is no help." (Psalm 146:3)**

I have learned that sometimes the temporary distancing of family and friends is the doing of God as He teaches us where *not* to place our trust, and corners our dependence on Him. In fact, the word *longsuffering, (*common in the writings of Paul, and synonymous with endurance) not only means "to suffer long," it often calls for us to suffer *alone.* As undesirable as suffering is, suffering alone when family and friends have forsaken and forgotten us is the worst! However, such times are extremely helpful to our relationship with the Lord, and valuable to our spiritual development. This is because the Lord does His *best* work on us when He has us *alone.* When most people make the decision to give their life to the Lord, they do it *alone*. Even if hundreds of people respond to the invitation to receive Jesus, the decision is made alone. The time that follows is almost always absent of many (sometimes all) family members, and old, unsaved friends.

This is a season of sanctification, as is the season of long-suffering. During these times the Lord may remove or not allow people to help us because sometimes the help of people can be a distraction from our dependence on God. A large part of our spiritual growth is in learning, and though the Lord uses people as vessels to help us, our hope and trust must rest exclusively in Him. Our understanding and arrival at this place will prevent us from being angry or harboring animosity toward others when they fail to meet our expectations.

If we don't protect our heart, we can prolong our residency in the city of trouble.

I am always amazed by the reaction of Jesus to Judas in the Garden of Gethsemane at the time of Jesus' arrest. While Peter probably wanted to kill Judas for betraying Jesus *(Malchus, the Roman soldier whose ear Peter cut off was just a casualty of closeness. I'm sure Peter preferred the ear…eyes, nose, throat, fingers and toes of Judas!),* Jesus kissed Judas *knowing* His disciple had betrayed Him. Jesus' kiss demonstrates to us how the condition of our heart should be toward those whom we *feel* have wronged us.

People disappoint us for only one reason: because they are people. People, like you and I, who are frail, flawed and prone to fail. We fail others, ourselves and even God sometimes. But in our aim and aspirations to be like God, we must be willing to forgive the mistreatment of others during our time of trouble—while we are yet in our time of trouble. *(Just as importantly, we must forgive ourselves for mistakes we have made that have contributed to our own trouble.)*

The heart of Jesus toward Judas as He kissed him was no different from His heart toward the other disciples who abandoned Him soon after His betrayal by Judas. His feeling of love toward them and Judas was not diminished by their betrayal or by their abandonment of Him in His time of trouble. Instead, Jesus treated them as if they had always only been helpful to Him. What a great lesson for us to learn and what a great example for us to live by!

We must forgive if we are to help ourselves during our time of trouble.

The apostle Paul was a mentor, a friend and a huge help to Timothy during his time of trouble. Paul encouraged Timothy with the encouragement he himself had received. Paul also shared with the young pastor what he had learned, and lovingly admonished "**you therefore must endure hardship as a good soldier**." The word *therefore* means "for this reason."

There are a number of reasons why we as Christians must *endure hardship*. While most of them apply to our personal development, purpose and promise possession, some of the reasons are about other people the Lord has placed in our life on whom we are to have a positive influence. This was the point behind Paul's persuasion for Timothy to hang in there.

"You therefore, my son, be strong in the grace that is in Christ Jesus. And the things that you have heard from me among many witnesses, commit these to faithful men who will be able to teach others also. You therefore must endure hardship as a good soldier of Jesus Christ."
2 Timothy 2:1-3

The apostle Paul pleaded with Timothy to "***endure hardship***" because others were depending on him to teach them what he had learned from Paul and elsewhere. Paul understood that if Timothy didn't hang in there and weather the storm of his troublesome times, generations of people could be without the Spirit-inspired teachings he had received.

It's the same with you and me. God has placed people in the path of our life who are counting on us to *endure hardship* and fulfill our purpose of being a blessing in their lives. It may be your spouse, your children, your grandchildren, other family members, church members, co-workers, neighbors or other men and women of God to whom your enduring power will help, encourage and be a blessing. Whoever it is, there are other people (whom you may or may not yet know) who are counting on you to hang in there!

"Therefore you <u>must</u> endure hardship," the well-being of others are depending on it!

In a previous chapter I stated that God never calls for, requires or expects anything of us that we're not capable of performing. We are always able to answer the bell because the Lord has already deposited *in us* that which He is seeking to withdraw *from us*.

The admonition of Paul for Timothy to "**...endure hardship as a good soldier**" is a Spirit-inspired admonition for us as Christians to do the same. Although admittedly, it is tough sometimes, we can indeed "**...endure hardship as a good soldier of Jesus Christ"** because God has already equipped us to do so.

Patience v. Endurance

Although the two are related, somewhat synonymous and sometimes interchangeable, it is important to understand that there is indeed a difference between the words *patience* and *endurance.* I consider endurance "the big brother of patience." Though both are *weapons of our warfare*, patience is the tank while endurance is the battleship. Both are athletes in the spiritual sport of *waiting*—patience is the middleweight, while endurance is the super heavyweight. Endurance is patience on steroids—a *lot* of steroids! Endurance is what enables us to hang in there, "**fight the good fight of faith,**" go the distance, and get the victory after patience got tired and couldn't answer the bell for the final round.

Patience is waiting for something to come to pass while everything else is fine. Endurance, on the other hand, is waiting for something to come to pass while *everything* else is extremely difficult, and little, if anything, *is fine*!

Comically, I have used the example of growing up in Chicago and waiting for the bus in the summertime versus the wintertime. In the summer when the weather is nice, waiting on the bus is simply about having patience. It's no big deal because it's warm, you're texting, talking or listening to music on your cell phone and looking at the pigeons pecking and plucking the feathers off each other while fighting for a piece of popcorn on the ground. Because everything is fine with the weather, all you need is *patience* in waiting for the bus.

But if you're waiting on the bus in the wintertime when it's freezing cold and your heaviest coat feels like it decided to stay home; your fingers, toes and nose feel like they are going to break off; your chattering teeth sound like an S.O.S. Morse code message; the wind chill factor has the flu; and even the snowflakes are complaining about the temperature—that's not just patience; *that's endurance!*

It may sound strange but often in order to arrive at desired places, we must first endure undesired places and undesirable circumstances. Despite the fact that it was freezing cold and I didn't want to, I *had to* endure the weather and wait on the bus if I was going to arrive at the place it promised take me—a place I desired to be. And waiting under those conditions wasn't just about having patience; it was about having endurance.

Endurance is weathering the undesirable—knowing that the desirable waits at the end of our endurance.

Endurance is long being in a difficult situation—while yet believing that better lies before us.

Endurance is hanging in there during the temporary death of the good because we believe in resurrections.

It is being without for so long that you can't remember being with, but not giving up because you know being *with* again is within time's reach.

It is continuing to believe through the tenth disappointment and the rejection of another job you were certain you would get.

It is continuing to believe that the marriage God endorsed will work well again—though it seems to be falling apart piece by piece, day by day.

Patience is waiting for the scheduled wedding day to arrive; endurance is continuing to believe God to make you ready for a mate though you have made mistake after mistake after mistake.

Patience is waiting in line at the grocery store; endurance is waiting in line for an organ transplant when you have been sick for years.

Patience is waiting for the extra money from the promised promotion to begin; endurance is continuing to trust God when you have no money and your time in your home has come to an end.

Endurance is continuing to believe that the ministry God has called you to will one day thrive though today it hangs by a thread.

Endurance is continuing to believe that your wayward child (or children) will be saved though they sit celled in some ungodly situation.

Endurance is continuing to believe God for the best when a little less than the worst has been the best as of late.

Endurance is continuing to live right and do right even when all your right seems to be rewarded with wrong.

Endurance is continuing to walk with, serve and believe God even though you have experiences you never expected He would allow.

Patience is hanging in there when all else is well; endurance is continuing to trust God when all else is not well, and there is no *well* in sight.

As Christians, we must all weather some sort of season of adversity. And that's what endurance is—weathering the worst of winter, *knowing* that better weather is on the way. It is also helpful to know that the storms of life are not without purpose as we have previously stated. The reality is that in order to possess the best of life, sometimes we must endure what seems to be the worst of life without giving up on life or the meaningful things in life. The undesirable things we endure ready us for things we will enjoy.

The greatly desired arrives after we have endured great difficulty.

There are many examples of endurance exhibited by people in the Bible who experienced extremely joyful and rewarding lives after weathering the season of bad weather. But there are none greater than what we find in Jesus.

> **"Therefore we also, since we are surrounded by so great a cloud of witnesses, let us lay aside every weight, and the sin which so easily traps us, and let us run with endurance, the race that is set before us, <u>Looking to Jesus</u>, the author and finisher of our faith, who for the joy that was set before Him <u>endured</u> the cross, despising the shame, and has sat down at the right hand of the throne of God.**
> **Hebrews 12:1, 2**

When the Word of God speaks to us about the death of Jesus on the cross, I don't believe it is speaking *only* of His time on the cross, though that was certainly a part of it. I believe it is also speaking of everything Jesus experienced leading up to the cross. The combination of everything Jesus experienced leading up *to* the cross contributed to His death *on* the cross. His death was not just the result of His betrayal, the lies, and the emotional humiliation, but the physical abuse as well—the slapping, the punching, the 39 lashes with a cat-o'-nine-tails, His beard being ripped from His face and every other wound and bruise.

(Before writing this, I had never thought about the fact that, because Jesus received 39 lashes with a cat-o'-<u>nine</u>-tails, that was actually 288 wounds when we multiply 39 by 9. And even more

if we consider the fact that each cat-tail had a number of pieces of broken glass and sharp stones.)

In the Hebrews passage, not only do we find a portrait of endurance, we also find an encouragement for us to be like Christ in enduring hardship. No, we don't have to endure the cross He endured (thank God, Jesus endured that for us!), but we all have a cross of different sorts to endure—just as our Christ endured His cross for our sin and for our sake.

In **Matthew 16:24** wherein Jesus says, **"…If anyone desires to come after Me, let him deny himself, and <u>take up his cross</u>, and follow Me."** He is saying that there will be times and things in life we will have to endure just as He endured the cross. But after Jesus endured the cross, He fulfilled prophecy and brought the promise and possibility of salvation to pass. As we follow His path of endurance, prophecies, promises, and blessings are also fulfilled for us and through us!

Endurance is patience to the tenth power.

"You have need of endurance…."
Hebrews 10:36

Our "**need of endurance**" does not mean we are without enduring ability—it simply means we *have need* to *exercise* that ability. The exercising of endurance brings about blessings and positions us to receive the things God promises us in His Word. In fact, the receiving of those promises is what the remainder of this verse teaches:

"For you have need of endurance, so that after you have done the will of God, you may receive the promise."
Hebrews 10:36

Endurance not only brings to pass the promises of the Word of God, it also plays a significant role in any word of prophecy to us coming to pass.

Endurance is the *ticket* that prepares us to operate in prophecy, and grants us access to the promises of God. When we don't endure difficult times and give up prior to the promises of God coming to pass, we deprive ourselves of the exceeding precious promises of God and do not allow endurance to equip us for the prophecy.

Prophetic fulfillment and many of the *exceeding, great and precious promises* are products of endurance. Some promises come through patience, while others simply come by God's grace. But special promises, *big* blessings and the completion of the prophetic all come by way of endurance.

"For when God made a promise to Abraham,
because He could swear by no one greater,
He swore by Himself, saying, 'Surely
blessing I will bless you, and multiplying
I will multiply.' And so, after he had
patiently endured, he obtained the promise.
Hebrews 6:13

The "promise" Abraham obtained was the birth of Isaac—the son he and Sarah, his wife, prayed and longed for. Isaac was a promised blessing that was prophesied. But the birth of the promise, the blessing, and the prophetic were born out of Abraham's endurance—his ability to hang in there and continue to believe God—even when he and his wife experienced difficult times.

Not only was Isaac's birth by endurance, the very first prophesied promise of blessing the Lord gave to Abraham (whose name was Abram at the time) came to life after having to endure hardship.

**"Now the Lord had said to Abram:
'Get out of your country, from your
family and from your father's house,
to a land that I will show you.
I will make your name great;
and you shall be a blessing.
I will bless those who bless you
and I will curse him who curses you;
and in you all the families of the earth
shall be blessed.' So Abram departed
as the Lord had spoken to him...."
And Abram was seventy-five years old.
Genesis 12:1-4**

First of all, understand from this passage that as far as God is concerned, we are never too old to be used by Him! Some people are called by God early on in life to do certain things. We find this with David who received the prophecy from Samuel about becoming king of Israel when he was a teenager. Such was the case with Joseph who may have been even younger than David when the Lord gave him two prophetic dreams about being used in a great way. But sometimes people are called by God to do things certain things once they are older. This was the case with both the apostle Paul and with Abram.

Abram was 75 years old when God approached him with the prophecy and promise of blessings. However, it wasn't something that quickly came to pass. Abram had to endure hardship before the prophecy and promises were realized.

**"So Abram journeyed, going on still
toward the South. Now there was
a famine in the land, and Abram
went down to Egypt to dwell there,
for the famine was severe in the land."
Genesis 12:9, 10**

What??! A "famine"? A *severe famine?!* Abraham may have been thinking, *"Come on, God! What happened to making my name great and blessing me to be a blessing? Not only is my name not great, people are laughing, joking and rejoicing in my demise. They're talking about how I didn't hear from You and how I should have never left my country, extended family or my father's house! I'm not being a blessing to anyone. I'm not even feeling very blessed myself! We have no home, and we hardly have any food to eat! What about the prophecy, and the promises? Where are the blessings?!"*

At some point during the time of trouble, I think we, as God's children, have all felt this way. In the sixth chapter of the book of Judges, the **"Angel of the Lord"** approached Gideon and said, **"The Lord is with you, you mighty man of valor!"** Gideon's respectful response was, **"O my Lord, if the Lord is with us, why then has all this happened to us? And where are all His miracles…?"** I have asked questions similar to these. "Lord, if…why then is…?" How about you?

God made promises to Abraham—promises He eventually made good on—but not until after Abraham *endured hardship,* which is actually the only type of endurance there is. The very need to endure is an indication that some degree of hardship is involved. In fact, the word *suffer* is used to define *endure,* and *survival* is synonymous with *endurance*. Enduring is surviving the suffering of hard times. But again, we can endure hardship because God has placed within us the ability to do so. Abraham did, and he afterward received the promises. Remember, the promises that await us at the end of our endurance are not your ordinary, everyday, run-of-the-mill promises. They are the, **"exceeding great and precious promises!"**

Not only did Abraham have to endure hardship before possessing the promises and living out the prophetic, so did Joseph and David and a number of others in the Bible. Everyone who accomplished something worthy of noting in the Bible endured days of difficulty, times of trouble, and seasons of suffering on the way.

Great promises, blessings and fulfilled prophesies are all products of endurance.

Sometimes we can be doing the *right thing* and experience what feels like a *wrong thing*! The *wrong thing* would be anything that is contrary to a reward for our obedience to God—much like what Abraham may have felt after obeying God and experiencing a famine.

When we are doing the *right thing* in obeying God but what we are experiencing in response seems to be contrary to what God has promised, it is then also that we must *endure.* We must endure what seems like the reward for the wicked because even the wrong we experience while doing right plays a role in bringing about good.

> **"And it happened on the next day that the distressing spirit from God came upon Saul, and he prophesied inside the house. So David played music with his hand, as at other times, but there was a spear in Saul's hand. And Saul cast the spear, for he said, 'I will pin David to the wall!'**
> **1 Samuel 18:10, 11**

> **"Now the distressing spirit from the Lord came upon Saul as he sat in his house with his spear in his hand. And David was playing music with his hand. Then Saul sought to pin David to the wall with the spear, but he slipped away from Saul's presence; and he drove the spear into the wall. So David fled and escaped that night."**
> **1 Samuel 19:9, 10**

In both instances, David was doing right in the right situation, but the treatment he was experiencing was wrong! Why did David go back after Saul tried to kill him the first time? *(I would have gone back too…with 200 highly trained soldiers! And I would have left the harp behind!)* David went back because he was enduring the difficult season so that he could come into his prophesied and promised season.

(Please don't misunderstand enduring to mean that a wife, a child or even a husband should return to a home where their life or physical well-being is in jeopardy. As it pertains to the husband and wife relationship, ***1 Corinthians 7:15*** *says,* ***"… God has called us to peace."*** *The Lord never "calls" us to places He doesn't want us to be, and He has not called wives, children or husbands to remain in war zones where their lives and health are in danger. What we find with David is much different and would be considered work-place hostility.)*

We would say David was crazy for going back and hanging in there, but he knew his place of problems was also his place of promise. What do you do when you're being mistreated, but your place of problems is also your place of promise, prophecy, or appointment by God? You endure!

Years ago, after finally coming to grips with the fact that the Lord was calling me into the Word ministry (like the vision He had given my mother prophesied), and after the Lord would not let me rest about the matter, I remember going to my pastor two years later. To be honest, I was hoping his response would not be favorable because I didn't *really* want to preach or teach God's Word. In his wisdom and experience in dealing with young, would-be ministers, my pastor told me to come back to him in 90 days if I still felt as if I was being called by God into the ministry. I was relieved because I felt as if I had done what God was urging me to do in sharing with my pastor, and because I wouldn't have to deal with the matter again—at least not for 90 days.

After another year passed, I felt the same urging to return to him, and I did. This time I was willing and ready! However, my pastor was not as willing and ready, and the negative response I had hoped for the first time, I received this time. "Brother Bailey, I don't know if you are called to preach. If so, I don't know if you are called to preach here." Although I don't believe that he meant me any harm or heartache, those words were pretty hard to handle! I would later understand that his response was because of different doctrinal views we shared. Not long after our meeting I figured it was time for me to leave the church because if I was called to share the Word of God but could not do so there, there must have been another church who would accept me, teach me, and help me to fulfill my calling. But I was wrong. God wanted me to remain there and He made it plain by working out a situation where I became the assistant teacher of the men's Sunday school class. And then a year or so later, I became the primary teacher of that same class.

It was not lost on me that I could not have occupied either position with the approval of my pastor. Whereas it had initially appeared that he was against me sharing the Word of God in the church he was the senior pastor over, he obviously was not. Sometimes we mistake "no", as "never", when "no" more often means "not yet". And sometimes God is behind the "no" we receive from people; but when God is ready for them to say "yes" they cannot resist Him because their heart is in God's hand and God turns it *whichever* way He wills, *whenever* He wills!

Three years after I had initially, reluctantly approached my pastor about my calling, and after nearly three years of teaching in the church as a Sunday school teacher (and a monthly singles' class), one Sunday morning during service my pastor, unbeknownst to me, announced that I would be preaching my first sermon! Needless to say, I was shocked, somewhat surprised, and I was happy! I am also grateful to my pastor for the role he played in my calling to the ministry.

My point is that, I had to endure what I initially thought was unfair treatment, and I had to remain in the place God had appointed me before the promise and the prophecy of me preaching came to pass. A part of me enduring was overcoming being offended and staying in the place God had given me purpose and had plans to prepare me for my destiny. As it turned out, having to wait three years before I was allowed to share the Word of God with the entire congregation was the best thing for me in that situation; because in that three years God taught me how to study His Word and how to recognize revelation. In that time God also taught me how to layout and deliver a message and He had made me extremely comfortable with sharing His Word in front of people. But the Lord did these things *during* the season of endurance! The season of endurance is difficult, but it is also purposeful!

The season of endurance is difficult, but it is also purposeful!

David knew that if he was going to possess the promise and fulfill the prophecy, he had to endure the presence of problems in the appointed place! Such is the case with us. And remember, we can endure because we have seen others who have endured.

"We are bound to thank God always for you brethren, as it is fitting, because your faith grows exceeding, and the love of every one of you all abounds toward each other, so that we ourselves boast of you among the churches of God for your patience and faith in all your persecutions and tribulations that you endure."
2 Thessalonians 1:3, 4

Here again we find believers needing to endure difficult times, and actually enduring them to the point where it caused Paul to boast about their endurance to other churches. Obviously, these people were believing God for some things that were not happening when or how they expected. But they didn't shout, pout and complain; rather, they endured. They hung in there until that which was promised came to pass, and they were no doubt rewarded for their patience under pressure!

"You therefore, my son' be strong in the grace that is in Christ Jesus. And the things that you have heard from me among many witnesses, commit these to faithful men who will be able to teach others also. You therefore must endure hardship as a good soldier of Jesus Christ."
2 Timothy 2:3

Notice that Paul says, **"You therefore must endure hardship..."** Paul's use of the word "therefore" tells us that there is a reason Timothy must hang in there and overcome difficult times. The reason is that the people referenced in verse 2 are counting on him.

Represented in this verse are countless generations of Christians who would ultimately benefit from Timothy enduring hardship and sharing the Word and other things he had learned from Paul. If Timothy had not endured, he would not have been in a position to share those teaching with "faithful men," and they would not have had those things to share and teach to others, who would not have had those things to teach to others, and so forth.

It doesn't matter whether or not we, like Timothy, are ministers of the Gospel; it is the same with you and me—people are depending on us to endure troublesome times because within us is something that has been designed and deposited by God to help and bless people—maybe even people for generations to come. To further make this point, let me do so in conclusion with what the apostle Paul goes on to say to Timothy:

> **"But you have carefully followed my doctrine, manner of life, purpose, faith, longsuffering, love, perseverance, persecution, afflictions, which happened to me at Antioch, at Iconium, at Lystra—what persecutions I endured. And out of them all the Lord delivered me. Yes, and all who desire to live godly in Christ Jesus will suffer persecution. But evil men and impostors will grow worse and worse, deceiving and being deceived. But you must continue in the things which you have learned and been assured of, knowing from whom you have learned them…."**
> **2 Timothy 3:10-14**

This passage was purposed to further encourage Timothy to hang in there and endure his time of hardship. In these verses Paul places Timothy in remembrance of some things and encourages him to recall other things. He encourages him to *recall* the things he has been taught in times past, as well as the things of which he has been assured. He does so because times of trouble have a way of obstructing our mental view of past victories, past teachings, and things we have been convinced of in past times. Because of Timothy's familiarity with the Scriptures from his **"childhood"** Paul knew he had learned, and been persuaded at some point of the faithfulness of God during the time of trouble, and how He had delivered others in times past. Paul also encouraged Timothy to bring these things to mind because remembering things we have been taught, and the things others have gone through and come through, will help us to endure.

Paul references his life experiences with trouble to allow Timothy to know that his trouble was not uncommon. But also, in recounting his time of trouble to Timothy, Paul was allowing him to know that if *he* was able to endure and overcome all that confronted him, Timothy undoubtedly was able to do the same, because the same Heavenly Father Who loved Paul and the same Son Who died and lived to make intercession for Paul, and the same Holy Spirit Who helped Paul, was present to help Timothy as well.

The words of Paul to Timothy were written by Paul to Timothy, but at the same time, they are Words of God written by God to us. What applied and enabled Timothy to endure his difficulties can do the same for us as we remember that others are depending on us to endure. We must also remember that the troubles that were overcome by saints in the past provide a pattern and a point of reference of God's faithfulness to help and deliver us. We must not lose sight of the fact that the Lord changes not; He *still* loves us, He is *still* interceding on our behalf, and He is *still* fulfilling His promise to comfort us, and to help us in our time of trouble. Because of Who He is, what He has done in times past, and what He promises to do even now, we are *equipped to endure*!

Chapter 13
The Helpfulness of Hopefulness

**"It is good that a man should both hope and quietly wait for the salvation of the Lord.
Lamentations 3:26**

When Jeremiah writes in this verse about waiting "**for the salvation of the Lord,**" he is referring to being delivered by God from a time of trouble. This *quiet wait* is a *patient wait.* The importance of patience during the time of trouble was addressed in a previous chapter—but in building upon the importance of having patience, Jeremiah says it is "**good**" to be patient, or to "**quietly wait**" for the Lord's salvation from the season of adversity.

Jeremiah says also that "**hope**" is "**good.**" And if the level of importance is revealed by the order in which "**hope**" and "**quietly wait**" are offered, *hope* is more important than *patience.* By no means does the order minimize the importance of patience, for patience is unquestionably an ally during times of adversity. However, *hope* helps to produce *patience*, and the producer of a thing is greater than the thing produced—just as the Crea*tor* is greater than the crea*ted*.

Hope is "confident expectation." *Hope* is "a firm, non-wavering belief that God is faithful to keep His Word and that He will aid us during our time of trouble and will ultimately deliver us from trouble." Hope is continuing to believe this truth even when the outlook is dim, and all the odds are against us. Like faith, hope is not the product of what we *see*, but what God *says*. It is not baseless, but it is not based on the facts or the evidence of our circumstances. Instead, our hope is built on God and the evidence in His Word of how He has delivered others from their time of trouble.

The Bible is not only the living Word of God, it is also a book of testimonies—testimonies of how the Lord showed up in the lives of others to sustain them during their times of difficulty before delivering them from those times. The testimonies of others are extremely important because they give us hope to help on our way to victory over trouble. When we are hopeful, or are *confidently expecting* God to help us, there is a help in that hope that cannot be had through anyone or anything else.

"Happy is he who has the God of
Jacob for his help.
Whose hope is in the Lord his God."
Psalm 146:5

Notice the connection between *happy, help and hope* in this verse. There is a *happiness* that is produced when we place our hope in God's help—a happiness that is imprisoned when hopelessness rules in our heart. Sometimes trouble can weigh on us so heavily that we cannot find humor or pleasure in anything. But as crazy as it may sound, *happiness* can be had *during* the time of trouble because hope in God frees the area of emotion that enables us to enjoy things that are enjoyable—even when other things are not so enjoyable. This is why Solomon, the preacher of **Proverbs 10:28,** said from his wealth of wisdom: **"The hope of the righteous shall be gladness...."**

King Solomon also said, **"Hope deferred makes the heart sick..." (Proverbs 13:12).** The Hebrew word for *sick* also means "worn, weak, afflicted and grieved." If a delay in hope causes the heart to be sick or grieved, it stands to reason that the presence of hope causes the health of the heart.

Hope helps release happiness in our heart—even in the midst of adverse happenings.

Hope is good because hope is helpful. Hope is helpful also because hope is faith, and faith, like hope, pleases God. When God is pleased, out of His pleasure He helps, pleases and blesses His children. Consider these passages as proof:

"The Lord takes pleasure in those who fear
Him, in those who hope in His mercy."
Psalm 147:11

"Blessed is the man who trusts
in the Lord, and whose hope is the Lord.
For he shall be like a tree planted by
The waters, which spreads out its
roots by the river, and will not fear
when heat comes; but its leaf will
be green and will not be anxious
in the year of drought, nor will
cease from yielding fruit."
Jeremiah 17:7, 8

According to this passage, hope not only brings the blessing of the Lord, it also helps in fending off fear and worry, which are both enemies of the peace of God that **"guards our heart and mind through Christ Jesus."** Hope helps because it protects our peace which protects our heart and mind. Solomon, son of David and the third king of Israel, penned in **Proverbs 4:23, "Guard your heart with all diligence, for out of it spring the issues of life."** Hope is helpful because it guards the guard which guards our heart.

Hope is the guard that guards the guard which guards our heart.

According to Jeremiah, hope also has a strengthening and stabilizing effect on our heart. The *roots* of a tree not only serve as straws from whence trees drink water and grow, *roots* also help to strengthen and stabilize the tree. The deeper and more spread out the roots, the stronger and more stable the tree. As a result, when storms come and are accompanied by strong winds, they may blow away leaves, spoil the fruit and break the branches, but the tree itself is not moved. Unmoved trees grow new branches, produce new leaves, and bear new fruit. This is what the roots created by hope do in the life of the believer—that believer who has an unrelenting trust in the Lord his God!

If the roots run deep the fruit will return.

In the midst of his mistaken rebuke of Job, Job's friend Zophar actually got something right when he said,

"And you shall be secure because there is hope; yes, you would dig around you, and take your rest in safety."
Job 11:18

This verse teaches that hope helps *because* it provides an emotional security that protects us from what our circumstances say to us. Thoughts of gloom and doom are silent words spoken to us by our circumstances in an attempt to attack us with the weapons of discouragement and depression. The phrase *"dig around you"* illustrates the idea of a moat or a trench that is dug around a city to provide protection from enemies. In the same way, hope surrounds and protects us by placing us out of the reach of the enemy elements of fear, doubt and worry—all of which causes discouragement and contributes to depression.

During a particular time of trouble, David's confidence in God compelled him to write a word of encouragement to believers about the helpfulness of hope. *(As with the apostle Paul's letter to the church in Philippi, I am interested in hearing words of hope written by people during their time of trouble because people who write about hope while they are in trouble know something about hope's help—something that will help the hearers.)*

"Oh, love the Lord, all you His saints!
For the Lord preserves the faithful…
Be of good courage, and He shall strengthen
your heart, all you who hope in the Lord."
Psalm 31:23, 24

To *"be of good courage"* means "to encourage ourselves." We encourage ourselves when we remind ourselves of the good God has done in times past to help us. Remember, whatever the Lord has done to help us in the past wasn't just about helping us in the past. What the Lord has done to help us in the past is also about providing something for us to reflect back on and from which to draw encouragement in the future.

When David was **"greatly distressed"** and **1 Samuel 30:6** says he **"encouraged himself,"** he did so by reminding himself of the goodness and faithfulness shown by God in days of old. In **Psalm 77:2** David wrote reflectively from another difficult time in his life: **"In the day of my trouble I sought the Lord."** After revealing his many thoughts of torments that stole his hope and discouraged him, David then shares what helped to encourage him:

"And said I, 'This [the negative thoughts] is my anguish; but [instead] I will remember the [good] years of the right hand of the Most High. I will remember the works of the Lord; Surely I will remember Your wonders of old. I will also meditate on all Your work, and talk of Your deeds.'"
Psalm 77:10-12

In the verses that follow, David goes on to repeat with his mouth what he remembered in his mind. And in doing so, he encouraged himself and rebuilt his hope.

"Who is so great a God as our God? You are the God Who does wonders; You have declared Your strength among the peoples. You have with your arm redeemed Your people...."
Psalm 77:13-15

Praise places us in remembrance of Who God is and the mighty things He has done. As we engage in praise vocally, what we remember and speak with our mouth ministers to us and strengthens our soul—our inward man.

"Bless [speak well of] the Lord, O my soul; and all that is within me, Bless His holy name! Bless the Lord O my soul, And forget not all His benefits; Who forgives all your iniquities, Who heals all your diseases, Who redeems your life from destruction, Who crowns you with lovingkindness and tender mercies, Who satisfies your mouth with good things...."
Psalm 103:1-5a

The Word of God encourages us *not to forget* the benefits of the Lord because for one, it helps us to be hopeful, and hopefulness is helpful. David also says we should remember the benefits of the Lord: **"So [that] your youth is renewed like the eagle's."**

The word "youth" represents a strength that is lost with aging. This verse teaches us that when we place ourselves in remembrance of the wonderful things God has done for us, those remembrances will renew our strength—making our strength like that of the eagle's. You may be wondering, "What is the eagle's strength like?" I welcome your wonder. The Bible provides the answer:

"Those that wait on the Lord shall renew their strength; they shall mount up with wings like eagles, they shall run and not be weary, they shall walk and not faint."
Isaiah 40:31

The eagle-like strength (that is renewed in us as we encourage ourselves by placing ourselves in remembrance of the good things God has done) is a strength that enables us to *mount up*, rise and fly above the effects of the storm. It is a strength that empowers us to run the race and not be to worn to finish though the race is long. It is a strength that allows us to walk through the war-torn times of tribulation without giving up before we get the victory.

Remembering, or recalling what God has done in times past, and the mercy and graciousness of His character is what led Jeremiah to say: **"It is good that one should hope…for the salvation of the Lord."** Listen to what led Jeremiah to this conclusion in the preceding verses:

"My soul still remembers [my trouble]
and sinks within me. [But] 21 This I recall
to my mind, therefore I have hope.
[I remember that] 22 Through the Lord's

mercies we are not consumed, because His compassions fail not: 23 They are new every morning; great is Your faithfulness. 24 'The Lord is my portion,' says my soul, 'Therefore I hope in Him!' 25 The Lord is good to those who wait for Him, to the soul who seeks Him. 26 It is good that one should hope and wait quietly for the salvation of the Lord."
Lamentations 3:20-26

When we encourage ourselves in the Lord by putting ourselves in remembrance of the powerful things He has done (and done to help us in times past), our self-encouragement gives us hope—hope that helps us, hope that strengthens us, and hope that pleases our God and King.

What Helps Us to Have the Hope That Helps Us?

Knowing that hope helps us is one thing, but knowing *how* to have the hope that helps is something else. A number of things help us to be and remain hopeful in our time of trouble, and a few of them have been addressed in previous chapters. Prayer and praise certainly aid us, as does church attendance wherein we fellowship and draw strength and encouragement from other believers, especially those whom have been through times of trouble and whose testimonies impart hope to us. We also talked about the importance and the helpfulness of the Word of God during trouble.

Although we receive the Word of God during church attendance, I have found that the more Word I receive, the more my hope was and is helped. Be it reviewing sermon notes, listening repeatedly to recorded church teachings, attending additional teaching services during the week, listening to sound Bible teachers by means of the Internet, reading doctrinally sound books on Christian living, or reading as much of the Bible (my personal favorite) as you can, brings hope! The more Word of God we deposit into ourselves, the more hope we will have and the more hope that will remain during trying times.

"Remember the Word to Your servant,
upon which You have caused me to hope.
This is my comfort in my affliction,
for Your Word has given me life."
Psalm 119:49

The psalmist credits the Word of God with comforting him and causing him to be hopeful in his time of trouble. God's Word does this because the Bible reminds us of how loving, kind, strong, faithful and powerful of a Deliverer He is. It never fails that when we feel down in the dumps and like our life's situation will never change, we read in the Bible a story about the Lord delivering someone who was also in a difficult way. Reading about God helping and eventually delivering them gives us hope because we are reminded of what type of God He is and that He is not a respecter of persons.

The Word of God
restores and helps our heart
to remain hopeful during
the time of trouble.

Have I mentioned that I love gifts? Well, if I have, I still love them! I especially love the gifts of the Holy Spirit. As heavenly things typically differ from earthly things that share the same title, spiritual gifts differ from natural gifts. The natural gifts we give to people are purposed to bless the receiver of the gift. But spiritual gifts given to us by God are given to us to be a blessing to other people.

**"There are diversities of gifts, but the same Spirit. There are differences of ministries, but the same Lord. And there are diversities of activities, but it the same God Who works all in all. But the manifestation of the Spirit is given to each one of us for the <u>profit of all</u>."
1 Corinthians 124-7**

I wish that all Christian churches would allow the operation of all of the gifts of the Spirit because their purpose is to *profit* the church by building up believers. I especially wish that all churches would permit the gift of prophecy to occupy a place in their fellowship because the gift of prophecy helps us to be hopeful. I realize that there is a legitimate concern about false prophets and false prophecy because Jesus said that as we approach the end times **"... many false prophets will rise up and deceive many,"** and also because the apostle John said, **"...many false prophets have gone out into the world."** Aside from deceiving people, false prophets destroy the credibility of the gift, causing people not to trust even in true prophets. Therefore, we have a right to be concerned and on guard against false prophets, but we should not be concerned or on guard to the extreme of prohibiting the *true* gift of prophecy to operate and bless the people of God. When we allow the fear of the *false* to keep us from operating in the *true,* yes, we keep out the *false,* but the *false* still hinders us only in a different way. It hinders us because it causes us not to allow in the *true* that will help us.

An age-old adage says, "*Don't throw out the baby with the bath water.*" The used bath water represents that which is of no value and should not be allowed to remain. But the baby represents that which is of value and should be kept. In throwing away the *worthless*, we must be careful not to throw out that which is *priceless.* Such is the case with not allowing the gift of prophecy. False prophets, their false prophecies, false doctrine, and false teachings should be avoided at all cost—*except* at the cost of the *true* gift of prophecy. We cannot allow fear of that which is false to cause us to cease our pursuit and embrace of that which is true.

"Let two or three prophets speak…
For you can all prophesy one by one,
that all may learn and be encouraged.
1 Corinthians 14:29, 31

Did you catch that? "**Let…prophesy…and be encouraged.**" It is good to **"let"** true prophets prophesy in the church because it helpful. But how do we keep false prophets from falsely prophesying in the church? Good question. The apostle John wrote, **"Beloved, do not believe every spirit, but test the spirits, whether they are of God [test them]; because many false prophets have gone out into the world." (1 John 4:1)** Unfortunately, many of these false prophets have found their way into our churches and into the favor of pastors. To avoid them, the first thing John says is, "**do not believe every spirit**."

I realize that **1 Corinthians 13:7** says love **"…believes all things";** however, Paul wasn't talking about believing *all* things about *all* people *all* of the time. If that were the case, we would buy every lemon of a car every dishonest car salesman tries to sell us. And we would fall for every scam. We don't because we know everyone isn't honest, and we don't believe everything they tell us. Not believing people all of the time does not mean we are not walking in love; however, it does mean we are walking in wisdom! Also, we know **1 Corinthians 13:7** doesn't literally mean to believe everything everyone says because John says, "**do not believe every spirit**" that is operating in every person because some people are inspired by *lying spirits*. John was inspired by the Holy Spirit to write this message because *lying spirits* are unclean spirits and are on assignment to deceive.

I am not suggesting that under-shepherds, who have a responsibility to protect the sheep from the wolves of false prophets, should assume everyone who claims to be a prophet is lying. I believe that John is simply saying we must be cautious and not quick to believe and permit people we don't *really* know to operate in the gift of prophecy in the church we oversee. In fact, a passage in Paul's letter to the church in Thessalonica confirms this where it says, "**We urge you, brethren, to <u>know</u> those who labor among you...**" **(1 Thessalonians 5:12).** The Greek word for *know* is also means: "to be aware; look, perceive, see, be sure, and understand." It is imperative that pastors take the time to observe and to be certain that those who claim to be prophets are *true* prophets before allowing them to labor in the church. Doing so will serve as protection from false prophets and their harmful intentions.

After saying, **"believe not every spirit,"** the apostle John continues, **"but <u>test</u> every spirit, whether they are of God...."** I find it interesting that instead of just taking someone's word about being called to the prophetic ministry, John says to **"test"** them. The indication is that if they fail the test, they are probably a false prophet, and God is allowing that to be known in order to keep injury from occurring.

There are at least three ways to **"test the spirits"** or the person claiming to be a true prophet. The first, as mentioned by John, is their confession that Jesus Christ has come in the flesh. You would be surprised at how many people ignore this test in assuming that anyone who claims to be a prophet must believe and have confessed this at some point. Well, require them to confess it at another point—before you.

Another test is that of patience. This is a good test because the unclean spirits who operate in false prophets cannot be patient because patience is a fruit of the Spirit. Though they may initially appear to, false prophets do not consistently operate in fruit of the Spirit. They will not patiently wait for their gift to make room for them because the assignment of the unclean spirit in the false prophet is to deceive people. Deceivers will not waste time waiting around. And when people are not patient and do not pass the test of time, it's a sign that they're either 1) a false prophet, 2) a true prophet not called to your ministry, or 3) a true prophet who is presently absent of the patience required in waiting for his gift to make room for them.

Another test is that of orderly submission to authority. If people commence to prophesying and have not been authorized by leadership to do so, they are not led by the *Holy* Spirit and could very well be inspired the *unclean* spirit of the false prophet.

Another test is that of holiness. If there is unrepentant sin of some sort in the person's life, that's a problem because prophets hear from God what they share with the people. But if a so-called prophet has not himself acknowledged what God says about sin in his own life, chances are God is not speaking to him about what to speak into His people's life. However, the devil will because unrepentant sin provides him with *place.* And with that *place,* he inspires them to deceive people through false prophecies.

The point is that we should not prevent the gift of prophecy from operating because we are trying to fend off false prophets. If we test the spirits and they pass the test and prove to be true prophets, their presence will be a great asset to the ministry and a tremendous blessing to the people of God. This will be the case in part because the gift of prophecy is extremely helpful when it comes to people being hopeful.

"Pursue love, and desire spiritual gifts,
but especially that you may prophesy.
For he who speaks in a tongue does not
speak to men but to God, for no one
understands him; however, in the Spirit

he speaks mysteries. But he who prophesies speaks edification and exhortation and comfort to men. He who speaks in a tongue edifies himself, but he who prophesies edifies the church."
1 Corinthians 14:1-4

The gift of prophecy helps us to hope.

The Bible contains the *Words* of God, but prophecy is the *voice* of God spoken through those He has spiritually gifted to do so. The Words of God are very helpful when it comes to knowing the power of God, seeing how He has operated in the lives of others, and knowing what He has promised to us, but there is something about *hearing* the voice of God that helps us to be or to remain hopeful. Sometimes that hope comes via the still small voice the Lord causes us to hear from time to time or via prophecy spoken directly to us. Like many others, I have been blessed to have heard both, and they have both helped me to remain hopeful in my time of trouble because the Holy Spirit brought to my remembrance what I heard.

When Jesus told the disciples in **John 14:26** that the Holy Spirit would, **"...bring to your remembrance all things that I said to you,"** He was not talking about the written Word because the Words of Jesus had not been written yet. Jesus was talking instead about the Words He *spoke* to them—many of which were words of prophecy. The Holy Spirit not only gives the gift of prophecy, He also inspires what is prophesied, and after it has been prophesied, He brings those spoken words to our remembrance—often when we need them most.

Again, the written Words of God are also helpful, but the enemy has a way of causing us to question whether or not what we've read actually applies to us—thereby depositing seeds of doubt in our mind that sometimes brings forth fruit of unbelief. But when God *speaks* to us through His voice or the true voice of prophecy, there is no question of whether or not what He said applies to us. There is no soil for the seed of doubt to take root and bring forth fruit because we know what was spoken applies to us. After all, it was spoken *directly* to us!

We may sometimes question what was written by God, but we rarely, if ever, question what was spoken to us by God.

Much of what we find in the Bible as it pertains to the prophecies of God fall into one of two categories:

1) Repentance from sin
2) His good plans for our future

The role of prophecy being helpful in providing hope to the children of God isn't only a New Testament truth. Words of prophecy also helped many of the Old Testament saints survive their troubling times. Many of the verses in the book of Psalms reveal the *hope* David had during his days of difficulties, including the times when King Saul tried to kill him. David's *hope* was the product of a prophetic encounter he had with Samuel. That encounter revealed that David would be the next king of Israel.

"And Samuel said to Jesse, 'Are all the young men here?' Then he said, 'There remains yet the youngest, and there he is, keeping the sheep.' Samuel said to Jesse, 'Send and bring him. For we will not sit down till he comes here.' So he sent and brought him in. Now he was ruddy, with bright eyes, and good-looking. And the Lord said, 'Arise, anoint him;

for this is the one!' Then Samuel took the horn of oil and anointed him in the midst of his brothers; and the Spirit of the Lord came upon David from that day forward. So Samuel arose and went to Ramah."
1 Samuel 16:11-13

"So David saw that Saul had come out to seek his life. And David was in the wilderness of Ziph in a forest. Then Jonathan, Saul's son, arose and went to David in the woods and strengthened [encouraged] his hand in God. And he said to him, 'Do not fear, for the hand of Saul my father shall not find you. You shall be king over Israel, and I shall be next to you. Even my father Saul knows that.' "
1 Samuel 23:15-17

What Jonathan used to "strengthen" David in the Lord was the prophecy that he would become king over Israel. The Spirit undoubtedly inspired Jonathan to remind David of what God said to him because reminding David that he would be the *next* king meant he *couldn't* be killed by the *current* king. It didn't matter how long, how hard, how often or how many times Saul tried to kill David (and he tried over a dozen times); no weapon that was formed against David would prosper and prevent the prophecy from being fulfilled. Remembering that promise helped him because it gave hope to him. It gave him a confident expectation that despite what he was experiencing, the good God had promised would still come to pass.

The power of prophecy prevents premature death and strengthens our heart in the plan of God for our life.

During my time of trouble, what kept me hopeful was the two prophecies I referenced in a previous chapter. Those prophecies—received twelve years apart in two states I had never visited by two people I had never met—both spoke of the Lord using me to "be a blessing to thousands and thousands all around the world."

When things were tough and my time of trouble seemed not only to be never ending but actually getting worse, and when I had reason to think I wouldn't be a blessing to anyone much less "thousands and thousands," the Spirit began bringing to my remembrance what He had inspired to be prophesied to me helped me. Being reminded of what was said, made me know I was not where I would always be. I had a *confident expectation* of the future. The spoken words of prophecy gave me hope—hope that helped me, anchored me, and enabled me to hang on, *knowing* change was coming!

"This hope we have as an anchor for the soul...."
Hebrews 6:19

In the time of trouble, *hope* is confident expectation in the fact that the season of trouble won't last forever because according to His Word, God will not permit that to happen. Therefore, hope is undoubted assurance that our deliverance draws nearer with the closing of each day. Hope is continuing in that conviction—even when today seems worst than the yesterday and tomorrow doesn't appear to offer promise. This is the *helpfulness of hopefulness!*

Chapter 14
The Voice of God in the Time of Trouble

"Arise and go down to the potter's house, and there I will cause you to hear My Words."
Jeremiah 18:2

As helpful as it is to hear God speak to us, the reality is that we are not going to hear from Him about everything we experience. We will not hear from God about every single encounter simply because God does not literally speak to us about every single thing we encounter in life. This is important to understand because there were times during my time of trouble that I hindered myself by wondering if, "I missed *hearing God*" on something that would have caused me to avoid the trouble in which I found myself. To help me through the hindering of myself, the Lord began to share with me some lessons about hearing from Him. These lessons and truths have set me free from the fear of missing something God was trying to share with me.

Before I go further, let me first say that I *most certainly* believe in hearing from God, and I recognize the tremendous value of doing so. But I don't believe our hearing from God is as much *our* responsibility as it is His. I don't intend for that statement to sound disrespectful toward God in the least bit, and I apologize if it sounds that way to you. My point is, just as any parent who wants their child to do something has to make certain the child hears their desire, I believe God would also make certain that we *hear Him* when there's something He desires us to do.

How reasonable would it be for a father who wants his son to go to the store to whisper that desire from a closet with the door closed while his son is five blocks away at the park playing basketball? Would it be fair for the son to be in trouble for coming home empty-handed? Would the father have a justified expectation of compliance when he didn't give instructions to the son in a way that he could hear them? Some dads may be unfair in that way, but I don't think our Heavenly Father is one of them. He wouldn't discipline us, or allow trouble when He *knows* we didn't hear Him.

When our Heavenly Father desires something of us, or wants to get instructions to us, He does! Whether it is with a still, small voice, the voice of His Word, or the voice of a person He chooses to use, God knows how to get His desire to us in a way we know it's Him. And, He knows when we know it's Him.

When the Lord wanted Abram to leave Haran for Canaan, He spoke plainly and gave him instructions in a way Abram could both hear, and understand. Abram wasn't even a follower of God at that point. And when the Lord spoke, He did not introduce Himself to Abram. Neither did Abram have to wonder whether or not that was God speaking. Abram *knew* because God made him to know that He was speaking to him and *Who* was speaking to him. The Lord didn't leave Abram in the dark about what He wanted him to do.

What I find interesting is that Abram heard from God when it was time to leave and go to Canaan, but he did not hear anything from God when it came to the severe famine he and his family encountered not long after leaving his homeland. Could Abram and his family have avoided the financial crises had he simply *heard from God?* I don't think so because God didn't speak to him about the famine. He didn't speak to Abram about the *trouble* because God wanted him to experience the trouble. The trouble allowed by God had purpose in fulfilling God's plan for Abram and his family.

When Moses was in exile from Egypt and in fear of facing manslaughter charges, God spoke to him about going back to Egypt to lead the Israelites out of captivity. When the Lord spoke to him, it was *impossible* for Moses to have missed God. He left no questions about whether or not Moses heard and understood Him. There was something God wanted Moses to do, and God obligated Himself to making certain that Moses heard His desire and instructions. This was not only the case with Abram and Moses, the Lord spoke plainly to a number of other people to whom He wanted to get instructions because He *really wanted* them to hear from Him and know His will for them.

When God chose to use Jeremiah to get a message to the Israelites who had been misbehaving, the Lord gave him instructions and told him He would give him further instructions later.

"The Word which came to Jeremiah from the Lord saying, 'Arise and go down to the potter's house, and there <u>I will cause you to hear My Words.'</u> "
Jeremiah 18:1, 2

The first thing we see in this passage is, "**the Word... came to Jeremiah.**" He didn't have to sit in silence for 65 minutes and 16 seconds in order to hear from God. God sent His Word to Jeremiah in a way that he couldn't miss it—even if he wanted to. Secondly, as it pertained to further instructions, God said He would, ***"cause*** **[Jeremiah]** ***to hear*** **[His] Words"** indicating that God was placing the onus of Jeremiah's *hearing* Him on Himself—not on Jeremiah. The word ***cause*** means "that which produces an effect." God Himself *produced the effect* of Jeremiah hearing His Words—not Jeremiah. The word *cause* also means "the reason something takes place," and "to make happen." The *reason* Jeremiah would be able to hear further instructions from God was because of God's ability to get the Word of instruction *to* him—not Jeremiah's ability to get the Word of instruction *from* God. The Lord *made happen* his hearing.

Another good example of this with somewhat of a twist takes place in the story of the apostle Paul's (who name was originally Saul) conversion to Christianity while he was on the way to Damascus to persecute Christians. After his life-changing encounter with Jesus wherein he was blinded by the light that shined from Heaven and he found himself on the ground, the Bible says Saul…

"heard a voice saying to him, 'Saul,
Saul, why are you persecuting Me?' "
Acts 9:4

Saul, who wasn't even a Christian at the time Christ confronted him, heard the voice of the Lord questioning him. His ability to hear from God was definitely not because of some elevated state of spirituality or Christian maturity. It was because the Lord *caused* him to hear Him. Now if God can, did and does cause unbelievers to hear Him, why wouldn't God cause His children, whom He loves dearly and deeply, to hear Him when He speaks? He does! However, when He doesn't, it doesn't mean He allows us to go without our knowing His will via some other means.

"And he said, 'Who are You, Lord?' Then the Lord said, 'I am Jesus, whom you are persecuting. It is hard for you to kick against the goads.' So he, trembling and astonished, said, 'Lord, what do You want me to do?' Then the Lord said to him, 'Arise and go into the city, And you will be told what you must do.' "
Acts 9:5, 6

The next thing we find Saul being "told" was through a fellow named Ananias to whom the Lord had spoken to about Saul. Notice two truths about this verse:

1) God also caused Ananias to hear His voice when it was necessary, as He did with Abram, Moses, and Jeremiah.

2) God further instructed Saul on what he must do through the voice of Ananias.

This latter point says that the voice of God is sometimes heard through the voice of spiritually trustworthy men and women of God. This is one reason why it is extremely important to have such people in our life. The Lord will speak to us directly about a situation on one occasion, and then He will speak to us through anointed people about the same situation on another occasion. The *main* point is that God doesn't always speak audibly or directly to us about everything in our life—even when it pertains to times of trouble. When He does, He will make certain that we hear Him.

"Out of Heaven He made you to hear His voice, that He might instruct You…."
Deuteronomy 4:36

"The Lord God has given Me the tongue of the learned, that I should know how to speak a word in season to him who is weary. He awakens Me morning by morning, He awakens My ear to hear as the learned."
Isaiah 50:4

Once again we find God causing, or making His people to hear His voice. We also see *how* He does it: "**He awakens [or opens] our ears**," enabling us to hear His voice. God makes our hearing happen because He does not want us to be absent of the understanding of what He requires of us. God wants us to know His will so that we can do His will and reap the benefits thereof. But respectfully speaking again, making certain we hear Him when He speaks to us is an obligation that belongs to the Lord. And He is capable of accomplishing that obligation quite well.

If God caused heathens to hear Him, why wouldn't He cause His children to hear Him when He speaks?

Please don't misunderstand me. I am not suggesting that we shouldn't *seek* the will of God in making key decisions. We most certainly should because there are indeed some times of trouble that can be avoided by knowing God's will. However, seeking God's will doesn't always mean He will reveal His will through His voice. Even when we seek God's will and actually hear His voice, it doesn't always or automatically mean we will avoid trouble. In fact, sometimes hearing and following the voice of God will lead to trouble—trouble that He will no doubt use for our good, but trouble nonetheless.

One example of this is what happened with Abram hearing the voice of God and following that voice. The voice of God led Him and his family to a "severe famine." Although from there Abram and his family were led to great blessings, their initial experience in hearing and following the voice of God was trouble. This illustration is not to say that we will *always* find trouble when we follow the voice of God; more often than not, when we know the will of God (however we come to know it), it leads to directly to that which is good. But every now and then, before the good, there is a little trouble that prepares us for the good that *always* eventually follows doing God's will.

I don't think we talk enough about the *good trouble* (*good* because of what it ultimately accomplishes) that sometimes follows obeying God. Consequently, many believers wonder whether or not they are actually in God's will because they have *only* been taught that the purpose of hearing from God and knowing His will is to avoid trouble. In actuality and according to Scriptures, sometimes before the will of the Father leads to the good He intends, it leads to trouble. I think Jesus would also testify to this truth. This is helpful to know because sometimes when we encounter trouble in doing what actually is God's will, we jump ship, abandon the project or cease our pursuit—all because we've been made to believe that doing God's will is trouble-free, easy-going and great from the get-go! Sometimes that is the case, but that is not so in every instance. However, if we hang in there, our expectations of good will eventually be realized.

An additional example of having heard and followed the voice of God and it leading to trouble is found in the book of Judges. Therein we find the story of the children of Israel going to battle against the tribe of Benjamin because they were harboring criminals who had killed the concubine of a man from the tribe of Levi.

"Then the children of Israel arose and went up to the house of God to inquire of God. They said, 'Which of us shall go up first to battle against the children of Benjamin?' The Lord said, 'Judah first!' So the children of Israel rose in the morning and encamped against Gibeah. And the men of Israel went out to battle against Benjamin, and the men of Israel put themselves in battle

**array to fight against them at Gibeah.
Then the children of Benjamin came out of
Gibeah, and on that day cut down to the ground
twenty-two thousand men of the Israelites."
Judges 20:18-21**

By all accounts, the children of Israel did the right thing. They sought the will of God; they heard *the voice of God* and followed His voice, but they still found themselves in trouble—on the losing end of a battle. This account further proves that hearing and obeying the voice of God doesn't automatically mean we will avoid trouble, just as encountering trouble doesn't mean we missed God and didn't do what He wanted us to do.

**"And the people, that is, the men of Israel,
encouraged themselves and again
for the battle line at the place where
they had put themselves in array
on the first day. Then the children
of Israel went up and wept before
the Lord, saying, 'Shall I again draw near
for battle against the children of my
brother Benjamin?' And the Lord said,
'Go up against him.' So the children of Israel
approached the children of Benjamin
On the second day. And Benjamin
went out against them from Gibeah
on the second day, and cut down to the
ground eighteen-thousand more
of the children of Israel; all
these drew the sword."
Judges 20:22-25**

There it is again, the children of Israel sought, heard and followed the voice of God into battle against the Benjamites and suffered defeat, indicating that hearing from God doesn't guarantee a trouble-free outcome. This reality is important to know because many of us have sought God's will for family, finances, business, and ministry matters, and after having heard from Him, and followed what we heard, we *still* experienced the difficulties we hoped to avoid! More often than not we later learn the reasons, or come to understand why we encountered what we sought to avoid, but sometimes it remains a mystery—even after things eventually work out the way we initially believed they would. But what I like about this story and the lesson for us is that the children of Israel didn't stop trusting God because they encountered trouble—even when the trouble was found by following His voice.

After the first defeat, they trusted and sought God again—only to suffer the same outcome the second time. After the second defeat, I am sure some of the Israelites were questioning whether their leaders were actually hearing from God. In fact, I would not be surprised if the leaders may have been questioning themselves on having heard from God because of the trouble they had encountered. Many of us are conditioned to think that hearing from God is evidenced by immediate, positive outcomes. We think that because the will of God is *good, acceptable and perfect,* the instant result of following His will is *good, acceptable and perfect.* Sometimes it is; but sometimes it is not. Both the situation with Abraham and this story in Judges prove that point. Still, the children of Israel remained trustful in trouble, and sought God *again* after having been defeated in battle a second time.

"Then all the children of Israel, that is,
all the people, went up and came to the
house of God and wept. They sat there
before the Lord and fasted that day until evening;
and they offered burnt offerings
and peace offerings before the Lord.
So the children of Israel inquired of the Lord...
Saying, 'Shall I yet again go out to battle against
the children of my brother Benjamin,

or shall I cease?' And the Lord said,
'Go up, for tomorrow I will
Deliver them Into your hand.' "
Judges 20:26-28

I cannot help but wonder if this is from where the adage, *"If at first you don't succeed, try, try again!"* originates. Maybe not, but this account certainly says a couple of things to us:

1) When we have heard the voice of God about a matter (or know His will by some other means), we should not dismiss what we *know* to be His will just because it didn't work out like we expected the first or second time we tried it.

2) Knowing, hearing and following the voice of God is not always immediately accompanied by the success we seek. Sometimes the success we seek comes after setbacks, disappointments and unyielding trust in God.

Hearing from God and following His voice doesn't guarantee we will avoid trouble. Sometimes His voice leads us to trouble on the way to victory; and sometimes He leads us to victory without the involvement of His voice.

Sometimes we don't have to seek God's will; sometimes His will seeks us. In doing so He *causes* us to know what He would have us do. However, even in His response to our efforts to hear or to know His will about a decision, sometimes God speaks to us, sometimes He inspires us, and sometimes He just leads and guides us without us feeling inspired by Him, and without Him saying anything at all.

"Then Jesus was led up by the Spirit into the
wilderness to be tempted by the devil."
Matthew 4:1

The Father didn't speak and tell Jesus to go into the wilderness; neither does the verse say the Heavenly Father inspired

His Son to go. By the Holy Spirit the Father simply *led* His Son to where He wanted Him.

There is a difference between God leading us and Him inspiring us. When He inspires us (though He doesn't literally speak to us), He allows us to *sense* what it is He wants us to do. Still, we are required to actually do what He wants us to do. But when He leads us, we don't necessarily feel, or hear anything. Inexplicably, we just find ourselves doing what He wants us to do!

This isn't to say that we cannot make mistakes by not knowing the will of God because we can. However, even *if* the mistakes we make in not knowing the will of God lead to trouble, God will use that trouble to accomplish His purpose in our lives. A believer's purpose in the kingdom of God cannot be fulfilled with complete effectiveness without the role *trouble* plays. Trouble has a purpose in fulfilling purpose, and it helps the believer to be even more effective in their operation of purpose.

Not every mistake means we have missed the will, or the voice of God. Sometimes it means God hasn't spoken. And sometimes the trouble we encounter that we *think* is the result of a mistake is *not* the result of a mistake at all. Not every perceived misstep on earth is considered a mistake in Heaven. Just as the Holy Spirit *led* Jesus into the wilderness where He was *tempted* by the devil, the Holy Spirit sometimes leads us to places where we are *troubled.*

Consider this passage:

"The steps of a good man are ordered by the Lord...."
Psalm 37:23

Let me pause to say that this verse doesn't necessarily mean God gives us verbal orders on what steps to take. If that were the case, it simply would have said "*A good man is ordered by the Lord.*" The wording of the verse is saying that God orders our steps without revealing to our mind where He has ordered our steps to go. In other words, He sometimes leads or guides us to do certain things without actually speaking and literally telling us to do those things. And at times God is leading and guiding us through the routine doings of life, and we have no idea He is ordering our steps and orchestrating His plans for us.

For example, Joseph's fateful encounter that led to him being sold into slavery occurred because he obeyed his father Jacob and went to Shechem to check on his brothers. From Shechem "**a certain man found him**" and told him he could find his brothers in Dothan. So Joseph went to Dothan, found his brothers, and he also found himself in a pit a short time later! *(Crummy brothers!)* Joseph ended up in Dothan not because God spoke to him and told him to go there, neither because he was inspired directly by God to go there. He found himself where God wanted him to be simply by doing what he always did—obeying his dad. Joseph ended up in the place where God launched His plan for Joseph's life and he wasn't even aware that God wanted him in Dothan, or that God's plan was being carried out in him being there.

The point is that God often orders our steps without our mind having any idea of what's going on. Because this is the case, we should rest assured that we cannot miss out on the plan of God for our life while we're living for Him, because He is at work fulfilling His will for our life. Sometimes He tells us what to do, making us aware of His movement; sometimes He does not. And sometimes, His orders lead to trouble. Notice what the passage in Psalm 37 goes on to say:

"The steps of a good man are ordered by the
Lord, and He [the Lord] delights in his way
[the steps taken by the good man].
Though he [the good man] fall, he
shall not be utterly cast down;
for the Lord upholds him with His hand."
Psalm 37:23, 24

Understand that the *good man,* whose steps were *caused by* God when they were *commanded by* God, led to his *falling,* or him finding trouble. It seems odd, but the Bible says that the Lord *delighted* in the way the man went—even *though he fell* and found trouble. The Lord did not delight in the fall itself but in what He knew would be accomplished in the fall, by the fall, and after the fall—the fall the Lord led the *good man* to.

Every Christian should take note of at least four points from this passage as it pertains to *hearing from God:*

1) The Lord leads and inspires some of the decisions we make and the roads we take without verbally instructing us to make or take them.

2) Those roads and decisions sometimes lead to trouble.

3) That trouble is not a mistake because God does not make mistakes. He was the One Who led us down that road (or to that decision), and He purposes to use wherever it led to help and bless us.

4) As troublesome as those places can be, God *delights* in them because He knows they will eventually bring delight to us.

Sometimes the Lord verbally instructs us, but He also inspires us to do His will without speaking to us. When we consider the existence of the Holy Scriptures, this should not come as a surprise to us. There are portions of the books in the Bible where the Lord literally told the author what to write. However, there are other places where the Lord inspired what they wrote without telling them what to write. It works the same way with us in life; we simply must come to trust this about God.

Not every perceived misstep is actually a mistake.

What I find interesting is that nowhere throughout the story of Joseph, from Genesis chapter 37 through Genesis chapter 50, can God be found saying anything to Joseph or of Joseph having heard anything from the Lord. However, we do find the fingerprints of God greatly upon the life of Joseph—especially during his time of trouble. We also find the following statements:

- **"...the Lord was with Joseph...."**
- **"...the Lord made all he did to prosper...."**
- **"...the Lord was with Joseph, and showed him mercy, and gave him favor...."**
- **"...God sent me...."**
- **"...God has made me lord of all Egypt...."**
- **"...God has given me...."**

But not a single reference to God saying or speaking anything directly to Joseph can be found. Still, Joseph arrived at the place God had shown him years earlier in a dream, trouble notwithstanding. That trouble was *not* encountered as a result of not hearing from God; rather, that trouble was a part of God's preparation process in readying Joseph for purpose.

It would be easy to wonder why God did not give Joseph a heads-up on Potiphar's wife so he could have avoided jail. Surely God knew what she was up to, and what she would do when she didn't get her way. It would have been easy for Joseph to think that he missed hearing from God about her, as well as his hateful brothers. But we know he didn't *miss* anything because God didn't *say* anything about either situation. Why wouldn't God speak to him about them and the trouble they were planning to cause him? It's simple! It was because God had plans of His own. He had plans to use their actions that led to Joseph's trouble, for Joseph's good! If the Lord had told Joseph of his brother's plot, and the mental problems of Potiphar's wife, he may have avoided the trouble, but he also would have also avoided the wonderful plan of God for his future. God doesn't always warn us when we're headed for trouble because the trouble for which we are headed, plays a key role in the destiny He has planned.

I touch on this subject in hopes of helping you avoid the self-inflicted emotional trauma that can accompany thinking you have missed hearing God, are not in His will, or believing that something is wrong with your relationship with Him just because you are not *hearing from Him*. Be encouraged! When God has something to say to us, He is not hindered by anyone or anything when it comes to making certain that we *hear* His voice. Neither is He hindered in making certain that, as we live whole-heartedly for Him, we are going to end up living out His great desire for our life!

I cannot recall reading anywhere in the Bible where God spoke to someone, and that person *missed Him* and consequently found himself in trouble. However, I know of plenty of places in God's Word where people found themselves in trouble because they *did hear* God and simply refused to obey Him.

But, if you have a heart for God and are truly living to please Him, don't be concerned about not hearing from Him, or missing Him. God is not always speaking His will to us in an audible fashion. When He does, He knows how to cause us to hear Him. And even when He isn't speaking to us and telling us what to do, He is inspiring, leading and guiding us to do His will. Even when we can't see how, or know that He's working, He is using other people, and the routine, mundane things of life to order our steps to the place where He will meet us and carry out His good, acceptable and perfect plan for our life!

"I will instruct you and teach you
In the way you should go;
I will guide you with My eye."
Psalm 32:8

Chapter 15
This Is Only a Test

"But He knows the way that I take,
when He has tested me,
I shall come forth as gold."
Job 23:10

This is one of my favorite verses in the entire Bible as it pertains to the difficulty of days and their eventual end. At some point during his time with trouble Job somehow realized that his season of suffering would not last always; and that it was only a test.

One of the good things about "tests" is that, though they are purposeful, they are *not* purposed to last forever. A good example of this is a test that a student takes in school; they are not designed to last longer than the school week, or to outlive the school year. The test is only designed to be a meaningful fraction of much longer periods of time. It is the same with us as Christians and the tests of life we face, in that they are only intended to occupy a fraction, or a portion, or a season of our life, and not our entire life.

Job came to understand that and out of his understanding he declared that his trouble—as difficult as it was—was only a test and would not span the remainder of his life. In the same way, the trouble we encounter as Christians is *only a test.* I don't say "only" to minimize or to make light of the difficulty of our troublesome times. I say it to impart understanding of three points made evident in the life of Job:

1) We will not forever experience what we are currently experiencing.

2) Our life will be better when our trouble is over.

3) Our trouble is not a sign that God doesn't love us, or that He is against us, or that something is seriously wrong with our relationship with Him—all of which we are capable of thinking with the aid of our enemy.

Although trouble could signify a problem in our relationship with God, it does not *automatically* mean something is wrong with our relationship with God. Our trouble is only a test—a test that is not without the purpose proving.

"In this you greatly rejoice though now,
for a little while, if need be, you have been
grieved by various trials [tests],that the
genuineness of your faith, being much more
precious than gold that perishes, though
it is tested by fire, may be found to praise honor,
and glory at the revelation of Jesus Christ."
1 Peter 1:6, 7

In this verse, the apostle Peter shares what may be the main and most important purpose of tests—to *prove* "**the genuineness of our faith**." This is the most important purpose because only *genuine faith* is *saving faith*—the faith we want to be *found* in possession when Jesus comes, or when we go.

There are other purposes for the tests we encounter, and those purposes will also be looked at later in this chapter, but beforehand understand that tests are common occurrences in the life of the child of God. They always have been and they always will be. Throughout the Bible we find the footprints of testing in the lives of those who faithfully followed God. And sooner or later—if not sooner *and* later—*every* Christian will undergo testing under the watchful eye of the Master Teacher. This is why Peter also wrote:

Beloved, do not think it strange concerning the fiery trial which is to try you, as though Some strange things happened to you;
1 Peter 4:12

In this verse Peter speaks of the commonality of tests when he says, "...**think it not strange....**" The apostle was saying to the people that what they were experiencing was not foreign to the life of all those who were followers of God. Undoubtedly Peter had in mind his own times of testing and that of other disciples as well as those about which he had read in the Old Testament Scriptures.

"Now it came to pass after these things that God tested Abraham...."
Genesis 22:1

"He sent a man before them—Joseph— who was sold as a slave... The Word of the Lord tested him."
Psalm 105:17, 19

"...God withdrew from Hezekiah, in order to test him, that He might know all that was in his heart."
2 Chronicles 32:31

"Then Jesus lifted up His eyes, and seeing a great multitude coming toward Him, He said to Philip, 'Where shall we buy bread, that these may eat?' But this He said to test him, for He Himself knew what He would do."
John 6:5, 6

The Lord also tested the Israelites a number of times after bringing them out of bondage to the Egyptians. The reason for their many tests will be addressed later, but I could not keep from wondering if their repeated testing was *retesting* because they kept failing the tests God gave them.

Peter was also inspired to write, "**Beloved, do not think it strange concerning the fiery trial which is to try you…**" because the Scriptures tell us that God tests us.

**"I know also, my God, that You test the heart
And have pleasure in uprightness."
1 Chronicles 29:17**

**"The refining pot is for silver
and the furnace for gold,
but the Lord tests the hearts."
Proverbs 17:3**

**"I, the Lord, search the heart, I test the mind,
even to give every man according to his ways,
according to the fruit of his doings."
Jeremiah 17:10**

**"You have tested my heart; You have
visited me in the night; You have tried me
and have found nothing; I have purposed
that my mouth shall not transgress."
Psalm 17:3**

**"But as we have been approved by God to be
entrusted with the gospel, even so we speak,
not as pleasing men, but God
Who tests our hearts."
1 Thessalonians 2:4**

Peter tells the Christian several times not to be surprised by tests because tests (of different types) are an ordinary part of life for the child of God. A Christian thinking a test to be strange is equivalent to a student thinking a test to be a strange thing.

What you are going through is what thousands of others like you have gone through and have been going through for many millenniums. Tests have always been a part of the child of God's relationship with Him, and they always will be—but that is not bad considering what testing accomplishes.

"Beloved, do not think it strange concerning the fiery trial which is to try you, as though some strange things happened to you; but rejoice to the extent that you partake of Christ's sufferings, that when His glory is revealed, you may also be glad with exceeding joy."
1 Peter 4:12, 13

Along with reminding us of the common occurrence of tests for Christians, Peter tells us to **"rejoice."** I know what you're thinking because I have thought it also: "*How in the world am I supposed to 'rejoice' when so much has and is going wrong?!*" Believe me, I understand. But we are not to rejoice in or over what hasn't gone right but in what is forthcoming *after* the time of testing. Peter talks about **"the fiery trial,"** and then he says, **"rejoice"** so that "**when His glory is revealed, you may also be glad with exceeding joy.**" The word **"when,"** in this context is a reference to a future time after the test is over. When we recognize that our troubles won't always last and our times of testing will end having produced something pleasurable, it's easier to rejoice. It is easier to rejoice also if we understand that the best of God for our life exists on the other side of our troublesome times. In all of the good Abraham, Joseph, David, and others experienced from God *before* their time of trouble, none of that "good" was as good as the good that was to come after their adversity came to an end. In addition to all we have identified trouble as being, trouble is also a sign that the *best* of God for our life has yet to come!

Peter wasn't the only New Testament writer to understand and encourage rejoicing over testing—James does as well.

"My brethren, count it all joy when you fall into various trials, knowing that the testing of your faith produces patience. But let patience have its perfect work, that you may be perfect and complete, lacking nothing." James 1:2, 3

James says there is something the Christian should *know* about being tested. He says we should be joyful over trials, *knowing* that they *produce patience.* Patience works to produce mature, fulfilled Christians who are ultimately **"lacking nothing."** The future things that are being accomplished for us *through* our times of testing are good reasons to rejoice *when* we're being tested. We don't have to like the test in order to trustfully rejoice over what it is producing.

I didn't like the cod liver oil my mother used to make me take growing up. And although I didn't know to rejoice, I trusted that going through the trouble of tasting it would bring about something that was in my best interest. And it always did.

My point is that with the testing of the Lord, we can and should rejoice because through His Word He allows us to know from the beginning that at the end of the test, something wonderful will be produced. Peter and James understood this end result, and this knowledge compelled Job to declare, **"When He has tested me I shall come forth as gold."**

In the same way that school teachers never test students without first teaching them on the material to be tested, the Lord never allows our testing without first giving us the answers and having deposited into us what we need to pass the test.

Teachers test students to detect how much of what has been taught has actually been learned or retained. It is different with the testing of God. The Lord does not test us so that *He* can know what's in us; He already knows because He placed it there. God is completely aware of our previous intellectual intake, therefore He doesn't test us to learn something about us. Instead, the Lord tests us for two major reasons:

1) His desire is to reveal to *us* what's in us.

2) He desires to provide us with an opportunity for spiritual promotion and/or advancement in His kingdom.

Consider again the prophetic words of Job:

"...When He has tested me,
I shall come forth as gold."
Job 23:10

Although Job received some gold after at the conclusion of the test, (Job 42:11) when he said, "I shall come forth as gold," he was saying that he would come out of his time of trouble possessing that which was more spiritually valuable than what he had possessed prior to trouble's testing.

One may ask, "*How can we know this is so when the story of Job ends right after he comes out of trouble?*" Great question! We know that Job increased spiritually and in spiritual value because God is *still* using his story to bless untold millions today! God only blesses the lives of so many others with the life of a person who has increased in spiritual value by passing the test of troublesome times. This is why God allows trouble, and this is why it is important for us to weather the storm of suffering. God wants to use us to touch others with *our life*, and that is exactly what He does when we pass the test and *come forth as gold*!

God knew what was in Job when He allowed Satan to attack him. The devil's attack was a test—a test the Lord knew Job could pass, and *would* pass! The Lord allows the testing of His children not because He thinks or knows we will fail, but because He knows He has placed within us the ability to pass. The Lord *only* allows us to be tested with what we can pass, harassed by what we can withstand, or attacked by that which we are more than capable of overcoming. And when we pass the test, withstand the harassment and overcome trouble's assault, we are rewarded with spiritual increase, spoils of war and other awards and prizes for test passing.

Trouble is a sign that the *best* of God for our life has yet to come!

I apologize if it appears as if I am making a mockery of the matter or seemingly equating it to a visit to the carnival. That most certainly is not my aim. It is simply a statement of fact that there are blessings we receive after passing the test of trouble that we would not receive otherwise.

As evidence of this certainty, let's consider the fact that God not only gave Job more children, but He also gave him *double* the substance he had lost during his season of setback. These blessings came *after* Job passed the test. Take also into account what can be seen with Daniel and the three Hebrew boys after they passed the test of trouble:

"Then the king promoted Shadrach, Meshach, and Abed-nego…."
Daniel 3:30

"So this Daniel prospered…."
Daniel 6:28

The two points are made in the lives of these four friends; these points also apply to you and me:

1) God knew it was in them to pass the test of trouble that confronted them.

2) They were rewarded after passing the test by staying on track.

It should not be a surprise that God rewards the passing of tests because the world rewards the passing of tests with academic and career advancement, as well as with the promotions and increase in pay that accompany such advancements. In fact, the world adopted this way of operation from the kingdom of God. This is one of the realities that falls beneath the umbrella of, **"...Your will be done on earth as it is in heaven." (Matthew 6:10)** In this verse, "earth" represents "the world", or society, and "heaven" represents the "kingdom of God", or sphere in which He operates. The idea of rewarding the passing of tests originated with God and has been embraced by the world. Before rewarding the passing tests became the practice of society, it was a principle of God's kingdom here on the Earth. We know this because we see it in His Word long before its performance in the world.

Therefore, neither the suggestion nor the expectation of being rewarded for staying on track and passing the test of trouble should be thought of as offensive or off-base. The idea as well as the expectation of such provides both hope and incentive hope and incentive that aid us immensely in overcoming the test and coming forth *as* gold, and maybe even *with* some gold!

The Lord allows us to be tested because He knows He has placed within us the ability to *pass* whatever the test is.

Again, sometimes God permits us to be tested because it reveals to us where we are with Him. Some tests reveal that we are not as trusting or committed to Him as we think. In response to the news from Jesus about His forthcoming arrest,

Peter was extremely confident in his commitment to Christ when he said,

"Even if all are made to stumble because of You, I will never be made to stumble...even if I have to die with You, I will not deny You!"
Matthew 26:33, 35

The arrest of Jesus was a test for His disciples—a test of the depth of their loyalty, a test that would reveal to Peter and to each of them that they were not as committed as they thought or wanted to be. By no means is this comment intended to be a criticism; rather, it is an observation—an observation that can be made about most of us (if not all of us) concerning some area of our relationship with God. I have failed tests during troublesome times that I didn't believe I would fail before the testing came. In even considering being confronted with the idea of being tested in certain areas and failing my attitude was, "Me, fail *that* test? Please! There is no way that *I* would fail that test!" But like Peter and the rest of the disciples, when the time came to prove my confident commitment, I failed! In failing something was proven to me, about me—I wasn't completely who, or where I thought I was spiritually at that time.

Thank God that failing a test at one time does not mean that we must forever be held back, permanently disqualified from promotion. God retests! Although Peter and the other disciples failed the test when they fled and forsook Jesus at His arrest (Peter would probably want us to believe he ran because he didn't want to be arrested for cutting off Malchus' ear!), they all passed the retest on the day of Pentecost. Though they were in the midst of many of those who were responsible for the death of Jesus and were hostile toward the Gospel, Peter passed the retest by boldly declaring Jesus to be the Christ—without fear of the consequences. Consequently, *about 3,000 souls* received Jesus that day, and millions of others have been and will be receiving Him since that day—not because they passed the initial test, but because they passed the *retest*!

Failing a test at one time does not mean that we will be permanently disqualified from promotion.

Sometimes tests reveal that we are not as strong as we think, or would like to be; but sometimes tests reveal that we are stronger than we thought we were. The testing of Job revealed he was stronger spiritually and more committed to God than he knew he was. Shortly after his trouble began, Job said,

"The thing I greatly feared has come upon me,
And what I dreaded has happened to me.
I am not at ease, nor am I quiet;
I have no rest, for trouble come."
Job 3:25, 26

I cannot help but believe that Job was not only fearful of what ultimately took place, but that he was also fearful how he would respond to such tragedy, and what it would mean to his relationship with God. When we consider what Job's testing apparently did to his wife's relationship with God, thinking Job feared the same result is reasonable.

Job's decision to hang in there with God despite all the Lord had allowed to take place in his life was a surprise to everyone except God because He knew what was in Job. By the twenty-third chapter, Job also knew what was in him and that he was stronger and more committed to God than even he thought he would be under the circumstances. The fact that Job decided at some point to persevere and pass the test of trouble is made known in his comments, **"My foot has held fast to His steps; I have kept His way and not turned**

aside. I have not departed from the commandments of His lips; I have treasured the Words of His mouth more than my necessary food." (Job 23:11, 12) These are comments of a child of God who is committed to sticking with God through thick and thin. Job getting to the point of realizing what was in him also explains the confidence of his comment, **"When He has tested me, I shall come forth as gold!"**

I love this verse for a number of reasons. I love it because it reflects Job's confidence that God would not leave him in those circumstances but would bring forth a better, new and improved Job. I also love it because of *when* it is rendered—right smack-dab in the middle of Job's season of testing! Even though he was in trouble, Job was not in doubt of the fact that God would deliver him and bless him! In fact, it was this belief that caused God's man to make such a bold confession.

In quoting Psalm 116:10, the apostle Paul stated, **"'I believed and therefore I spoke, we also believe and therefore speak" (2 Corinthians 4:13).** While this saying was put into words by the psalmist, and later by the apostle Paul, it was put into practice by Job long before the psalmist or Paul even lived. *In the middle* of his time of testing by trouble, Job **"spoke"** that he would **"come forth as gold"** because he **"believed"** he would **"come forth as gold."** Jesus says in Matthew 12:34, **"...out of the abundance of the heart the mouth speaks."** Despite the trouble in his life, *in his heart* Job abundantly believed his trouble would not last always and *when* (not *if*) it was over, he would be a better servant, and he would be in a better situation.

Troublesome times test us and reveal through our mouth what is *really* in our heart about our God and His faithfulness to us. Our words, especially during times of difficulty, are extremely important so we should be careful of what we say. Like Job we should make confessions out of our confidence in God, and guard against complaining because of the crisis. Our words do indeed make a difference—they make a difference in whether or not we pass the test and possess the prize of the promises of God, or *how long* it will take to do so.

For good reason, **Proverbs 18:21** is one of the most popular verses in the Bible when it comes to speaking about the importance of our words and what we confess. However, the verse that precedes this verse also helps to make our point.

"A man's stomach shall be satisfied
from the fruit of his mouth;
from the produce of his
lips he shall be filled."
Proverbs 18:20

The terms "**fruit of his mouth**" and "**produce of his lips**" are speaking of a person's words. But the word "**stomach**" is symbolic of one's being (or his life); while the expression, "**be satisfied**" means "to be filled." A person's life will be filled with the words of his mouth or with what his lips *produce.* Verse 21 supports and further spells out this truth as it goes on to say:

"Death and life are in the power of the tongue,
and those who love it will eat its fruit."
Proverbs 18:21

The "fruit" of our tongue—our words—play a crucial role in the quality of our life, in the outcome of our times of trouble, and in the length of our times of trouble. Consider this: "**death and life are in the <u>power</u> of the tongue (our words)"** meaning that our words are able to give life or bring death. When it comes to our time of trouble, there are two examples of this truth that we can follow and experience the outcome thereof or, "eat its fruit."

One example is that of the children of Israel after they had been led from bondage in Egypt and purposed for the abundant life in the Promised Land of Canaan.

"Then the whole congregation of the children of Israel complained against Moses and Aaron in the wilderness. And the children of Israel said to them, 'Oh, that we had died by the hand of the Lord in the land of Egypt, when we sat by the pots of meat and when we ate bread to the full! For you have brought us out in this wilderness to kill this whole assembly with hunger.' then the Lord said to Moses, 'Behold, I will rain bread from heaven for you. And the people shall go out and gather a certain amount every day...' "
Exodus 16:2-4

Herein is an example of the children of God having been saved by God, having a promise from Him of a better quality of life, and being prepared for this better quality of life by a time of trouble. Instead of trusting God and confidently confessing things that were consistent with what He had promised, they complained. They complained about the present problems as if they had no future promises. When we complain, we are praising our problems instead of placing our trust in the promises of God.

One of the notable, interesting aspects about the above referenced passage is that God responded to their complaint and fed them sustaining bread in the wilderness, but *because* of their complaining they never enjoyed milk and honey in the land of Canaan. We must be careful not to confuse God's provision in complaining as His acceptance of complaining. Complaining is *always* accompanied by negative consequences—even if we don't realize them or know what they are. Complaining deprived the children of Israel of God's good desire for them. It also caused them to wander in the wilderness for 40 years—never making it into the place that

God had already planned, prepared and appointed for them to be pleasured by.

We must be careful not to confuse God's provision in complaining as His acceptance of complaining.

The *power* of their tongue worked against them to prolong their time in the place of trouble and testing because complaining also has a *trapping* affect. Remember, *traps* impede progress, and keep us from going forward.

"The wicked is ensnared [trapped])
by the transgression of his lips,
but the righteous will come
through trouble."
Proverbs 12:13

The opposite of being **ensnared** or *trapped* is "**coming through"** or "being able to go forward." When our lips sin by complaining, we are kept from the progressing in the predetermined time frame of God. In many cases complaining will cause people to *never* come out of the wilderness and experience the promised land the Lord has planned for them. Consider the previous *words* of Israel's complaint and their ultimate outcome:

"Then they said to Moses, 'Because there
were no graves in Egypt, have you taken us
away to die in the wilderness? Why have
you so dealt with us, to bring us up out of Egypt?
Is this not the word that we told
you in Egypt, saying, "Let us alone that
we may serve the Egyptians?"For it would
Have been better for us to serve the Egyptians
than that we should die in the wilderness.' "
Exodus 14:11, 12

"And the Lord spoke to Moses and Aaron, saying, 27 'How long shall I bear with this evil congregation who complain against Me? I have heard the complaints which the children of Israel make against Me. 28 Say to them, "As I live," says the Lord, "as you have spoken in my hearing, so will I do to you: 29 the carcasses of you who have complained against Me shall fall in this wilderness, all of you who were numbered, according to your entire number, from twenty years old and above. 30 Except for Caleb the son Jephunneh and Joshua the son of Nun, you shall by no means enter the land which I swore I would make you dwell in.' "
Numbers 14:26-30

Despite having an assurance of God bringing them out of their time of trouble in the wilderness and taking them into the Promised Land, the complaining words of the children of Israel ultimately gave birth to their future—but not the future the Lord had in store for them. Their complaining allowed their season of trouble to live longer than God had planned because their negative words *fed* and provided *power* for their negative circumstances to have longer life.

Remember, our words—be they negative or positive—are empowered to give life. Complaining and negative words give life, or longer life to negatives, while confessing the Word and promises of God will not allow seasons of trouble to live on beyond their purpose. Positive words or life-giving words will instead steady us in trouble and bring us *through* trouble and into the places of promise.

Their complaining not only allowed the wilderness to exist longer than necessary, it was also the reason God gave for their dying in the wilderness and not making it to the Promised Land.

Notice that in their complaining, on different occasions they said, **"For you have brought us out in this <u>wilderness</u> <u>to kill</u> this whole assembly with hunger…Because there were no graves in Egypt, have you taken us away to <u>die in</u> <u>the wilderness</u>…it would have been better for us to serve the Egyptians than that we should <u>die in the wilderness</u>."**

"Dying in the wilderness" was nowhere in the plan, promises or Word of God for them; that idea was *given life* to by the **power of their own tongues** through complaining. In Numbers 14:29 when God said, **"The carcasses of you who have <u>complained</u> shall fall [die] in this wilderness,"** He was simply saying that they would eat the *produce* their lips produced.

"For the Lord had said of them,
'They shall surely die in the wilderness.' "
Numbers 26:65

The adverb "surely" meant they would *definitely* partake of their own complaining—the fruit of their own mouth. It wasn't God's will; it was their *words* that prolonged their stay in the wilderness. And it was their continual complaining that eventually put to death for them the promises that waited outside of the wilderness.

The children of Israel's complaining spanned approximately 39 years—from 1462 BC (the year they were delivered out of Egypt) until 1423 BC (the year Joshua, Caleb and the younger generation entered the Promised Land).

Question: Who complains 40 years??
Answer: People who spend most of their life in the wilderness and never make it through the time of testing and into the Promised Land.

When we complain, we are praising our problems instead of placing our trust in the promises of God.

Another more positive example of eating or living in the fruit our lips, and words produce, is taken from that same group of people, the Israelites. Unlike most of the children of Israel, Joshua and Caleb would exit the wilderness and enter the Promised Land because instead of complaining about the conditions of the wilderness that was testing them and preparing them for purpose, they were confidently confessing the promise God had made to them and His power to bring it to pass.

"Then Caleb quieted the people before Moses, and said, 'Let us go up at once and take possession, for we are well able to overcome it.' "
Numbers 13:30

"Joshua the son of Nun and Caleb the son of Jephunneh ...spoke to all the congregation of the children of Israel, saying, 'The land we passed through to spy out is an exceedingly good land. If the Lord delights in us, then He will bring us into this land and give it to us, a land which flows with milk and honey.'"
Numbers 14:6-8

Joshua and Caleb ate from the fruit of Canaan because of the fruit of their lips. Having the same promise from the same God, and faced with the same time of trouble as those who died in the wilderness, Joshua and Caleb were able to leave the place of testing and live in the place of promise. They were able to do so because their words helped put their trouble to death, and gave life to the good God had long ago planned for them.

Such was also the case with our difficulty-enduring hero, Job. Although he went through some rough patches early on in his time of trouble, Job rebounded and began to speak differently about his future and his belief in what God was doing. He believed the Lord was testing his loyalty, and he also believed that when he had passed the test he would "**come forth as gold**." It was as if Job quieted his spirit from the chaos of the trouble, and realized his trouble was only a test.

Troublesome times test us and reveal through our mouth what is in our heart about our God and His faithfulness to us.

The Lord allows us to be tested to reveal where we *really* are with Him and what's *really* in us. Some of us know where we are and what's in us even before trouble comes. The arrival of trouble merely presents an opportunity to demonstrate our character and commitment to Christ. We sometimes *think* we know what's in us only to be proven mistaken when trouble comes. What is *truly* in us isn't revealed when all is well, it's revealed when the weather of life is not so fair.

Like Job, sometimes we don't become conscious of what's in us *until after* troubles comes and we have taken its best shot and are still standing. A little wobbly for the wear but we're weathering the storm and sticking with the Lord because we know passing the test will produce something precious, and spiritually priceless!

Passing the test of trouble also rewards us with the realization that we are stronger and more committed to God than we imagined.

One thing that is required in the passing of *every* test is having learned about the test subject. It is impossible to pass a test of any sort without first having learned some things about the area of testing. The Lord never allows us to be tested without *first* teaching us on the subject, or making it an *open book (Bible) test.*

It is important to understand that, though connected, there is a difference between *teaching* and *learning. Teaching* is "the providing of information" but *learning* is "the comprehension and retention of that information." Teaching requires a teacher to provide information, while learning requires the student to retain the information provided. If students are to benefit from what teachers teach, they must not only retain the information, they must also apply it at the appropriate time. In other words, the student must also put the information into operation!

It is possible for two students to sit beneath the exact same *teacher* and receive the exact same *teaching,* and yet only one of them *learn* and enjoy the fruits of learning. This *two student* analogy can be seen with the children of Israel versus Joshua and Caleb. They both had the same Teacher, and both were taught the same things. However, only Joshua and Caleb actually learned, applied what they learned toward passing the test of trouble, and were rewarded with the promise.

There are a number of good Bible teachers in churches all around the world. But they are only of good value to good learners—people who will consistently put into practice the things that are taught by living by them. When the test of trouble comes, it's not what we have been *taught* that will determine whether or not we receive a passing grade; it's what we have *learned* that will make that determination.

Passing the test of trouble
not only *proves* something,
it also *produces* something.

There are lessons to learn that prepare us *for* times of trouble, lessons to learn *from* our times of trouble, and there are also some important things to learn that will be helpful *during* our times of trouble. In previous chapters I wrote about the helpfulness of prayer, praise, the Word of God, and church attendance. But there is something else the apostle Paul learned to be helpful to him during his troublesome time of testing—something that will be tremendously helpful to *any* Christian who is going through their own troublesome time of testing. In Philippians 4:11 Paul wrote, ***"I have learned in whatever state I am in therewith to be content…."***

While penning this epistle to the church in Philippi from prison, Paul said he had *learned* how to be *content* during his time of trouble. Such a lesson must have served Paul well when we consider the fact that he was encouraging contentment even while he was in a time of trouble.

(To further make a point on an earlier point about the work God does in us and through us even if we are in a season when it appears we are not making progress, rational thinking would consider Paul's time of imprisonment such a season for him. However, with this letter to the church at Philippi, as well as letters to the church at Ephesus and Colosse, and a personal letter to his friend Philemon, we see that the Lord did a great work in Paul while he was incarcerated and could not go forth. If Paul had not been imprisoned and experienced a season of seeming stagnation, it is very likely that these letters, [which were a blessing to

the intended recipients and millions of others like you and I who were unintended recipients} would have never been written. But even in a time of literal imprisonment God was doing something great! Such is the case with us in the stand-still season of circumstantial stagnation—God is doing a great work; we just don't know it yet!)

Although the apostle Paul had no idea his letters would be used by God as a part of the Holy Scriptures, in his letter to the saints in Rome he wrote of learning from the Scriptures and the lives of those spelled out therein. I have previously referenced the following verse a few of times; but let's look again at a point I believe to be important.

"For whatever things were written before were written for our learning, that we through the patience and comfort of the Scriptures might have hope."
Romans 15:4

Just as Paul taught about learning from the lives of those in Scripture who preceded him, we can learn from the life of Paul who, like David, was no stranger to troublesome times. In his second letter to the church in Corinth, while making his case for the authenticity of his apostleship, his commitment to the cause of Christ and answering the claims of his critics, Paul lists the various difficulties he faced while traveling and sharing the gospel:

"Are they Hebrews? So am I. Are they Israelites?
So am I. Are they the seed of Abraham? So am I.
23 Are they ministers of Christ?—I speak as a fool—
I am more: in labors more abundant, in stripes above
measure, in prisons more frequently, in deaths often.
24 From the Jews five times I received forty stripes minus
one. Three times I was beaten with rods; once I was
stoned; 25 three times I was shipwrecked; a night
and a day I have been in the deep;

26 in journeys often, in perils of waters,
in perils of robbers, in perils of my own
countrymen, in perils of the Gentiles,
in perils in the city, in perils in the wilderness,
in perils in the sea, in perils
among false brethren; 27 in weariness
and toil, in sleeplessness often, in hunger and thirst,
in fastings often, in cold and nakedness—
28 besides the other things, what come upon
me daily: my deep concern for all the churches."
2 Corinthians 11:22-28

This catalog of Paul's trials allows us to know that trouble not only varies in source and type, it also varies in tenure. Paul had certainly experienced the gamut from mistreatment by so-called friends and foes, from beatings on land to boat wrecks at sea, from heartache to hardship, from being without food and water to being without clothes and shelter, and troubles that lasted from minutes to many years. But through it all, the apostle Paul says he *learned* how to be content.

As great, anointed, and knowledgeable of a teacher as the apostle Paul was, it was what he learned about contentment that may have helped him as much as anything else during his many times of trouble. Along with the importance of prayer, praise and patience, there is no more important lesson to learn while in trouble than that of *contentment.*

The idea of contentment in trouble can sound ridiculous because contentment suggests that we have to be satisfied with our time of trouble—without the expectation of different. And the last thing we are, or should be in trouble is *satisfied*! Contentment *in* trouble is different than being content *with* trouble. Contentment in trouble is the ability to limit ourselves in what we require and desire for the duration of the trouble, while maintaining an expectation of trouble's expiration. Contentment does *not* mean that we must hopelessly resign ourselves to not experiencing better days. Although the apostle Paul spoke of being content while in prison, surely he wanted to be free. His contentment didn't require him to be satisfied with prison to the point of not wanting the *better* of being free.

Contentment is an internal strength that does not require the external aid of all being well in order for us to be at peace. It is the state wherein we consider sufficient whatever we have no matter how slender it may be—realizing that the state is as temporary as it is slender. Contentment is the place that doesn't call for abundance or more than what we currently have in order to be emotionally healthy. Contentment does not mean we do not desire more; it means we can cheerfully make do without more until more comes. Contentment is also that which causes us to remain good with God—even if things don't change. Contentment is the mental muscle to be satisfied with *whatever* God supplies.

Contentment is one of the "weapons of our warfare" and a Christ-like characteristic. Discontentment must therefore be a weapon of the devil's warfare against us, and a trait of his character. We know this to be true because Lucifer was not content with who God created him to be—even though he was one of the highest ranking angels, unequalled in beauty or talent. And of course it was discontentment that led directly to his demotion as well as his eternal demise.

For the Christian, contentment is a tremendous ally during the testing of trouble because it aids us in the fight against frustration, stress, and worry. Contentment paves the way for peace. This is why in the same breath in Philippians 4:6 and 7, Paul was able to talk about *not being worried,* but being *thankful* and *peaceful.* This is also why Paul said, "**… godliness with contentment is great gain." (1 Timothy 6:6)**

In passing the testing of troublesome times, it is extremely helpful to learn as much as possible from the apostle Paul, including how to be content in our state of tribulation. The key to being content is being grateful. Regardless of the type of trouble we experience, there are yet things for which we have to be thankful.

*Dis*contentment distracts us from the good that exists in our life, and causes us to focus instead on what we don't have, or on all that is wrong. But when we consistently thank God for all that is good, thanksgiving will not only cause us to remain focused, it will also encourage us, create contentment within us, remind of God's goodness, restore our hope, and increase our peace. Outside of the Prince of Peace Himself, *nothing* is more valuable than inward peace during outward warfare. Priceless is the peace of God in the time of trouble! This is why the apostle Paul encouraged the Philippians to focus on the good things.

> **"Finally, brethren, whatever things are true, whatever things are noble, whatever things are just, whatever things are pure, whatever things are lovely, whatever things are of good report, if there is any virtue and if there is anything praiseworthy—think on these things. The things which you learned and received and heard and saw in me, these do, and the God of peace will be with you."**
> **Philippians 4:8, 9**

There is a *presence of God* that is *with us* when we *think, thank and praise* God for the wonderful things He has done for us, including placing helpful people in our life.

***Praise* and thanksgiving create peace and contentment.**

If you are struggling with being content (signified by impatience, complaining, envy, worry or a lack of peace), it will help you to make a list of the people, things and doings of God in your life for which you are grateful. And on a daily basis, make a practice of choosing a few of those things and begin to thank God, expressing *why* you are thankful for them.

Once our praise and thanksgiving to God has created contentment within us, that contentment will assist us in passing the test of troublesome times, and possessing the promotion that accompanies doing so. Your trouble is *only a test* and you have what it takes to pass—even if it requires retesting 15 or 20 times! For **He [God] knows the way that you take; and when He has tested you, you shall come forth as gold!**

Chapter 16
Trustful in Trouble

"Though He slay me, yet will I trust Him."
Job 13:15

The Hebrew word used for *trust* in this verse is a word that also means *"to be patient, hope, stay, and to wait."* In his assertion that he "would trust" God, Job was also vowing to stay connected with God, to be patient, and to continue to wait for his *change* to come. In fact, it is the exact same Hebrew word that is used for *wait* in 14:14 where Job says, **"...All the days of my hard service I will wait, till my change comes."**

In a previous chapter, I explained that the only time we wait is when there is an anticipation of an arrival. We don't wait for things we don't think are coming. Job was trusting, and he waited because he was anticipating the arrival of a new season wherein his troubles would become a memory of the past.

I also talked about the meaning of the word *hope,* and how Biblical *hope* is not a *wish* or a mere desire for something specific to take place. Instead, the Hebrews 11:1 *"hope"* that is used to help define faith is "confident expectation." Trust is therefore *confidence* in God. It is having a confidence that:

1) God has our best interest at heart.

2) God will exercise His sovereign power and authority on our behalf.

3) Whatever He allows, He will help us through, and He will use whatever has been allowed to fulfill His purpose, His good plans *for us*, and His great promises *to us*.

I realize that in times of trouble, trusting or continuing to trust God can be an extremely tall order—especially when we have trusted Him to keep things from getting to where they have gotten and when things haven't work out the way we hoped. If we were forced to express our sentiments about God not staving off our trouble, we would have to confess that it feels as if He has failed us by not doing what we asked of Him in prayer. It is difficult to trust anyone when we feel we have been failed by them, the Lord notwithstanding.

It can be *extremely* difficult to trust God when we feel He has failed us because we know He had the power to prevent our problems, but He didn't use that power on our behalf. Just as our best buddy standing by and watching us get beat up on Tuesday makes it tough to trust that he will help us in the rematch on Thursday, trusting God after He has allowed trouble to beat us up can also be tough to do.

For Job, at the writing of this verse, all that could have gone wrong *had* gone wrong. And it *went wrong after* He had come to expect and experience the goodness of the Lord. Job had been extremely blessed with a wonderful family, plenty of land and livestock, substance and good health. But as the story tells, he lost it all!

Maybe the greatest hurdle in trusting God again after feeling He has failed us is the fear of feeling disappointment again—the disappointment that always accompanies unfulfilled expectations. And the greater the expectation, the greater the frustration when our expectations are unfulfilled. It is the feeling of great frustration that fosters distrust. Frustration and distrust team together to dismantle our faith—seeking to keep us from accomplishing and possessing the things of God that are obtained by faith.

What impresses me and what impresses me enough to emulate, is Job's commitment to *yet* trusting God despite the tragedies that had taken place in his life. Possessing this kind of trust should be the target for every Christian. At some point, if not already, we will not only have to trust God *for the good*, we will also have to trust Him *through the bad.* The aim of every Believer should be to grow and get to the place where we find Job stating that he will continue to trust God beyond misfortune, heartbreak and disappointment. Even if God were to be responsible for the worse possible occurrence in his life—his death—Job had vowed to still trust in the Lord with all of his heart.

In Job expressing his commitment to trusting God even if God caused his death, he was also saying he would continue to trust God in everything short of his death—which would be every other happening in his life. This level of trust is a product of realizing that our life is *"not our own, we have been bought with a price"*, and the Purchaser is free to do with us as He pleases. And though we don't and won't always like the things the Purchaser permits, we continue to believe that what pleases Him will lead to that which pleasures us.

Job trusted God, but I don't believe he understood why God allowed what He allowed. In fact, I am certain that Job did not understand because he didn't even understand that what was happening to him wasn't the doing of God, though it was allowed by Him. We know Job didn't understand this fact because in Job 1:21 he mistakenly stated, **"The Lord gave, and <u>the Lord has taken away</u>."** In fairness to Job, you and I have the luxury of knowing *how* his troubles came about and *who* was responsible for them. We know it was *not* our Lord who took away Job's family or possessions during his time of trouble. Neither was it the Lord who caused Job's sickness. Job, however, was not aware of *how* his troubles came about, or *who* was responsible for them. But the point is, in even *thinking* that God was responsible, Job was *still* committed to trusting Him. And although Job did not understand why God would do such things, the integrity of God's past faithfulness caused Job *yet to* trust Him—even though the toughest of all troubles had found him.

Our aim as believers should be getting to the place in God where we continue to trust Him no matter the misfortune, heartbreak, disappointment or setback we suffer.

Job did not rely on understanding God before he committed himself to continuing to trust God or perhaps, even trusting God again—and neither must we. We must not base our trust in God on having an understanding of why He allowed what He allowed, or how what He allowed will work together for our good. Trust under such circumstances is not trust at all; it is *suspicion suspended. True* trust, on the other hand, is confidence in God to bring good out of a bad situation—even in the absence of understanding *why* He allowed the bad situation, or *how* He will make the bad situation *good.* If we must possess a pre-understanding of why God is doing what He is doing before we trust Him, we are walking by sight and not by faith—that is out of order and will lead to a broken belief.

Out of supernatural, God-given wisdom King Solomon wrote:

**"Trust in the Lord with all of your heart,
and lean not on your own understanding."
Proverbs 3:5**

"Our own understanding" does not always allow us to know how God will work out a situation. But as we continue to follow His Word, we are trusting that He *will* work out things somehow—probably in a way we cannot imagine, though we try. We must not wait until we understand how, when, or what God is going to do before we trust Him. Trust Him on the credit of His impeccable track record.

Don't wait until you understand God before you trust Him. Faith is trust that is absent of understanding!

Our trust in the Lord is revealed not only by the mental aspect of believing, it is also revealed by our faithful following of His Word—especially when following His Word would appear to be more harmful than helpful. However, when we demonstrate our trust in God by doing what He says, His hand begins to move on our behalf.

The Bible is full of stories wherein children of God demonstrated their trust in God by obeying His Word. In every story of trouble, the element of trust can be found. And in every episode when people trustfully followed God's Word, the God of the Word showed up miraculously on their behalf.

In the book of First Kings, chapter 17, during the time of famine (trouble), Elijah went to the Brook Cherith, and later to the city of Zarephath at the instruction of the Word of the Lord. He did so *trusting* that God was leading him to that which would help him. And God was. God exercised the power of His lordship over all of creation and commanded a bird to feed Elijah. *(I guarantee you that in trying to figure out how God would provide for him during the famine, using a bird never crossed Elijah's mind!)*

In the same chapter when the widow of Zarephath obeyed the Word of the Lord and fed Elijah with the last of her flour and oil, she did so *trusting* that God would still somehow provide for her and her son. And He did! He did so by exercising the power of His lordship over the matters of flour and oil, speaking to them and causing them to supernaturally replenish. And I am certain she had no idea how God would cause "**the bin of flour to not be used up**" or how "**the jar of oil would not run dry.**" Although she did not *understand,* she still trustfully obeyed. Her trustful obedience caused the Lord to move miraculously on her behalf. And He will do the same for you and me as we demonstrate our trust by following His Word.

A sign of true trust in God
is obeying Him,
without understanding Him.

Sometimes our faith in obeying God leads to trouble. I realize this statement doesn't sound so *good*, and therefore it probably doesn't inspire motivation to obey the Word of God. However, it is a true statement. But what is also true is that, when our trustful obedience leads us into trouble, the power of God moves mightily in such situations to deliver us and bless us. *(The only thing I love more than being delivered from trouble is being blessed on top of being delivered!)* Consider an abbreviated version of the following stories that each prove this point:

- In Genesis chapter twelve, Abram trustfully obeyed God's Word to leave his country, kindred and father's house, and it led him to a severe famine. But from there, it led him to a place where he left *very rich.*
- In Genesis chapter thirty-nine, Joseph trustfully obeyed God's Word and did not commit adultery with Potiphar's wife. The prize for his trustful obedience was prison! But prison was the place Pharaoh found him and ultimately made him second in command over all of Egypt.

- In Daniel chapter six, Daniel demonstrated his trust in God by refusing *not to* pray when praying had been made illegal for a period of time. For his trust he found himself in a den full of hungry lions. But shortly after he was delivered from the lions' den, the Bible says Daniel *prospered* for years to come.
- In Daniel chapter three, the three Hebrew boys trustfully obeyed the Word of God by not bowing down and worshiping King Nebuchadnezzar's false god. Their reward? A burning fiery furnace! But the end result of their trustful commitment to God's Word was deliverance and a promotion. In fact, the same king who ordered them cast into the furnace was forced to acknowledge the effect their trust had in the matter when he said, **"Blessed be the God of Shadrach, Meshach, and Abed-Nego Who sent His angel and delivered His servants who <u>trusted in Him</u>... then the king promoted Shadrach, Meshach and Abednego."**

In each of these situations, the principal characters were trustful *before* trouble because it takes trust in God to obey His Word. Even after their trust landed them in trouble, they remained trustful in God. The same trust that led them *into* trouble, led them *out of* trouble and into the blessings God had already planned and put in place for them. This was also the case with Job. His trustfulness in God led him to trouble. But even from the podium of trouble, Job declared, "...**though He slay me, yet will I trust Him."**

The trust that sometimes leads to trouble will always lead to blessings.

"How long, O Lord? Will You forget me forever? How long will You hide Your face from me? How long shall I take counsel in my soul, having sorrow in my heart daily? How long will my enemy be exalted over me? Consider and hear me, O Lord My God; Enlighten my eyes, lest I sleep the sleep of death; lest my enemy say, I have prevailed against Him"; lest those who trouble me rejoice when I am moved.
Psalm 13:1-4

"Awake! Why do You sleep, O Lord? Arise! Do not cast us off forever. Why do You hide Your face, and forget our affliction and our oppression? For our soul is bowed down to the dust; our body clings to the ground. Arise for our help, and redeem us for Your mercies' sake."
Psalm 44:24

Have you ever felt like this? I most certainly have! I have been in a season of trouble for so long I have wondered if I was a candidate for deliverance or if I had been completely abandoned by God. David obviously had similar feelings, and he seemingly had them on more than one occasion.

One of the things I admire about the Psalm 13 passage is having a short-lived glimpse of David's momentary frailty of faith in wondering if God had forgotten about him. If we were to be honest, we have also probably wondered the same at some point in our time of trouble. Also like David and I, you too have probably spent days with a sorrowful heart, wondering if things would *ever* get better.

Another thing I like about this passage is that right in the midst of David's wondering about whether or not the Lord had forgotten about him in his time of trouble, David's tone takes a turn. Even during the days of his unhappy heart, he begins talking about his *trust* in God. Listen to what he wrote in the following verses:

> "**But** [despite all that is going on and going wrong]
> **I have trusted in Your mercy; My heart shall**
> **rejoice in Your salvation. I will sing to the**
> **Lord because He has dealt bountifully with me. '**
> **But I have trusted in Your mercy;**
> **my heart shall rejoice in Your salvation.' "**
> **Psalm 13:5, 6**

Let me pause and share something I have noticed for the first time. What was written by David in Psalm 13 is extremely powerful! We know the Holy Spirit inspired the writing of the Holy Scriptures, but we see Him here spontaneously inspiring thoughts of encouragement and trust at the very moment David was deeply discouraged and feeling abandoned. David wasn't writing this from the standpoint of looking back into the past and recognizing what the Lord had done—like he had done in other Psalms. Psalm 13 was a spur-of-the moment, *"what-I-am-feeling-right-now"* writing from David. In the very moment that David was writing about feeling deserted by God, the Holy Spirit stepped in and reminded David of God's past goodness and reawakened his trust in God. David also wrote of that! Notice when he began writing, he opened with a gloomy "**How long, O Lord? Will you forget me forever?"** introduction. In a very short five verses later after the Spirit had inspired him, David was writing about singing to the Lord—**"Because He has dealt bountifully with me."** How awesome is that?!! Nothing had changed in his situation between verse one and verse six—only his heart had changed when the Holy Spirit reminded David of the trust factor.

This is exactly the same way the same Holy Spirit works in you and me! Right when we are feeling forsaken, boom! The Holy Spirit will bring something to our remembrance that will rejuvenate our trust in the God we serve! I love that attribute of the Holy Spirit!!

I have trusted in Your mercy;
My heart shall rejoice in Your salvation.
Psalm 13:5

The word *mercy* used in Psalm 13:5 means, "God's loyal love and faithfulness to care for His people", and *salvation* means, "help in the time of need or deliverance from a distressing dilemma." On the heels of questioning whether or not the Lord had forgotten about him, and during the days of his heavy heart, notice David's confidence in God. David begins to speak confidently when he seemingly emphatically states, "**My heart shall rejoice**"! The confidence exuded by David was a product of his trust in God. David was saved from his time of trouble because he trusted that God's mercy cared enough for him *to* deliver him, and that God's power over his circumstances *would* deliver him.

Trust is revealed in obeying God. Trust is also reflected in our words—which are products of what we *believe* about God's mercy and His power to deliver.

"When Jesus departed from there,
two blind men followed Him,
crying out and saying, 'Son of David,
have mercy on us!' And when He had come into the
house, the blind men came to
Him. And Jesus said to them, 'Do you believe that I am
able to do this?' They said to Him,
'Yes, Lord.' Then He touched their eyes, saying,
'According to your faith let it be
to you.' And their eyes were opened."
Matthew 9:27-30a

The blind men *trusted* that a merciful Jesus *wanted* them to be delivered and that His power *could* deliver them from what troubled them. Their trust prompted their pursuit of the

Lord and caused them to *believe* that He would deliver them, and He did!

There are a few interesting points about this story—none more noteworthy than the fact that neither of the blind men who received mercy from Jesus had a personal relationship with Him. This lack of relationship is made apparent by the term **"son of David,"** which they used to get His attention. The term **"son of David"** is used to describe a number of people in the Bible—from Absalom, Amnon and Solomon, the biological sons of David to Joseph the stepfather of Jesus. And while it was one of respect, it was somewhat of a general term—not one used to signify a close and intimate relationship as were the terms "Lord" or "Master."

The point is that, if Jesus honored the trust of the two blind men who *did not* have a personal relationship with Him at the point of their approach, how much more will He honor the trust of those of us who *do* have a personal relationship with Him? **"...shall not God avenge His own elect, who cry day and night unto Him, though He bears long with them?" (Luke 18:7)** Yes, He will!

"The Lord also will be a refuge for the oppressed, a refuge in the time of trouble. And those who know Your name will put their trust in You; for You, Lord, have not forsaken those who seek You."
Psalm 9:10

Until it leads to our deliverance, our trust plays other significant roles in the mean time—roles that are extremely important to our ability to hang in there and not become wearied and worried.

"You will keep him in perfect peace, whose mind is stayed on You, because he trusts in You."
Isaiah 26:3

There is a peace that is produced by our prayer and praise life. Then there is a *"perfect peace"* that is not predicated upon the positivity of circumstances, a peace that is produced by our trust in God—our unshakable confidence that He will deliver us and bring our troublesome season to a close.

"Those who trust in the Lord are like Mount Zion, which cannot be moved, but abides forever."
Psalm 125:1

Mount Zion was a huge, strategically located mountain that was used as a fortress and considered impenetrable. Although many armies lost battles and were removed from the mountain, the mountain itself was immovable. The Spirit-inspired psalmist says those of us who place our trust in the Lord will be like the mountain of Zion. Though we face battles, we will not be moved by the battles we face. Instead, our trust in our King will lead His people to victory!

"Trust in the Lord and do good; dwell in the land, and feed on His faithfulness. Delight yourself also in the Lord, and He shall give you the desires of your heart. Commit your way to the Lord, trust also in Him, and He shall bring it to pass."
Psalm 37:3-5

"Many sorrows shall be to the wicked; But he who trusts in the Lord, mercy shall surround him."
Psalm 32:10

Certainly, God does many things because He is a gracious God. Still, a great deal of what God does is based on what we trust and believe Him to do. He still moves by faith—which is trust and confidence in Him. If your faith, trust, belief, or confidence in God is waning or has completely disappeared, check your Word intake because "**faith comes by hearing, and hearing <u>from</u> the Word of God" (Romans 10:17).** It is vital to the strength and the existence of our trust that we have a daily ingestion of God's Word. Reading stories about God's mercy and trust will help us to trust in God's mercy.

A great deal of what God does is based on what we trust and believe Him to do.

" 'My God sent His angel and shut the lions' mouths, so that they have not hurt me, because I was found innocent before Him; and also, O king, I have done no wrong before you.' Now the king was exceedingly glad for him, and commanded that they should take Daniel up out of the den. So Daniel was taken up out of the den, and no injury whatever was found on him, <u>because he trusted in His God</u>."
Daniel 6:22, 23

We looked at Daniel's situation in one of the earlier chapters and said that though the Lord did not prevent the trouble of him being tossed into the lions' den, the Lord did not permit trouble to do what it was intended to do—which was to have Daniel eaten alive by a bunch of greedy lions! Daniel probably believed God to keep him out of the lions' den, but when God chose not to, Daniel did not desert his trust.

Psalm 62:8 says, **"Trust in Him at all times, you people...."** This would undoubtedly mean trusting God before *and after* trouble has come. This is important because trust provides a protection *from* trouble while we are yet *in* trouble. Daniel was in trouble while he was in the lions' den, but his trust kept him from the trouble of being in the lions' mouth!

Daniel's deliverance from trouble without trouble doing what it was purposed to do was tied to his trust, or his belief in God's loyal love and faithfulness to care for His people—even during the time of trouble. Although Daniel, like David, was in trouble; also like David, Daniel continued to believe God. Both David and Daniel escaped trouble's ultimate desire *because* they remained *trustful in trouble.*

Proverbs 3:5 also encourages us to *trust in the Lord with our heart*—not to *trust in our heart.* There are a number of problems with placing our trust in our heart. One such problem is that our heart is the author of *our own understanding.* Therefore, trusting in our heart will lead to us *leaning on our own understanding.* If our understanding was reliable and uninfluenced by the *sight* of things, that would be acceptable. However, because our heart is not only easily influenced by the natural appearance of things, it is also **"deceitful above all things, desperately wicked" (Jeremiah 17:9)**, and spiritually distrusting by nature—and this is on a good day!

Don't wait until you understand God before you trust Him. His integrity is deserving of our trust without our understanding.

Trouble often leads to some of the biggest blessings in life. After being blessed there is a tendency to think that the Lord could have brought the blessing and left the trouble behind. But there are things that take place in trouble that are instrumental to the arrival of the blessings.

In **Isaiah 55:8,9 the Lord says, "...My thoughts are not your thoughts, Nor are your ways, My ways...as the heavens are higher than the earth, so are My ways higher than your ways, and My thoughts than your thoughts."**

There are things that God *knows* and *ways* that He goes about accomplishing things that are different from how you and I see them, or would go about accomplishing them. For example, the humility created by times of extreme trouble is in part purposed to keep us grounded and humble when times of extreme blessings come. Though we may *think* we would be humble if God blessed us greatly without the trouble, we must understand that if God chooses to humble us before He blesses us it is because He *knows* humbling us will help us to handle the blessing—even if we don't *think* the humbling is necessary. His *thoughts are higher than our thoughts* simply means God knows more about us than we do. Of this truth David sang:

"O Lord, You have searched me and known me.
You know my sitting down and my rising up;
You understand my thought afar off.
You comprehend my path and my lying down;
And are acquainted with all my ways."
Psalm 139:1-3

Because the Lord knows us, we should trust Him in the trouble He allows, and be confident it will lead to blessings of some sort—without the blessings causing us to elevate the estimation of ourselves.

God knows everything about the trouble He allows, what it will create in us, and to what it will lead. We never know everything about our seasons of trouble. Job not knowing the particulars of his trouble, indicates that we can be people who are "**blameless and upright...who fear God and avoid evil**" and yet not know *why* we face the trouble we face.

It is important we understand that no matter how spiritually mature or close to God we are, there are some things He does, or allows that He simply doesn't let us in on. Because He's God, He is under no obligation to reveal His reasoning to us before or after our trouble. *(This reminds me of times when I would ask my mother why she wanted me to do something and her response would be, "Because I'm the Mama!" which was simply a nice way of saying, "Do it because I'm the boss, and I said to do it!" That always turned out to be a good reason to do whatever she had asked. Avoiding the consequences of not doing it was another good reason.)* As good, loving, kind, gracious, and merciful as God is, He is still *the Boss,* and as *the Boss*, He is not required to fill in His children on the particulars of the *what, how and why* of things.

It's not an indictment against Job's spirituality; neither is it remarkable that he didn't know who was responsible for his trouble. As upright and blameless as Job was, he was still human and limited in his ability to know everything that took place—even in his own life. As it pertained to his season of difficulty, Job did not *miss* anything he should have heard from God that would have helped him avoid his trouble because God didn't speak anything to him *about* his upcoming trouble.

What *is* remarkable, however, is that despite the fact that Job was under the erroneous impression that it was God Who had taken the life of his children, his possessions and his livelihood and had caused the sickness and trouble he was experiencing, Job's commitment caused him to declare of God, "… *still* will I trust Him."

At face value, and from a *natural-man* mindset, if the "He" and "Him" were anyone other than God, this verse wouldn't make sense. It wouldn't make sense because we don't typically trust people who we believe have greatly injured us in some way; or who we believe possess the propensity to do so. *(We should forgive them, but forgiveness doesn't always or automatically require us to trust them again.)* We find Job not only purposing in his heart to stay on track with God, we also see him pledging his commitment to trust in God—despite being under the impression that it was God who caused his time of trouble.

After he lost his children, his home and his income, and when his sickened self was all he had left, Job said of God, "**Though He slay** **me** (all that remains), **yet will I trust Him.**" Job was saying he had lost everything of value to him except himself—but if God chose to take him too even that would be acceptable. Job was going to continue to trust God.

Like all of the *things of God* (prayer, praise, church attendance, etc.), trusting God in the time of trouble can also be challenging. It can be challenging because there is a part of us (typically the whisperings of the enemy) that silently reminds us that we trusted in God not to allow trouble to come upon us, yet it did. That thought alone—without knowing or considering the good that God will make trouble accomplish in us through us and for us—can cause us not to trust God in trouble.

Whereas that would make sense in dealing with humans, it's different in dealing with God. Even after He has permitted trouble to enter our home and upset our life, the Lord is still worthy of our trust because He is still God. And as God, He still possesses the power, after the fact, to change our stormy seasons of rain into a fruitful seasons of reaping. In truth, we have no other *good* choice except to continue to trust God in trouble—or, to trust Him again if we have stopped trusting Him *because* of trouble.

Aside from Job, the Bible has many wonderful stories (testimonies) of people who continued trusting God after trouble and terrible times had taken place with them. And though the scenarios differ, each of these stories share in common the fact that their continued trust paid off—God came through for them in a *mighty* and *miraculous* way!

One such story is that of Mary and Martha and their brother Lazarus.

"Now a certain man was sick, Lazarus of Bethany, the town of Mary and her sister Martha. It was that Mary who anointed the Lord with fragrant oil and wiped His feet with her hair, whose brother Lazarus was sick. Therefore the sisters sent to Jesus saying, 'Lord, behold, he whom You love is sick.' "
John 11:1-3

It goes without saying that the purpose of their sending word to Jesus about the sickness of Lazarus was so that He would come and heal him. After all, Jesus had been traveling the region and healing other people—many of whom He did not know. Very few, if any, had the type of intimate relationship Mary, Martha, and Lazarus shared with Jesus. Surely He would come and heal Lazarus; thus they trusted. But initially, Jesus did not come and Lazarus did not live—even though the sisters trusted God that both would be the case.

"So when Jesus [finally] came, He found that Lazarus had already been in the tomb four days.
18 Now Bethany was near Jerusalem,
about two miles away. 19 And many of the Jews had joined the women around Martha and Mary, to comfort them concerning
their brother. 20 Now Martha, as soon as she heard that Jesus was coming, went and met Him, but Mary was sitting in the house.
21 Now Martha said to Jesus, 'Lord, if You had been here, my brother would not
have died. 22 But <u>even now</u> I know that whatever You ask of God, God will give You.' "
John 11:17-22

The first time I ministered in my hometown of Chicago at my mother's home church—the place people prayed for me years prior when I was wayward heathen in need of salvation—I shared a message from this passage entitled, "Even

Now." In that message I talked about the power of God to change, repair and restore things *even after* the worst has seemingly occurred with them.

This is what Martha understood when she declared to Christ the words "**even now**." She was contending that even though the trouble they were hoping to avoid has made its visitation, *even now* Jesus was able to rebuke the storm, right the ship, repair the damage and restore everything that had been lost in the process. In other words, despite the fact that Jesus had allowed the worst to take place by not showing up and healing Lazarus, Martha *still* trusted in the Christ! She continued to trust in Jesus—not with the idea that He *would* bring Lazarus back to life—but with the idea that He was still Lord of all, and that Jesus *could* bring Lazarus back to life if He chose to do so!

On what is our trust of God based? Is it based on what He *would* do, or what He *could* do? I would say it should be based on both what He would do *and* what He could do. If we base our trust *only* on what God *would* do, what happens to our trust when He *doesn't* do that for which we believed Him? Our trust goes out of the window. But if our trust doesn't end at what He *would* do but continues to what He *could* do, it means our trust doesn't die when God does not come through with that for which we initially trusted Him.

This is what we see with Shadrach, Meshach and Abednego when they were brought before King Nebuchadnezzar and maintained their refusal to bow down and worship the image he had created. When the king made certain they knew they would be cast into the burning fiery furnace should they *not* bow down, he sarcastically asked, "**...Who is the God who will deliver you from my hands?" (Daniel 3:15)**

"Shadrach, Meshach, and Abed-nego answered and said to the king, 'O Nebuchadnezzar, we have no need to answer you in this matter. If that is the case, our God whom we serve is able to deliver us from the burning fiery furnace, and He will deliver from your hand O king.' "
Daniel 3:16, 17

Surely the Hebrew boys were trusting God to keep them out of the burning fiery furnace because they knew He *could*. However, just in case He didn't and they found themselves in the furnace, they still trusted that God *would* deliver them—even if it got to the point they were hoping to avoid. What this allows us to understand is that our trust in God should not be limited to one thing, desire, or expectation. Shadrach, Meshach, and Abednego trusted God for protection from the furnace, but at the same time, they realized that the Lord might allow them to be cast into the furnace. They then shifted their trust from *protection* from the furnace to *deliverance* from the furnace. It was the same trust—merely a different area of application.

If they had abandoned their trust when God did not protect them from the furnace, it's possible that they may not have been delivered from the furnace. There was a connection between their trust and Jesus' pre-incarnate presence in the furnace. His presence was a product of their trust. When they said to the king, "**...our God whom we serve is able to deliver us from the burning fiery furnace, and He will deliver us from your hand, O king,"** that expression of trust in God's *after-the-fact* delivering power moved the Father to send His Son to meet them and to deliver them from the place from which He did not protect them. For this reason we cannot trade our trust for despair when God hasn't protected us from something we hoped to avoid. Hold on, it's not over! Don't toss out your trust because even in what God has permitted to take place, trust is still a kingdom commodity that will prove to be extremely valuable.

"Therefore do not cast away your confidence, it carries great compensation of reward."
Hebrews 10:35

Remain trustful in trouble. You'll be glad you did!

Conclusion

Regardless of the type of trouble you are going through, you will come out victorious! Through Christ Jesus you are more than a conqueror. The Lord is a present help during your days of difficulty, and He will deliver you out of your times of trouble!

God has begun a good work in you and He will complete it, using your time of trouble as a tool to build a better you, and a better future for you, in Him. Your trials, no matter what type or how tough, are simply a part of the process. Hang in there! God has great things in store for you!

Endure hardship as a good soldier, being mindful that the end of your endurance is the beginning of the good that God, Who cannot lie, has already planned for you. You will one day awaken to find that all of the trouble was worth the exceeding great and precious promises being fulfilled in your life.

Jesus said of a woman who was experiencing the pain and trouble of giving birth to a child, "…when she is in labor, she has sorrow because her hour has come; but as soon as she has given birth to the child, she no longer remembers the anguish because of the joy of the child being born…." In the same way, you are experiencing the pain of your troublesome times. But when the promises of God are birthed into your life, the pain of your problems will be a thing of the past, and the joy of the promises will flood your heart, and your life!

Continue to pray and praise. Continue to attend church, singing and giving to God, and getting His Word into your heart! Even if the labor pains become a little more intense, continue to trust and believe God. Don't cast away your confidence in Him, because it carries great reward. Be encouraged. Your trouble will not last forever! The sun is rising, darkness is fleeing, a new day is dawning, and God is preparing you to triumph over your trouble!

Great is the faithfulness of our Heavenly Father! Great is the love of our Lord and Savior! And great is the grace of our God and King!

CPSIA information can be obtained at www.ICGtesting.com
Printed in the USA
BVOW05*0742240314

348554BV00001B/1/P

9 780989 782609